ECHOES From ETERNITY

Arvin S. Gibson

Second Printing, October 1993

International Standard Book Number
0-88290-468-X

Horizon Publishers' Catalog and Order Number
1040

Printed and distributed
in the United States of America by

**Horizon
Publishers
& Distributors, Incorporated**
P.O. Box 490 Bountiful, Utah 84011-0490

Acknowledgments

This book would not exist save for the efforts and encouragement of many people. First among those is the marvelous lady, Carol Gibson, whom I somehow was wise enough to marry forty-three years ago in Berkeley, California. Carol continues to be my right arm. She assisted with the many interviews in the research for the two books (*Glimpses of Eternity*, and *Echoes From Eternity*), and she offered helpful comments throughout.

Duane Crowther urged me to expand the research effort begun with the previous book, and he offered useful suggestions throughout the effort. His encouragement—and courage in offering to publish another book on near-death experiences—were vital in getting me to continue with the substantial effort necessary to complete a second book. He, and his people at Horizon Publishers and Distributors, contributed much to the finished product.

Florence Susan Comish was gracious in providing the beautiful painting *A Child's Savior* that graces the jacket cover of this book. The story of how that painting came to be was sufficiently pertinent to the theme of the book that I included it as a part of Chapter 2.

Dr. Lynn D. Johnson, a practicing psychologist in the Salt Lake City region, generously wrote a foreword for the book. Dr. Johnson's perspective is especially appreciated because of his own research in the field of near-death experiences (NDEs).

Rose Mari Finter, as with *Glimpses of Eternity*, again labored to improve my grammar and writing style. Her careful attention to detail helped me avoid embarrassing mistakes.

Marian Bergin, a clinical psychologist practicing in the Provo, Utah area, assisted me in a difficult technical area. She provided the scientific material needed to better understand an issue of importance to the book.

Several people read a draft of the book and offered helpful comments. Included in that group are: Norman and Helen Herzinger, Janice Ridges, Pat Pexton, Grant Bishop, Randle King, Fred Beckett, Bill and Leslie Starkweather, Bill English, Thomas Greenburg, and Lorin L. Richards. I am grateful for their diligence in rapidly reviewing the early draft.

Grant Anderson from the LDS Church Historical Department provided information useful for historical perspective. This was helpful in detailing some of the background information for the book.

The Utah Chapter of the International Association for Near-Death Studies (IANDS of Utah) was a fertile source of help. The officers of that group were supportive of my effort, and many of those selected for interviews came to my attention during local IANDS meetings.

Without the freely offered experiences by the many people Carol and I interviewed, there would be no book. These people touched our lives in ways that cannot be expressed by a simple thanks. They changed the way we thought about those things we cherish most. Their unselfish giving of themselves, often under significant emotional strain, helped me to better understand the NDE phenomenon. Their stories should provide sustenance to many people.

My sons, Craig, Aaron and Dale Gibson, and their wives, Janis, Sue, and Lori; and my daughter, Leah Gibson, provided encouraging support. Gary Gillum helped again with this book, by acquainting me with an individual who had an unusual NDE.

All of us doing research in the near-death field are indebted to those pioneers that initiated the research work and first brought it to the attention of the world. Foremost among the early researchers was Dr. Raymond A. Moody, Jr., in his book *Life After Life*. Other pioneers in the field included Dr. George G. Ritchie and Dr. Kenneth Ring. Dr. Ring was one of the founders of the International Association for Near Death Studies (IANDS).

Echoes From Eternity is primarily the result of my work and my judgment. In exercising that judgment I attempted to do the research and to present the material in as accurate a manner as possible. It is my fervent desire that the material so presented will provide others with the same feelings of love, wonder, and hope which I felt as I listened to people tell of their experiences. I desire, also, as readers explore Part II of the book, that they gain some of the peace and joy that I experienced upon discovering scriptures which related directly to many of the events described by those having gone through the experiences. May this book prove to be a source of knowledge and understanding to all who read it.

Arvin S. Gibson

Contents

CONTENTS

Foreword

What can you gain from reading this book? There is a story of a famous Japanese warrior, a samurai who was without peer on the field of battle. When asked how he had become a great swordsman, he replied that as a youth he had asked an experienced soldier what he must do to be a good samurai. The wise old man replied that a true samurai must never be afraid of death.

This bothered him greatly, since he did fear his own death. So he meditated about death for several years until he could truly say that life and death were the same to him. Only then did he become an excellent swordsman; only then did he begin to live.

Over the past ten years, as I have studied persons who have had a near-death experience, this has been happening to me. I remember the first time this experience (the NDE) ever was explained to me. I had interviewed my own grandfather, tape recording his recollections about his life. At the end he told me about an unusual experience which had greatly affected his life. He concluded, "Never fear death. It is the most wonderful thing you can imagine."

I had always trusted my grandfather and found him to be an impeccable person. But I did fear death, and his instruction was difficult to carry out. Only with the help of unselfish, loving persons like those you will meet in this book did I begin to come to a point where I was at least closer to the truth that life and death are parts of the same eternal plan and that death is nothing to fear.

I study NDEs for several reasons, but I think this is the most important one: I want to learn to really be alive. If death—my death or the death of a loved one—if death is something I fear, then I am less alive. I then am fearful, constrained, and worried, not joyful, loving and hopeful.

For how can we be hopeful if we expect that some horrible fate implacably awaits us? How can we feel joy if we believe we face annihilation tomorrow? As our brothers and sisters who have stepped through death's door return and speak to us, the fear disappears and we live again ourselves.

In the pages of this book, you will meet some people with extraordinary experiences. And while they are ordinary people, their messages are fascinating and worth pondering.

11

There are many people who are disturbed, even enraged by the NDE reports. What they hear about does not conform to their ideas so they reject the reports, rather than consider there may be greater truth in what they are hearing. We can all understand such a reaction, for we are all susceptible to that temptation. I have often wished to keep my ideas rather than accept what life tells me to accept. And we should be cautious about this. Only a foolish person will accept unthinkingly whatever report someone tells him or her.

But if several independent sources report the same thing, one is obligated to at least consider that one's own perspective is too limited. In this book there are several experiences that Arvin Gibson might have left out or ignored. After all, he writes from the perspective of a faithful, active Latter-day Saint. And here in these pages you will find two instances of a minister of another faith administering a powerful blessing which had spiritual reality. Arvin's LDS background does not interfere with the telling. He does not flinch or step back from reporting what he has learned. I think this shows his greatness of spirit, and makes the book worthy of your careful consideration.

And in fact, we ought to expect such openness from ourselves as well. Didn't Jesus tell us that we cannot imagine the things that God has prepared for us? And this is a mark, for me, of a genuine NDE. Almost every one I have interviewed has a sense of awe, a sense that he or she is telling us, "This happened, and *I never had imagined it would be so.*" Even an experience by someone who had studied NDEs himself before his own experience occurred was surprising to him. And when you study it, I suppose you will be surprised too.

It is almost as if God were saying to us, "Yes what you think, what you believe is good and true in many aspects. But there is more, there is so much more that you cannot comprehend it, except in bits and pieces at this time."

Arvin Gibson extends to you this invitation: come and learn some of what he has learned. Sit with these good people, and hear them tell you things that you had never imagined. And see if what I found is true for you: As the fear of death fades, the ability to love and live in joy increases.

What better gift could you receive?

Lynn D. Johnson, Ph.D.
Psychologist

Introduction

Ann's Angel

. . . I felt so tired that . . . that I simply wanted to get to sleep. I lay there for a moment waiting to go to sleep when I noticed a light coming into the room. It was a beautiful golden-white light which seemed to appear in the wall to the left of my bed. . . .

I wasn't afraid, just curious about the light. It was about three feet up from the floor and mid-length of the bed, which was located near the wall. As the ball of light grew, the pain and feeling of illness suddenly left me. I had no idea what was happening, but I felt at peace.

I sat up and watched the light grow. It grew rapidly in both size and brightness. In fact the light got so bright that it seemed to me that the whole world was lit by it. I could see someone inside the light. There was this beautiful woman, and she was part of the light; in fact she glowed.

Her body was lit from inside in a way . . . it's very hard to explain what she looked like. It seemed as if she were a pure crystal filled with light. Even her robe glowed with light as if by itself. The robe was white, long-sleeved, and full length. She had a golden belt around her waist and her feet were bare. Not that she needed anything on her feet since she stood a couple of feet off the floor.

I had never seen such kindness and gentle love on anyone's face such as I saw in this person. She called me by name and held out her hand to me. She told me to come with her—her voice was soft and gentle but . . . but it was more in my mind. Communication was easier than when you verbalize thoughts. At the time I thought of it as 'mind talk.'

I asked her who she was and she explained that she was my guardian and had been sent to take me to a place where I could rest in peace. The love emanating from her washed over me so that I didn't hesitate to put my hand in hers.

As soon as I was standing beside her we moved through a short darkness to a beautiful, even brighter, light. And then I saw . . . there was this astonishingly beautiful world before me. It was like nothing

13

else I have since seen on earth. Somehow I knew, inside of me, that the earth had been left behind. I had no idea where I was, and I didn't care. I felt a deep, profound peace . . . no, it was more than that. It was a world of peace and love.

The new world looked sort of like the world I had left behind, but it was also very different. Everything glowed from the inside with its own light. The colors were beyond anything on earth--they were more vibrant, brilliant, and intense. And there were colors I had never seen before—don't ask me what they were. There were shrubs, trees and flowers, some of which I had seen on earth, like evergreens, and others which I hadn't seen before, and I haven't seen since. They were beautiful, beautiful. . . .

Ann was a four-year-old girl, with leukemia, when she had this remarkable experience. Upon returning from the beautiful world of peace and love that her angel took her to, she was cured of leukemia.

My wife, Carol, and I first heard Ann's story when she visited our home, as an adult, in 1991. Ann's was one of the forty firsthand accounts from people we interviewed who had undergone near-death experiences (NDEs), or other out-of-body or analogous spiritual events. Those experiences are documented in the book *Glimpses of Eternity,*[1] the predecessor to this book.

Why Another Book on Near-death Experiences?

Glimpses of Eternity was written to offer new accounts of NDEs, and to attempt to provide meaning for the new experiences, and others from the literature, by reviewing the events in the light of available LDS scriptures and teachings. The research, and other work associated with that book, proved to be rewarding to Carol and me, principally because of the choice people we met. Those people, and the stories that they told, exposed us to an ethereal adventure—and led us on a spiritual journey—that was totally unexpected.

Our journey took us to the banks of a river; a river of knowledge—knowledge of things as they are, things as they were, and things as they are to come. We drank briefly from the waters of that river, but the drink was most refreshing. Our thirst was only momentarily quenched, however, and we sought again to drink from those crystalline waters.

To quench our thirst—to find further meaning from those who had glimpsed eternity—we launched ourselves on a continuation of the journey we began some three years ago. We were unsure of what we would find on our continuing odyssey, except to observe that it would be exciting.

This book, *Echoes From Eternity*, then, represents an effort to drink, again, from the river of knowledge that we previously found. The book's major purpose is to continue the exploration of the world of NDEs, and to expand the knowledge revealed by the preceding work. In addition to recording and preserving many firsthand accounts of NDEs and related spiritual events, we have attempted to provide additional meanings, in the second part of the book, for the various accounts.

The Search for Truth

As with the earlier effort, our drink from the river of knowledge was refreshing, but brief. It seemed that the more we learned of the other world, the more we wanted to know about it. It was as if our thirst for knowledge, once activated, became unquenchable. We continued to look for evidence that paralleled previous findings, and we sought insight from completely new findings.

A marvelous thing happened in our journey, this time. We suspected that we had found certain truths during our work on *Glimpses of Eternity*. And we did, in fact, receive further confirmation of some of those truths during the creation of *Echoes From Eternity*. The very name *Echoes From Eternity* was taken from one of the truths. While we were interviewing a lady, Elane Durham, who had an extensive NDE, she said: ". . . and as I listened to those young Elders it was as if I were hearing an echo of the spiritual being I had met on a high place in a different world." The Elders that Elane was listening to were young Mormon missionaries, and they were teaching her the Gospel of Jesus Christ, as they understood it.

We heard this truth revealed again, in a slightly different manner, when a young mother, Berta, explained how her four-year-old son, Rocky, fell from a second-story window onto his head on the concrete below. As Rocky gradually recovered from that tragic fall, he described an encounter with Jesus in a different world. Equally amazing, he began to quote scriptures from the King James version of the Bible—scriptures that he had not previously known of.

A major truth that these anecdotal incidents hinted at was that the Gospel of Jesus Christ, as given in the Bible and in latter-day scriptures—and as taught by Prophets throughout the ages—is the foundation for life after this life. And it is the key to happiness in this life.

Other truths were exhibited as Carol and I drank from the river of knowledge. We listened, enchanted, to individuals overcome with emotion explain what they had seen and heard on the other side of the veil. Most of the people were unaware that they were divulging patterns of thought, from another world, that mirrored patterns others had also divulged. Many of these thought patterns duplicated, in detail, information from the Prophets as recorded in the scriptures.

When Carol and I finished research for this book, we found that our journey was still incomplete. Our drink, though refreshing, had not quenched our thirst for knowledge. Light had illuminated some truths—truths that we had dimly understood—but ultimate knowledge eluded us. We had merely succeeded in building a few more sign-posts to aid us in the journey through life.

For most of us, including those who have experienced NDEs, we still must grope our way through life—with faith. We must stumble along, seeking truth as we go, but having ultimate faith in the goodness and love of an eternal God. We are destined, in this life, to be like Paul of old, "for now we see through a glass, darkly; . . . now I know in part." But we may have hope, and faith, as Paul did, that ". . . then face to face; . . . then I shall know even as also I am known."[2]

Carol and I offer this book, with the additional sign-posts it contains, to aid you in your journey through life. As you drink from the waters of knowledge as we did, our hope is that you, too, will enjoy the thrill, the love, and the peace that we felt as we listened to echoes from eternity spoken by those we interviewed. And may you gain a greater appreciation for that greatest of all adventures—the transition from this life to the next.

How the Research Was Conducted

The research for this book was performed in much the same manner as for *Glimpses of Eternity*. Firsthand accounts were sought and documented from individuals who had undergone NDEs or analogous spiritual experiences; the near-death literature was reviewed again to learn what new findings others had uncovered; and the resultant data were compared with LDS teachings and scriptures.

Candidates for interviewing were found by a number of methods. As with the previous book, I advertised in local papers and publications, and I relied upon referrals from friends, relatives and associates. There were a few, this time, who sought me as a result of reading *Glimpses of Eternity*. I found others who were active in a local chapter of the International Association for Near Death Studies (IANDS).

All of these methods were fruitful. Initially, I did not actively pursue people for the purposes of starting a new book. Instead, I interviewed those who wanted to tell me of their experiences, mostly for the purposes of understanding what they had to say and to help them understand their own experiences. This gradually led to new findings, and these findings, in-turn, suggested further research. The information base thus grew and ratcheted itself into the outline for a new book.

Each candidate who was interviewed met with me—and where women were involved, with my wife, also—and told their story as I recorded it on tape. They were instructed to give background information on themselves and then to tell, in their own words, what happened during their NDE. We had previously prepared a list of questions that should be addressed before the interview was completed. As the interview proceeded, we listened to their account; then, in as open-ended manner as possible, asked questions that had not been addressed during their initial account.

Upon completion of the interview, I used the tape to type up each experience—without editorial comment. The candidates were then asked to review the written record, edit it so that it fully corresponded to what they remembered experiencing during their NDE, and then send the corrected copy to me. Alternatively, they could call me with corrections. In this manner, in an iterative fashion, each account was tailored so as to be as accurate a record as possible of the individual's memory of the NDE.

Some of those interviewed preferred to be recognized with their true identity; others preferred a pseudonym. For those desiring complete identification, I used their full names; others wanting anonymity were assigned a pseudonym for a given name, with no surname.

The interviews took place from the summer of 1992 through the spring of 1993. Twenty-nine candidates, whose firsthand stories were selected for inclusion in the book, were interviewed. Of those, twelve were male and seventeen were female. By reason of the location of the interviews, in the greater Salt Lake City region, most of the people who were interviewed (69%) professed membership in The Church of Jesus Christ of Latter-day Saints. The rest were from various other religious backgrounds and faiths.

Other phases of the research for this book involved reading the available new literature on NDEs (literature up to 1992 had been reviewed for the previous book), and marking appropriate sections for later use. Applicable LDS scriptures and teachings were also studied and marked for later reference.

Are the Stories True?

There are several questions concerning the research that I am repeatedly asked. They are: "Are the stories true?", "Why do people tell you their stories?", and "Do you think their experiences are real?"

These questions are asked with sufficient frequency that I have decided to devote an entire chapter, in Part II of the book, to their answer. For those who insist on knowing the answers to these questions before reading further, I ask you to turn to the chapter in Part II that addresses these questions. For all others, I ask you to patiently read through the book based on my belief, and assurance, that the stories in this book are true accounts of real experiences.

During the interview process, Carol and I observed the demeanor of those we were talking to. There was an awe about them and an attitude reflective of having undergone a profound experience—one that affected their understanding of who and what they were. There was no need for these individuals to embellish the reality or truth of what they had experienced. They knew what they had experienced, and they could not, or would not, alter the facts to suit other people's preconceived notions of what might have happened.

The accounts are anecdotal by their very nature, and not subject to some of the normal tests for repeatability that characterize other scientific investigations. Nevertheless, there are patterns of thought and activity that can be scrutinized for parallelism, and there are other tests of accountability that can be used to separate fact from fiction. These, and other more spiritual tests, are discussed in Part II.

Why the Comparison with LDS Scriptures?

Many books on the near-death experience have been written since Raymond Moody's renowned *Life After Life*.[3] The sheer size of the bibliography attests to the popularity of the subject. Relatively few, however, have been written from the LDS perspective, particularly books that include new research on the subject. One of the earliest, and best, LDS oriented books was *Life Everlasting* by Duane Crowther.[4] First published in 1967—even before *Life After Life*, which was published in 1975—*Life Everlasting* is still being published.

Other books on the near-death experience by LDS authors have been published. None of these more recent works, however, provide the depth of research or the timeliness that are attempted in *Glimpses of Eternity* and *Echoes From Eternity*.

As an active member of The Church of Jesus Christ of Latter-day Saints I was, of course, familiar with the teachings of that church and of the LDS scriptures relating to life after death. Those teachings and scriptures are, for the most part, in harmony with what people having NDEs said they had experienced. Indeed, many of the teachings of the Prophet Joseph Smith, writings from the *Book of Mormon*, and writings from the *Doctrine and Covenants* give details that parallel some of the NDEs to a remarkable extent—and usually these teachings and writings provide additional information as to causes, effects, and ultimate outcomes.

I wrote this book, then, to fulfill a perceived need by relating *new* NDEs to the available LDS scriptures and literature. The book builds upon the foundation and expands the research that was carried out for the book *Glimpses of Eternity*. In relating the research to the LDS perspective, I hasten to explain that I do not, and cannot speak for The Church of Jesus Christ of Latter-day Saints—that privilege is reserved for the Church's Prophet and other General Authorities. Rather, I speak as a person who has spent a lifetime as a member of the Church, and I speak as one who is convinced that the LDS Church is true in its doctrinal claims. Any analysis of the data, which I present, is made in that context.

How This Book Is Organized

Part I, which follows this Introduction, includes printed accounts of the interviews of respondents largely as they were recorded on tape. The interviews are reported, including background information, in their totality and with as much detail as practical. In some instances considerable background information is given, either because the information is directly pertinent to the experience, or, equally important, because it adds to a better understanding of the individual. The reader can review the interviews without the interjection of editorial comment and can thus obtain a better feeling for what the respondent was saying in the setting of the total experience.

Part II provides an analysis of the Part I data in the context of LDS scriptures and teachings. References from other NDE books are also cited where appropriate. Part II also contains some observations and speculations, by me, which are the results of observing the respondents during the interview process and of studying the accounts of their experiences. Data from the sixty-eight respondents' accounts (from the two books) of their experiences are tabulated and analyzed in Part II. Patterns and parallels from the analyzed data are discussed.

Part I

The Experiences

Ye worlds of light and life, beyond our sphere;
Mysterious country! let your light appear.
Ye angels, lift the veil, the truth unfold,
And give our Seers a glimpse of that bright world;
Tell where ye live, and what is your employ,
Your present blessing, and your future joy.
Say, have you learn'd the name, and tuned the lyre,
And hymn'd the praise of Him—the great Messiah?

> Parley P. Pratt, "The World of
> Spirits," *Key to the Science of
> Theology*, Ch 14, p 128.

Chapter 1

TWO LEFT—ONE CAME BACK

Eloise Weaver

Background and an Early Experience

Eloise Weaver was a short, cheerful lady with curly auburn hair. She exhibited enthusiasm—none of the nervousness sometimes evident in interviews of this type—when she visited our home in July 1992. Carol and I greeted her and the interview commenced.

Eloise informed us that she was born in Evanston, Wyoming on August 14, 1942. She was raised as a first child in Wyoming where her father was a barber, and where her grandfather had also been a barber and a mayor. Her parents moved to Davis County, Utah, when she was a senior in high school. There she met her future husband, David, whom she married at age 17. They subsequently had six children, four girls and two boys.

Eloise was raised as an active member of The Church of Jesus Christ of Latter-day Saints. Her mother was a convert to the church, and her father was a member all of his life.

Eloise began telling of her experiences: "The first unusual experience I remember was when I was nine or ten years old. I was in bed with rheumatic fever, which I'd had for about three months, and I was very sick. We lived on a corner where there were no lights and no other houses around us. My parents had just taken my brother to the doctor because of something he swallowed, and I was alone and frightened.

"My parents told me to keep the door locked and to stay in bed. I was scared and crying, and I remember praying for help. All of a sudden a great light filled the room. Standing there by me in the light was Jesus. He put His hands on my head and I felt this enormous outpouring of love.

"Jesus was all dressed in white, and he was very handsome. His eyes were the most wonderful blue, and there was the most warm, wonderful feeling emanating from him. I don't remember Him saying anything—just His hands on my head. It seemed that He was there for a long time, and the room was very bright. Then He left, and the room was dark again.

"When my folks came home, I told them what had happened. And they . . . you know how parents are, they just sort of patted me on the head and told me to go to sleep. They took me in for a test later that week, though, and all of my tests were absolutely wonderful. The doctor said I was almost completely well."

Eloise paused as though in thought, and I interjected: "You said that when the room got bright you saw Jesus standing there. How do you know it was Jesus?"

"Oh, I knew it was Jesus. His beautiful face, His countenance, His hair, it was . . . it was a beautiful brownish-golden color. And those wonderful big blue eyes. He had a little beard—and when He put His hands on my head I felt His strength. It was a strength that I felt through my whole body. I'll never forget the feelings that I had in His presence."

"What were His clothes like?" I asked.

"They were white; they covered His arms down to his wrists, and they were open at His neck a little way. They were flowing, and white; and the room was gold and blue and pink. It was radiant—it was just wonderful."

"Did He glow too?"

"Oh yes, there was just a . . . it was like an aurora coming off of Him. And the feeling. I'll never forget the feeling of His hands on my head.

"I never had any other experiences of that nature as a child."

A Premonition

"In May 1990, my husband and my children and I were living in Layton, Utah. My husband and I decided to take a trip to Missoula, Montana where we could go biking. We were both bikers, and we felt that it would be a short second honeymoon. Four of our six children were still living at home and we felt that we needed a break by ourselves. We were busy getting ready, and Dave had the car all packed, and . . .

"Did you ever feel that things weren't what they should be—sort of a premonition of something wrong? We were supposed to leave at 10:00 a.m. with a group of people we would be traveling with. The car was all packed from the previous evening, and Dave said, 'I'm ready to go.'

"It was 8:00 a.m. and I mentioned that there was still time before ten o'clock when we were to meet the others. Dave repeated that he felt we should go, then.

"When we went to the car, the bikes weren't on the bike racks of his car where we had loaded them the previous night. Instead, he had unloaded them from his car and put them on mine. I asked him why he did that and he said that he felt that we should take my car.

"As we got ready to leave, my seventeen-year-old daughter came up and pleaded to go with us. She said that she really wanted to go. Dave explained that we needed to get away for a separate vacation. She continued to beg her dad. He smiled and said: 'Okay, if you want to go, climb in just as you are—no clothes or other packing.'

"I'm sure that my husband felt my daughter would not go with us when he told her to climb in without packing, but she did. She got in and we took off. Dave drove for a time, and then I drove.

"When we reached Dillon, Montana, we stopped for lunch. Dave seemed compelled to keep going. Normally we would have relaxed for a time during lunch, but he insisted on eating in the car while we were traveling. He said that he felt we should get there and then relax. He also took the driver's seat though it was my turn to drive. He argued that we would get there quicker with him driving."

A Terrible Accident—Strange Visitors

"About twenty minutes after we left Dillon, and while I was laying my head down on the passenger side, I heard Dave holler: 'They're going to hit us.' And that's when the car hit us—in the front-side of our car.

"It was two o'clock in the afternoon; we were on a highway without another car around, and this older couple, coming from the opposite direction, apparently fell asleep. They hit a guard rail and it redirected their car back onto the highway but toward us. Their car was airborne when it plowed into my husband's side of the car.

"Our car rolled over many times. We were all wearing seat belts so we stayed in the car. When the car quit bouncing I looked over at Dave, and he was slumped over. I thought he had left me, and I took a deep breath. I was totally awake, and as I attempted to take the breath I found that I couldn't breathe. Immediately, I knew that my neck was broken.

"Looking into the window I saw two personages. Who they were, I don't know. I could see them from their shoulders up. One of them said to me: 'Pull your legs up to your chest, hold them tight and breathe shallow, and you will live.' Then they were gone.

"I think they were two men, from the tone of voice of the one, and they were dressed in white. The white was as bright as . . . it was as bright as the snow when the sun hits it. And there was a warm, calm, sweet feeling in that light.

"I did as he told me; I pulled my legs up, and I held on tight. That action probably saved my life. Later I found that the first two vertebras in my neck were broken, my spleen was ruptured, all my ribs were broken, my lungs were collapsed, and my diaphragm was in fifteen pieces. When I pulled my legs up, though, it's a mystery why my spinal column didn't rupture. The medics said that I couldn't have pulled up my legs because I was wearing the engine of the other car underneath my arm and my chest.

"Nevertheless, I know those people were there, and I know what they told me and what I did. Someday when I meet them again I'll know who they were."

An Embrace Out-of-Body

"After the people in white left it was a while before anyone saw us. There was very little traffic on the highway. Three kids were on a hill, though, and they had binoculars. They were watching for a white fox which they had seen the previous day. As they were watching for the fox they saw our dust. It took them about ten minutes to get to us.

"The kids came and began talking to us. My daughter was screaming from the back seat. My husband was conscious by this time and he was telling them his name and address. Finally, after what seemed a long time, other help came and they began the process of trying to get us out. There were the police and the paramedics. They were frantic because it appeared that we were in danger of dying.

"The paramedics got my daughter out first. Then they began to pry on the door where my husband was. Dave kept saying how badly he hurt, and they were afraid he was dying. He turned toward me, and that's when everything in the car got really bright, very warm, and very quiet. I didn't hear my daughter screaming anymore, and I didn't hear any voices coming from outside the car.

"I felt Dave's presence very close to me, and suddenly we were above our bodies. He held me really tight, and he said: 'Hang in there babe; I love you.' That's what he always called me. Then he said: 'I'm being called home, and you need to go back and raise our girls.'

"I remember telling Dave that I really didn't want to go back without him, but he told me I had to return. Then the warm feeling left, and I was hit with pain—immense pain. The pain was more horrible than when the car first hit us.

"I could hear the people again, and I saw Dave as they were pulling him out of the car. He winked at me. Then they began doing CPR on him; I knew he was gone. I could feel his presence near me. He had a habit of brushing my hair off my forehead—I could feel him doing that, and I felt very calm.

"Dave lived as long as he did, I think, (three hours before they got him out) so that he could encourage me to live. I wouldn't have struggled to live as much as I did without him there to help me."

Further Questions About the Experience

"Eloise, can you describe the light you saw?" I asked.

"It was just radiant and brilliant; it was soft and warm. The experience was almost as if I were sitting by a mountain stream and hearing the creek babbling, and the little birds. It was the most peaceful feeling I have ever felt, probably more peaceful than sitting in the temple—just absolutely wonderful."

"Why did you use the word peaceful?"

"I felt so great. I didn't feel any pain."

"When you went out of your body could you see your physical body in the car?"

"Yes. I could see myself with my knees pulled up, and I could see Dave slumped over."

"As you were embraced by Dave how did your spirit body feel?"

"It felt just like me; I was exhilarated from the embrace."

"When you were out of your body did you see anything or anyone else?"

"No, I've read about other experiences, but I didn't see a tunnel, or flowers or trees, or . . . . There were just Dave and I and the soft, beautiful brightness. It was soft, just so soft."

"Why did you use the word *soft*?"

"It was kind of a pastel color—just soft. When I saw the two personages, they were radiant and breathtaking. But with Dave in the light, it was just a soft . . . it reminded me of a cloud that puffed around us in a soft, cuddly, warm way."

"Could you tell us a little more about the two personages? What did they look like?"

"I could see them from the waist up. When I first saw them I couldn't tell whether they were men or women, but after I heard the tone of voice of the one I assumed they were men. They were dressed in white—very, very white. Everything was white."

"After seeing Dave, when you were out of your body, do you remember going back into your body?"

"I just remember him kissing me and hugging me, and then the noise came back. The pain—it was so terrible."

"You said that you looked at Dave as they were removing him from the car, and he winked at you. He must have been back in his body . . .?"

"Yes, he must have been back too. They were just starting to take him out when he gave me that little wink that he always gave me. They pronounced him dead at the hospital, but I think he was dead right after they took him out. I felt him brushing my hair with his hand shortly after they got him out."

"After you reached the hospital what was your recuperation like?"

"We were in Butte, Montana, in the intensive care unit of the hospital. My daughter and I both had life-support systems on us. We were in that hospital for two-and-one-half weeks. Then they flew us to Utah, and my daughter went home. I went to the McKay Hospital in Ogden and stayed there for another two weeks."

"How did they treat your broken neck?"

"First they had to treat my internal injuries. Then they put a *Halo* on my head with screws to hold it in place. It was very painful, and I wore it for five months."

"Did you have any permanent damage?"

"I was paralyzed on my left side for a while. I have a stiff neck, still, and I often get headaches, but my recovery truly was miraculous. I think, because of the blessing my brother gave me, and because of my experience, my recovery has been almost complete."

"Did you have a feeling, other than what your husband told you, why you came back?"

"I think there were a couple of reasons. One was to raise my children. The other was to do genealogy work to trace my ancestors on my mother's side. When I was very ill in the hospital, shortly after the experience, my brother said I kept talking about all the genealogy I had to do."

"Did you have a feeling at the time that you had a choice to stay or to come back?"

"No. I felt I had to come back."

"After that experience did you tell many people?"

"Yes. I told my brother, my parents, my children, my Bishop, and my Stake President."

"Did those people believe you?"

"Oh, yes."

"Had you read anything up to that time on the near-death experience?"

"No, but I sure have since the experience."

Final Thoughts on the Experiences

"The experiences I have had have made me a much stronger person. I understand, now, that life is really short. We need to make the best of each day, to love our children, to have humility, and to have charity toward others. We also need to know that Heavenly Father loves us, and no matter how hard our difficulties are everything will be okay.

"My perspective on death has changed. I used to be a real coward about death. I think the fear that was in me—and that which is shared by many people—is, in part, because our body has a survival instinct; it doesn't want to give up. I now feel that death is a piece of cake. It doesn't scare me anymore."

Chapter 2

A CHILD'S VIEW OF JESUS

Cynthia Prueitt

It was a bright summer day in July 1992, when Cynthia Prueitt drove up to our house. Our yard, although not as colorful as it had been in the spring, still showed the results of my wife's tender care. Cynthia immediately took note of the flowers, shrubs and trees and commented on them to Carol. She pointed out that one of our shrubs was being attacked by a particular type of bug, and she recommended a corrective spray.

The source of Cynthia's expertise in this area became apparent as she entered our house and began to tell us of her background. She currently resided in Clearfield, Utah, and she was employed as the head groundskeeper for the Ogden-Weber Applied Technologies grounds. Her active interest in plants of all types was apparent as she admired our blooming orchid and our less-than-vigorous prayer plant.

Cynthia was born September 13, 1958, in Provo, Utah. She was raised in Los Alamos, New Mexico, where her father was a physicist at the Los Alamos National Laboratory. After high school she went to college in New Mexico and in Idaho where she got a degree in horticulture.

Her parents were still living, and she had four brothers and one sister. Her parents were both converted to The Church of Jesus Christ of Latter-day Saints, and the family followed that religion. Cynthia was not married at the time of our interview.

A Troubled Child and a Remarkable Experience

Cynthia began telling her story: "When I was about seven years old, and living in Los Alamos, I found myself one night very upset about many events. I slept in a lower bunk bed, and I wasn't supposed to wake my sister who was in the upper bunk, so I was sobbing into my covers. I was so distraught from the events of the day that I couldn't stop crying. I continued to cry, muffling the sobs in the covers, until about 1:00 a.m.

"My mind kept dwelling on my problems, wondering why it was happening to me, and I prayed to God for help. The next thing I remember was being introduced into a room that was completely and brilliantly white. There was a man sitting on a chair that resembled a chair-type throne.

"Seeing this man with a beard sitting there, I ran up to him and climbed onto his knees. He gathered me in his arms and began to . . . he just began to comfort me. He gave me such a warm, warm feeling of love, and . . . I've never felt anything like it. It was warm, it was love, it was joy—I didn't want it to end. It was the most thrilling feeling I had ever experienced before or since.

"This wonderful being wrapped me in his arms and held me close. I began to sob and tell him my problems. He comforted me with words of comfort. Then he began to talk to me about my life. He told me that I had certain things in this life that I had to do. He began to tell me what they were and how I was to accomplish these things. As he outlined what I was to do he asked me if I would try to accomplish what he had described, and I promised that I would.

"Then he said that it was time for me to leave. I began to bawl, and I told him that I didn't want to go. Crying helplessly, I pled that I might stay in his presence.

"I got off his knees, and I forget much after that—except I remember going back into my body through my head. I saw myself just before I entered. My body was still in the same position it had been before I left.

"I began to cry again as I returned. Crying for some time, I again made the promises I had previously made to Jesus Christ when I was on His lap. I promised that I would do the things He told me—no matter what it took to do them. And I stopped crying.

"For a long time after the experience I had a hard time dealing with it. I knew I had seen Jesus and I couldn't deny it, yet I couldn't tell others because I felt they wouldn't believe me. Furthermore, I couldn't understand why I was allowed to have such an experience. I sort of felt that only really righteous people, like in the Bible, had experiences such as this."

A Special Blessing

"It wasn't until I was sixteen that I started to understand a few things about the experience. Up to that time I put it behind me; I just shoveled it back into my memory. Then when I was sixteen, I was given the opportunity to have a patriarchal blessing.

"The man who gave me my blessing, Patriarch Harry Vearle Payne, of the Albuquerque, New Mexico East Stake, did not know me. He knew nothing of me, and I had never seen him before in my life. We lived in different cities in the State.

"When he placed his hands on my head and began to give me my blessing, it was as if I were back again on Jesus's lap. I heard the same words that He had told me—the words that detailed what I needed to do with my life. It was an extensive blessing and it included details of how I was to help others.

"As the blessing went on, I began to bawl uncontrollably. It brought everything back from my previous experience. I'm sure, to this day, the Patriarch has no idea why I was crying so hard.

"This blessing helped me understand my experience—and to know for sure that it was real. There is no way that the patriarch could have known what Christ told me when I was seven years old.

"Much later, when I was in my late twenties, I read some books on spiritual manifestations and on the near-death experience, and these books rang bells with me. My experience had many similarities to what I read in the books, even though I don't remember everything that happened when I was out of my body."

Analysis of the Experience

"When you were sitting on Jesus's lap and he told you what you should do with your life, Cynthia, do you remember, explicitly, what some of those things were?" I asked.

"They are all in my patriarchal blessing. An overview would be: to love my brothers and sisters, to help the less fortunate, and to bring joy into the lives of others."

"You served a mission for the LDS church, didn't you?"

"Yes, it was the Columbia, Bogota Mission."

"Do you feel that what you did there was, in part, responsive to what you were told?"

"Very much so. I was serving others, and I was testifying of Jesus Christ—I wanted everyone to know of Him."

"You mentioned that during your experience you sat on Jesus's lap. How did you know it was Jesus?"

"When I was there it just seemed logical. The being was everything that Christ should be. He was an all-knowing, all-powerful personage that . . . I just knew it. I don't know how I knew it."

"Can you describe in more detail what He looked like?"

"He was a handsome man with the most kind face I had ever seen. He had wonderful eyes; they were soft and kind, and . . . I forget the color. There were no time-lines in His face. His face was smooth and kind, with a beard. His hair was white."

"What were his clothes like?"

"I didn't think about His clothes while I was sitting on His lap. I didn't try to analyze what He was wearing, I just knew that I was in an absolutely white room. He seemed to be dressed in an effervescent, Clorox-white, robe which shone."

"And you were in a room?"

"Yes, someone opened a door, and I entered this white room."

"Did you see anything else?"

"Well there was one thing about how I saw me. When I was on his lap it was almost as if I were standing back and seeing myself on his lap. It was like there was a camera taking pictures, and I could review what was going on despite being a part of the picture. I don't know how to explain it other than I was there watching myself sitting on His lap."

"How did your spirit body feel?"

"I felt just like me."

"Did you feel Jesus when you were on His lap?"

"Oh my, yes. I could feel His hands. He had beautiful large hands and broad shoulders. It was the most wonderful thing to be held in His arms."

"Do you remember going through a tunnel when you left your body?"

"No."

"Do you remember coming back?"

"No. I remember seeing my body in the same position when I left and then entering through my head. I was crying again."

"Were you crying, this time, for a different reason than before you left?"

"Yes, I was crying because I didn't want to leave where I was. I wanted to stay with Him. I didn't want to leave that feeling of . . . that emanating power. The feeling that you have when you are with Him, it has no words, no description, but you know that you've been there. The feeling was so warm, and I never wanted to leave."

"What do you mean by warm—was it hot?"

"No, it was all encompassing, it made me feel so loved. He gave me so much love with his gentle hug. I felt so good, and I've never felt that way since. I've longed for a repeat of that feeling."

"Was it your choice to come back?"

"No, I was told I had to come back. I didn't want to."

"Even though you knew the things that you were supposed to do?"

"As a child, I guess I had some rebellion, but I knew I had to come back. The happiness I felt in that love kept me entranced and made it difficult to return.

"There's another thing about coming back, though. After returning to my body, and after having cried for some time about having to return, I again told Christ that I would help my fellow man and do what He had told me. I was wide awake during the entire experience—in fact during the whole night—it was no dream. I remember when daylight came, and I still remember making the commitments to my Savior as if it were last week."

"Do you have a copy of your patriarchal blessing that I could read?"

Cynthia gave me a copy of the blessing. It is too long for inclusion in this chapter, but a few excerpts would be meaningful:

Our Heavenly Father has a work in mind for you, and you covenanted before you came to this world that you would do certain things for the building up of His church and kingdom here upon the earth and for the help and betterment of your departed dead. . . .

. . . you will also be interested in the welfare work of the church. You will be interested in getting into the hearts and lives of other people. . . . You will be a friend to the friendless. Love and charity will be strong in your heart that you may be able to go among those who are less fortunate than you are and lend sunshine to their lives.

Final Thoughts by Cynthia

"I would like people to know that if they ever have an experience like this they shouldn't feel that they are strange. I didn't feel worthy of the experience I had, but for some reason our Heavenly Father granted it.

"People may not feel that they have much worth, or they may not feel loved, but I know that our Heavenly Father loves us. He cares about our aches, pains, sorrows, and even our childish woes.

"Christ's message to me was that I needed to love my fellow beings—all of his children. The experience I had has been a beacon in my life. That beacon has shined for me, since it happened, and it has helped me try to achieve the charity and love spoken of by Him."

Florence Susan Comish

Carol and I first met Susan in 1992 during the preparation of the book *Glimpses of Eternity*. We gave her a draft copy of the book and asked her to read it, select a story from the many stories in the book, and produce an oil painting that would represent the selected story and could be used on the book cover. The result was *Ann's Angel*, a beautiful painting of Ann, a little girl with leukemia whose angel visited her and cured her of the leukemia.

Susan had dark hair and a striking, cultured appearance and a gentle manner of speaking. Her home was a perfect reflection of Susan, with magnificent oil paintings throughout.

Susan was born in 1948 in Salt Lake City, Utah, and she lived in Berkeley, California in her early life. The family moved back to Provo, Utah, where she was raised as an active member of the Church of Jesus Christ of Latter-day Saints.

As a young adult Susan attended Brigham Young University and studied art. She met her husband at the University. At the time of our interview she had five children, three boys and two girls. Her husband was an airline pilot, and Susan devoted her time to her family, her church, and her painting.

One of the rewarding aspects of a visit to Susan's home was to be able to see many paintings of different subjects. She was a professional portrait painter, and her oil paintings of various people were fascinating. Her skill in depicting the character and emotions of the individuals was obvious.

An Interesting Painting

During my initial visit to Susan's house in 1992, when I was exploring the possibility of having Susan prepare a painting for our cover, she showed me a painting she had done some years earlier of a dream. It was a picture of the Savior with a little boy as the focus of the Savior's attention. The painting had an arresting way of directing attention to the two principal characters, even though there were several other characters in the picture.

As Carol and I have continued to interview people for *Echoes From Eternity*, it has become apparent that the Savior plays a more prominent role in many near-death experiences than we had originally supposed, particularly where children are involved. It has also become apparent that dreams can have substantial meaning in a spiritual context. For these reasons, with Susan's permission, we decided to interview her concerning her dream, and to use the picture she painted of her dream as the cover for this book. For the purposes of this book we have entitled the painting: *A Child's Savior*.

Susan's Dream

Susan began to tell us of her dream. "In April of 1983 we were living in Montana; my husband was a counselor in the mission presidency of the Montana Billings Mission, and we enjoyed traveling to the areas of the mission, giving talks, meeting the members and missionaries, and attending conferences. On a particular night I dreamed that I was in Heaven in a large building. My presence in the building was as a spectator, and I watched the Savior as he walked down a hallway followed by many important people such as Peter, James and John, other prophets and apostles. They entered a large room full of people.

"The Savior's back was to me as He moved through the crowd so I didn't see His face—only a profile. He stopped to look at a little boy who was standing in a tattered shirt, and who was somewhat unkempt. I could see the child's face clearly. He was looking up at the Savior, sweetly, and he was completely uninhibited. Wondering at the Savior's full attention on the little boy—despite all the seemingly *important* people who were there—I came to understand the great love the Savior had for a child which would have been completely unnoticed by the world."

Questions About Susan's Dream

"Did you have any special feelings during the dream, Susan?"

"Yes, the feeling of love from the Savior, that He cares for each of us, and we don't comprehend just how important we are to him individually."

"Did you see any landscaping or other features of the surroundings in your dream?"

"No. We were in a large building. Everything was white, and everyone was dressed in white. There were no furnishings of any kind—only a spacious building full of people."

"That's interesting. In your painting you showed landscape features such as a tree and clouds. Why did you change it from your dream?"

Susan laughed. "That's known as artistic license. To an artist, color is everything. I wanted to capture the Savior's attention to the little boy—especially the uninhibited confidence and natural sweetness that only a child could have in meeting the Savior. The background and color are there to complement and add interest to the painting."

"Was the dream significant to you?"

"Yes, it was very special to me. I wanted to portray the dream on canvas and share it with others."

Chapter 3

NEW BEGINNINGS

Barry E. Kirk

I had arranged to meet Barry Kirk, on August 7, 1992, at his office in the Family History Library in Salt Lake City. Barry was a tall, dark-haired young man with a gentle speaking manner. He smiled as I walked in, and he ushered me into a conference room where we conducted our interview.

Barry was born in 1949 in Vancouver, British Columbia, Canada. When he was eleven years old, his family joined The Church of Jesus Christ of Latter-day Saints. He does not remember much of his early youth for reasons that will be explained shortly. His high school education emphasized five sciences, and his university education emphasized French, Gerontology, Religion, and later Genealogy. While he was serving a mission for the LDS Church to France and Belgium, from 1969 to 1971, his father died.

Barry has one brother and two sisters. At the time of our interview he was married, had been blessed with five children, and his wife was expecting their sixth.

A Bad Accident

Barry began to tell his story: "In 1972, I was the Stake Young Adult Leader in the Vancouver, British Columbia Stake. In July of that year, just before my twenty-third birthday, we held a Regional Young Adult activity on Whitbey Island in Washington State. I took time off from my summer job at Wells Grey Park to attend. I drove from my work (100 miles north of Kamloops, which is 250 miles northeast of Vancouver), picked up some

38

friends in Kamloops, picked up my fiancée in Vancouver, and drove to the activity.

"Arriving late Friday night (7 July), I stayed in a tent with some friends. Saturday morning, after a long conversation, my fiancée and I broke up. That afternoon, even though I was feeling gloomy about the breakup, I participated in a pre-arranged football game. It was the 'touch' variety and was supposed to be no-contact, but it didn't turn out that way. My friend and I both went out to catch a pass and we collided—his knee hit me in the head.

"We didn't have helmets, of course, and I didn't think anything of it. Having been hit in the head many times before during athletics, I did not think it was that serious.

"Even though I was a little woozy, some other friends wanted me to join in a baseball game, so I did. The losing team asked me to pitch, and we won! But, the wooziness continued. It seemed to me that I was just tired from not enough sleep, so I went to a dance that night and to a church meeting the next morning. After the church meeting, I drove my ex-fiancée to Vancouver and my friends to Kamloops.

"After dropping off my friends at Kamloops, I drove by myself for the remaining 100 miles to Wells Grey Park, where I was working for the summer building new campsites. As I drove the final 100 miles, I had to keep stopping—my dizziness kept getting worse. I still thought my problem was lack of sleep from the weekend.

"My work was to begin at 6:00 a.m., and I finally arrived at the campsite at 5:45 a.m. My boss looked at me; I must have looked terrible, because he told me to go lie down and rest.

"I lay down and rested, and he looked in on me after a while. He decided I needed to have a doctor examine me, so they drove me back to Kamloops to the Royal Inland Hospital. There, hospital personnel took tests and X-rays which revealed that I had a blood clot on the brain.

"The blood clot seemed to be lessening, and the doctors thought I would improve in a few days; instead, I kept getting worse. They took more tests, including an angiogram, which showed that I had a tumor (or cyst) in the left side of my head that had ruptured when my head was hit during the football game.

"The ruptured tumor/cyst, together with the blood clot, was causing the pressure on my brain. They scheduled me for an operation on the following day, and I called my mother in Vancouver to let her know what was happening. She had not known, yet, that I was even in the hospital. I told her I would call her again on the following day after the operation. Because of what happened to me during the operation, I was not able to follow-through with the promised phone call to my mother."

Lost Memory, a Tunnel, and a White Light

"The operation was performed on July 26th, and, unfortunately, the tumor/cyst apparently ruptured again during the operation, destroying the memory cells on the left side of my brain. For the following four days, after the operation, it was touch and go whether or not I would make it.

"My mother phoned and found out what had happened. She came to the hospital and brought the branch president from the LDS Church at Kamloops, and he gave me a blessing on July 30th.

"Sometime between the 26th and 30th of July I had my experience. I was lying there in bed, and suddenly I was looking down on myself. As I looked down, I asked myself: *Is this for real?*

"While I was lying in the hospital bed I did not have my glasses on, and I normally cannot see well without glasses; in fact, I am almost totally blind without them. But I could see myself with perfect vision—from a point that seemed to be about twenty feet above my body.

"It seemed that I had gone in and out of my body several times. Then I saw this darkness; I felt as though I were traveling through the darkness in . . . in sort of a tunnel. Then there was . . . it was a yellow warmth which enveloped me. And I felt an unbelievable peace. It seemed to be a long time, and yet it probably was not a long time—I do not know how long it was.

"There was a peace I have never experienced since, except one time in the temple (in the Celestial room of the Salt Lake Temple). It was an unforgettable peace.

"That is about all I have been allowed to remember. But my mother told me later, after the blessing, that I talked about seeing my uncles who had passed on in the 1950s. That is about all I remember, though. I think one reason I may not remember very much, besides the damage to my brain cells, is because I would have wanted to stay there in that wonderful peace if I had remembered more."

A Twenty-three-year-old Baby

"When I returned, I was like a newborn baby in a twenty-three-year-old body. I could hardly make a vocal sound. I could not write, I could not read, I could not walk. My mother had to show me things a few times. But once my brain understood what it had once known it could do that function again; it was similar to a computer that had lost data and then had it restored. So, for example, when Mother showed me how to use a spoon she only had to do that once.

"The doctors told me that it would be four to six months before I could leave the hospital. Actually, after the blessing I was in the hospital for only fourteen more days. The total stay was five weeks.

"The doctors also told my mother that it would be four to six years before I would be back to a first grade level in education. Instead, I was back in the university in four months, and I realized a 3.21-GPA for that semester and did better later. I am convinced those abilities were restored through the power of the Priesthood—in the blessing."

Analysis of Barry's Experience

"Let me ask a few questions, Barry, concerning your experience. First, was the tumor/cyst which they removed malignant or non-malignant?"

"It was non-malignant. It turned out that I had been born with it. In a sense it was a blessing in disguise—that it happened the way it did rather than have it rupture while I was driving, for example."

"What was your feeling when you left your body and saw yourself?"

"I kept asking myself: *What's happening? What's going on here? Why are the medics over me?* It was almost like a dream in which I was looking at somebody, yet I could see myself lying there. I could recognize myself. The real me was way up near the ceiling—I was almost 'touching' the roof."

"Did you have any emotional attachment to the body lying beneath you?"

"I don't think so. In one sense I was relieved—I was fascinated by the aspects of the newness of the experience."

"How did your spirit body feel when you were out of your physical body?"

"It felt very versatile. At first I did not understand how easy it was to get around. Going back and forth, or 'traveling,' was so easy."

"Did you feel as if you did have a body with arms and legs?"

"Yes, I felt that there was something there. And it was versatile and elastic, with no pain."

"Could you see other people around your spirit body?"

"I do not remember seeing any person other than me. As I said, though, my mother told me that I kept talking about seeing my deceased uncles, but I don't remember that now."

"After you saw your body lying there, you said that you then went through this tunnel-like thing. Can you describe it?"

"After being above myself in the hospital room, suddenly it seemed to go dark. I felt sort of enclosed. I never thought of it as a tunnel until I heard Dr. Moody, in a talk at BYU, express it that way. It seemed a reasonable description of what I saw."

"You say it felt somewhat confined, though?"

"Yes, particularly as I went through it. It got more confining as I traveled—the walls got closer and closer. Not that I was touching anything, it just got closer. Almost as though it were a sticky day with high humidity. And through this experience I felt as though I were going somewhere even though I could not see much.

"Then everything seemed to stop, and this warmth enveloped me. It was a light of warmth. I cannot really describe it. It was a yellow color, but . . . but it was not really yellow, it was white-yellow; it was bright. And the peace! It felt as though everything were okay."

"Why did you use the word, *warm*? Was it hot?"

"It was not hot. It was pleasant-warm. Words do not really describe how it was."

"Why did you use the word, *peace*?"

"Because it felt as though all my concerns, all my pains, all my worries had left. A whole load had been taken off my shoulders. It was a relaxing feeling—as if someone cared. I did not feel alone; I felt as though someone were there who cared."

"Did you have a feeling of having a choice about returning to this life?"

"I do not remember."

"The next thing you remember was being back in your body. Do you remember entering it?"

"No. I remember opening my eyes, being back in the hospital room, and feeling pain again."

"Did you tell anyone about your experience when you came back?"

"Yes. When I got out of the hospital I was still very limited with speech, but I was excited about what I remembered of the experience; similar to a child who receives a new special toy. I wanted others to know about it, so I told my mother; and at first I told many others also. Then I found that many did not believe what I was telling them—some of them even scoffed at me. So I stopped telling the story except in special circumstances."

"How has your life changed as a result of your experience?"

"Well, of course, there is the problem of my early memory loss. In addition to that, though, I feel that I have been given bonus time (i.e. extra years of life). Because of that I often feel driven to make the most of each hour. Sleeping for eight hours in a night is difficult, for example. Usually I get by on six hours of sleep, or less. I also have a difficult time relaxing."

A Final Message—Importance of Personal Histories

"We never know when the time is for us to leave, so we had better keep our lives in order. From a personal point of view I feel that it is vital for us to keep a journal of our lives. I did not keep one very well before my accident, but where I did, such as on my mission, it helped me to reconstruct my memory. Other than my missionary journal and a one year diary in 1966, I had to rebuild my memory by interviewing people and having them tell me about my life.

"There is also an urgency, I believe, to build a genealogical history of our ancestors. In 1974, I became hooked on genealogy when I first found the marriage date of my great-grandparents. Now, as result of that interest and my academic pursuits, I work full-time in the Family History Library in Salt Lake City.

"So, my challenge to others is to ask themselves the question: if their memory were to be taken from them, without warning, what evidence would they have to describe who they were and what they had done? A record of their life experiences, no matter how simple, would be important to them and to their posterity."

Vern G. Swanson

Vern Swanson was the enthusiastic Director of the Springville, Utah, Museum of Art whom Carol and I met when we delivered a painting to the museum. The painting was *Ann's Angel* by Florence Susan Comish, and it was painted to depict an event described in the book *Glimpses of Eternity* in which an angel visited a little girl afflicted with leukemia. As we described the story to Vern he seemed curiously affected. He commented that he was interested in angels because of an experience he had undergone some years earlier.

I made arrangements to return later in the week to hear Vern's experience. As we began the interview Vern explained that he was born February 4, 1945, in the small town of Central Point, Oregon. He was the youngest of six children. His father worked in the lumber industry, and his mother worked as a seamstress and baked wedding cakes. Vern was athletically inclined during his youth, achieving "All-State" status in football.

The adults in the Swanson family were not associated with any religion. Vern's father was an atheist, and his mother was not religiously inclined. His brother, though, was active with Vern in the Pilgrim Holiness Church, a derivative of the Quaker Church. One sister was active in the Church of the Nazarene. When Vern was fourteen years old he met the Mormon Elders, and he, his brother Mike, and his sister Cherry joined the Church of Jesus Christ of Latter-day Saints. He has remained active in the church since that time.

From 1964 to 1969 Vern attended Brigham Young University on a football scholarship, and it was there that he met a Canadian girl named Elaine. He married her in 1970 in the Cardston, Canada, Temple, and they had a baby boy in 1972.

Vern majored in art at BYU and achieved his master's degree in art history at the University of Utah. After getting his master's degree he obtained the position of Assistant Professor of Art History at Auburn University in Alabama. In the fall of 1973 Vern moved to Alabama where he and his wife became the house parents for the Sigma Chi fraternity. In this capacity they helped supervise the young men of the fraternity.

A Tragic Trip

Vern began his story. "In April 1975, Elaine's brother, Gordon, was getting married in the Cardston Temple. My wife and another girl from our church branch drove, with our baby son, to Cardston, Canada. I was teaching school so I couldn't go with them.

"After the wedding, Elaine and her sister Robin with my son, Brett, began to drive south from Cardston toward Salt Lake City. They reached a place called Choteau, Montana, and they found themselves in a blizzard. As they were driving in this blizzard they collided head on with another car.

"The crash killed the lady in the other car and my wife. My sister-in-law was holding my baby son, and that probably saved her life, but my son died.

"About 11:00 a.m. my two home teachers from the church branch came to my office at the university. They walked in, and as I looked at them I knew exactly what had happened. Brother Hatch returned my gaze and said: 'Your wife and son have been killed in a car wreck.'

"I stood there for a moment, not moving, stripped of all thought as the enormity of what he had said penetrated my mind. I said: 'What do we do?' They told me that they would make arrangements to get me on a plane. I informed the Dean of the College and left work. The church branch was wonderful in helping me to make arrangements to leave for Montana.

"In Montana I visited with my sister-in-law Robin, in the hospital, and I saw the demolished car. Then I drove with my two sisters and my mother to Calgary, Canada, where the funeral was to take place.

"Up to this point I was running on adrenalin and I was doing well. My in-laws, though grieving themselves, had made good plans for the funeral and they did their best to prepare me for it. Because Elaine and Brett had been severely injured in the accident my in-laws prevailed upon me not to view the bodies. They told me that they wished that they had not done so themselves.

"At the funeral there was a single casket. Our son, John Brett, was two-and-one-half years old, and he was placed with my wife in the casket. As the funeral progressed, therefore, I only saw one casket, and it was not opened.

"It was a beautiful funeral, and when it was over I returned to Auburn. I resumed my teaching duties for the remainder of the school year. As the adrenalin wore off I had the normal relapse associated with grief, but then I recovered and took up my usual activities."

Problems of Severe Melancholy

"Our son had been such a delightful child, always laughing and singing, that I found myself often thinking of him. When my wife and son were alive and coeds would visit the boys at Sigma Chi, they would frequently wind up playing with our son instead of visiting with their dates. Brett was the life of every party.

"My wife was in her mid-twenties at the time of her death. Her loss was tragic, and I felt it sorely, but she had at least seen some measure of life with school, earning her Master's degree, marriage and a child. Our charming son, though, had no chance to experience much in life except for being born and then dying. This bothered me—more and more as time passed.

"Grieving almost continuously, I became morose, which was not like my normal nature, and I suffered severely. I didn't sleep or eat well, and I could tell that I was sinking into an unhealthy pattern, but I didn't seem to be able to control it.

"My teaching skills suffered as I struggled through the rest of the teaching semester. By the end of the summer, after the end of the semester, I was really going downhill. Others observed this, and I remember one student bringing me a small dog in an attempt to cheer me up. I couldn't bring myself to take the pet; I didn't want to be comforted. I was wallowing in my grief for Brett—and for myself.

"Intellectually, I knew that Brett was dead, but emotionally I couldn't accept his death—I hadn't actually seen him dead, nor had I seen a small coffin for him. I brooded on this, and it affected me in a very adverse way."

A Beautiful Visitor

"One night, about six months after Elaine and our son had died, I was lying restlessly in bed. Suddenly I looked up and I saw a light. Standing there in the light was my wife.

"As I remember, it seems as if I were instantly out of bed—just thuung! . . . and I was up next to her. It was the most interesting situation you could imagine, because she looked exactly like Elaine, yet she didn't. It's hard to explain.

"My wife, the woman, the angel in front of me was so peaceful, so beautiful. There was a light that came from within her so that she glowed. It wasn't reflected light; it was almost as if there were a bright candle inside of her.

"I had always thought that Grace Kelly, the movie star, was the most beautiful woman in the world. Elaine, standing before me, would have put Grace Kelly to shame. She was very white with that inner glow, and she was absolutely the most beautiful person I had ever seen. To this day I can remember how she looked, and I marvel at what I saw. Elaine, in life, was a good-looking woman, working as a model during college, but her earthly body was a poor shadow, an impoverished copy, when compared with that beautiful person before me—yet it *was* Elaine.

"As she stood before me I began to embrace and kiss her; I smothered her with kisses. When I touched Elaine, I was filled with joy from her white radiance—not a cold white, but a warm white.

"Then I looked down and I saw my son. Elaine was holding Brett in her arms. When I touched my son it was as if I had touched something that had been frozen, similar to cold clay. He looked dead.

"I kissed my son, and he felt cold and dead. Elaine sternly said: 'Vern, he is dead.' And I said: 'No, no, it can't be,' and I kissed him again. Elaine repeated a second time that he was dead.

"During this episode Elaine was very serious. She was most dedicated to delivering a message. There was no funny business about her; rather she seemed intent solely on the message. I kept telling her no, and I was crying.

"Repeating the message that he couldn't be dead, I said things like: 'No, no, he's okay. He'll be okay.' And I was crying.

"Then she said the third time, very emphatically: 'Vern, he is dead.'

"By the third time, similar to hitting a boxer with a one-two-three punch, it penetrated and I understood. I still didn't want to accept it, but I knew it was true.

"After Elaine said it the third time she disappeared, and I found myself sitting up in bed crying and sobbing. In my sobs I cried out: 'No, no, no.'

"As I heard myself I recognized that I was very loud, and the sound must be penetrating the thin walls that separated my room from the rest of the fraternity. The sun was out, it was breakfast time, so the fraternity boys were in the cafeteria next to my room.

"Usually the fraternity boys were noisy at breakfast, but this morning they weren't making a sound. They had heard me crying out."

Some Aftereffects

"This singular event caused me to ponder about it for some time. I am not a very revelatory person; I am got given to having epiphanies. Nothing like this had happened to me prior to the event, nor has anything like it happened since. And I remember it as though it were yesterday.

"I shall never forget what I regard as a personal revelation that was tailored to meet my needs. There probably is no other way it could have happened and still have had the same effect.

"From that moment on I ceased grieving about our son, Brett. Knowing that he was with Elaine, I understood that he would be taken care of—and Elaine was fine. I realized after that event that my son was gone, and that I was alive and I had to resume living. That very day my appetite for life returned.

"People noticed the difference in me and told me how fine I looked. Some of them asked me what had happened in my life to restore me to such vigor. I only told a few people about the event.

"In 1976 I met my present wife, Judy, and we were married in the Manti Temple. We have two girls who are now eleven and fourteen years old. Judy and our children are very close to Elaine's family. They visit us in Utah, and we visit them in Canada. They consider our children in Utah to be their grandchildren."

Questions about Vern's Experience

Vern paused at this point and I began to ask him some questions about the event. "Do you remember how your wife was dressed, Vern?"

"White."

"What do you mean, white?"

"This all occurred in my room, and I can just remember that she was dressed in white. I don't remember the type of garment she was wearing."

"How was her hair?"

"It was as it was in life. Her face was a little different from life, and it glowed. She was standing about twenty feet from my bed, and she was facing sideways. I had to travel to her in order to embrace her."

"How did she communicate? Was it by voice?"

"I don't remember her lips moving, but I remember her words being very solid and penetrating. She was very officious . . . but not mean. It was extremely forceful and it hit me in the heart. I really wasn't concentrating on watching her lips, though, since I was either kissing her or kissing Brett."

"Could you feel her?"

"Yes, just as normal. She was warm, and Brett was cold."

"Did it seem as a real experience, or more like a dream?"

"It was not a dream, it was absolutely real—more real than you and I sitting here. It was an astonishing event and it was charged. I was awed."

"You mentioned that before the event you had been very morose. Had you prayed to receive help?"

"Yes, I had. I prayed to know about eternity, and that I would feel better. Having been extremely active in the LDS Church, I read a great deal—from the scriptures and from religious writings."

"What were the circumstances that led you to meet your present wife?"

"I taught a third year at Auburn through the '74-'75 school year, and then I decided to go back for the summer to BYU—hopefully to find a wife. I made a lousy bachelor.

"At BYU I went to a special interest dance, and I saw a lovely girl that I wanted to meet. She was with another fellow though, and I had about given up when he walked her to the edge of the dance floor. I jumped at the chance and quickly asked her to dance. That dance led to marriage six months later."

Chapter 4

MULTIPLE EXPERIENCES

Julie

She came to our home to be interviewed on a beautiful fall day in September 1992. Carol and I had known Julie for several years. We were unaware, however, that she had experienced an NDE. After reading the book *Glimpses of Eternity* she told us that she had undergone several experiences that we might be interested in.

Julie is a slight, exuberant lady with dark hair and smiling eyes, and with a large zest for life. She was born in Ogden, Utah in 1950. She was the youngest, and only girl, of a family of five children. Her parents were members of The Church of Jesus Christ of Latter-day Saints, but they were not active. When she was fourteen years old, Julie became active in the Church after a challenge by her brother, Lloyd.

Julie graduated from Weber College where, on a ski trip, she met Steve whom she married in 1971. They have four children.

Visit by a Deceased Vietnam Soldier

Julie began to tell her story. "When I was seventeen years old, in January 1968, we were living in North Ogden. My mother and I had visited my sister-in-law over the holidays, and we had all viewed some slides of my brother, Dale, who was a fighter pilot in Vietnam. The war was on my mind as a result of seeing the slides.

"We returned to Ogden by train, and after I went to bed one night I started dreaming about the slides. And then, suddenly, I . . ." Julie's discourse was interrupted by her tears. After a moment she continued: "Then, I left my bedroom—it was no longer a dream. I was standing,

50

in my nightgown, in the doorway of our kitchen. I was drawn to the kitchen because it was full of light, a bright golden light. It's not something I can describe; it was very bright, but it didn't hurt my eyes.

"The thing I remember was that all of the burdens, all of the troubles, all of the cares, all of the concerns of this world were gone. There was just this . . . this overwhelming love. It was a breathtaking feeling of love with full acceptance. And yet, through it all, I was still me, and I was embarrassed.

"The reason I was embarrassed, aside from the fact that I was seventeen and easily embarrassed, was that I was in my nightgown and someone else was in the room. It was my cousin, Allen, and he was standing across the room by the telephone. I hadn't been thinking about him, although he too, was in Vietnam.

"It surprised me. He was in army fatigues and boots, and he was leaning against the kitchen counter with his head down. I said to him: 'Allen, what are you doing here?'

"He looked at me, and he talked to me without moving his lips. I thought that was really strange, and at first I did not understand. He repeated: 'I have come home.'

"I asked him what it meant that he had come home. I didn't understand what he meant. And then there was something inside me that . . . it was a feeling that I had to hug him.

"Now you should know that we were not that close. Allen was only a second cousin. His mother had been raised by my parents. He was somewhat older, and we had not been the hugging types. It surprised me, then, when I just ran to hug him. I remember distinctly feeling his body when I hugged him—and I was still embarrassed because I was in my nightgown.

"My feelings were confusing, and I didn't understand what he was telling me. When I asked him, again, what he meant, he repeated: 'I've come home.'"

Instructions About a Wonderful Place

"I stopped concentrating on Allen for a moment, and I looked around the kitchen. But it wasn't really the kitchen, it was just this light. Where the kitchen doorway should have been there was another person. It was another man. I don't remember how he was dressed or very much about him. I remember his face and his eyes; he had dark hair. His age appeared to be about nineteen or twenty. He was not standing directly in the light—he was in this tunnel, or darkness.

"We all stood there for a while, and somehow—and this is the part where there is a gap—I seem to remember picking up our conversation after it was mostly over. During the conversation I was giving Allen instruction, but I don't remember what the instruction was about.

"When I was through, and I was standing away from Allen, he had his head down, and he was sad. Or maybe I just assumed he was sad, but he wasn't the Allen that I grew up with—always the tease. He used to throw watermelons at me and things like that. Instead, as I saw him there, he was very serious and he had his head down.

"I said to him: 'Allen, this is wonderful.' That's where I remember the conversation picking up. I stood there, and Allen turned and looked at this other man, and I could hear him think: 'It's time to go, isn't it?'

"The other fellow, who was Allen's escort, said: 'Yes.'

"I then said to Allen: 'Now, Allen, remember everything I've told you. It's true. You are going to a place where there is no time. We will all be together again, and I want you to be happy. This is wonderful.'

"The joy that filled me at that time was overcoming. I was jumping up and down with ecstacy, urging him to be happy. I told him to pay attention to what I was saying and to learn. My words were words of encouragement.

"In an ecstasy of joy, I understood that I could not go with Allen. Deep inside me, I knew that I had to stay where I was, in the light. I stood as if in a line, practically, in the light, and watched them. At first the other fellow turned, and then Allen followed him; I watched them go while I was still jumping up and down—and telling him that I loved him.

"The last thing I remember, as I watched them move into the darkness, or tunnel, was Allen raising his head and looking at me. Hopping up and down, I tried to encourage him as they moved into the tunnel. Then they were gone."

Aftermath

"The next thing I knew I was back in my bed. It was about five o'clock in the morning and I woke up, or something. I thought to myself: *What has happened?* and I started yelling for my Mom. We were the only ones in the house; my Dad worked the night shift.

"My Mom came, and she must have understood that I had had some sort of experience, because she yelled at me: 'Is it Dale?' Later, she said that she didn't know why she yelled that message. Anyway, I responded: 'No, it was Allen.' As I began to tell her the story I felt completely exhausted, physically and emotionally; I could hardly move.

"Mom started to cry, and I told her the rest of what I had experienced. Then I went back to bed for the entire day. The experience had completely drained me.

"Mom immediately started calling my brothers; and she called Phyllis, Allen's mother; and she told them what had happened. Neither Phyllis nor Allen had been active, although they were members, in the LDS Church.

"Then, I'll never forget, there were five days, or maybe a week that went by and nothing happened. Not a word. By then I was starting to get teased by my brothers. They would say things like: 'Hey, Julie, have you had any more experiences you can tell us about?' They were really giving me a bad time.

"My brothers continued to find humor in the situation, and because of that, I began to doubt what had happened to me. Also, I still wasn't sure what Allen meant by the phrase: 'I've come home.' I thought maybe it meant that he would be coming back from Vietnam; he only had a couple of months and his time would be up.

"I was very uncomfortable about the situation and I wished that my mother had never told anyone. I also wished that I hadn't told my mother about it.

"Finally, after about a week, two military officers showed up at my cousin Phyllis's house and told her that Allen was missing in action. He and another fellow had been sent ahead to go through the jungle first, as scouts to look for snipers, and they had not returned. They dated the incident of his disappearance to when I had undergone the experience.

"After the officers visited Phyllis I had to repeat over and over what I had seen. Nobody could quite analyze what it meant.

"In about another week they found Allen's body. They shipped him home, and he was buried here.

"The feeling that I took away from that experience was that we really know a lot more than we realize. There truly is a veil over our minds."

A View of a Previous Existence

"The next experience I had was even more strange than the one I just told you about. I was about nineteen years old when it happened, and I was in college. It was in the middle of the afternoon, and my mind was occupied with studies.

"I had come home from school, Weber State, and I found that my Dad was home. He usually was at work in the afternoon, and I was a little surprised. We talked for a few minutes, and then he resumed watching TV.

"Sitting on the sofa, I leaned my head back and closed my eyes. I could hear the TV in the background and was aware of the presence of my Dad. And then . . . I don't know how to describe this.

"Suddenly I had a remembrance—that's all I can tell you—just a remembrance. I could see it as a scene, yet it was a memory of something that had happened before.

"I was in a long white dress, and I came through some large double doors, wooden and beautifully carved, into a large room. Chairs were arranged auditorium style on either side of the room. The chairs were empty when I came in. I went down a center aisle to . . . it's so hard to describe this.

"The room was like an amphitheater; it was slanted down. At the front of the room there was something that looked to be a table or an altar. As I looked at the front of the room I saw three men dressed in white.

"I knew where I was supposed to sit, and I came down the center aisle and sat on the left side, in toward the middle of the seats. All the chairs were padded, and they were hooked together.

"I remember looking at my hands on my lap, and . . . . It wasn't as though I were watching a movie, it was a memory as though I were feeling it while I was in that body. And my mind, being nineteen years old, questioned some of the things I saw. Yet it was *I*, and the thing that surprised me was my composure. I had the same personality that I had in this life—except it was significantly more mature; much more dignified and self assured than the nineteen-year-old that I was.

"Looking at my hands, I wondered why they seemed so small. Then I remember thinking: *It is going to be so strange to go to earth and forget home. I can't comprehend that. I understand exactly what I'm getting into and what I have to do. But I cannot comprehend forgetting home. Please let me remember this experience and this room.*

"When the double doors to the room would close, I knew that I would not remember what was behind those two doors—a veil would be placed over my mind. But I wanted to remember this room, and I studied it very carefully. That's what I remember.

"The three men at the front of the room, I understood to be in complete control of when I was to go through. When my time came I would know it, and I would move down the aisle and go through the white curtains that were across the front.

"The three men were reverently whispering, but I didn't pay any attention to what they were saying. I was studying the room—I did not want to forget it. Drapes were over the windows, and the ceiling was very tall.

"It seemed strange to be getting ready to go to earth. And when I thought about earth, it was as if I could see through the walls of the room and see the earth suspended out in space. I was not afraid, I just didn't want to forget.

"Then . . . it was as if a bolt of electricity went through my body. Just like that—a snap of the fingers. It was a jolt, and I felt my body jerk with the electricity. And I realized that I was on the sofa. My Dad was there and the TV was still on. I didn't know how long the experience had been. I was astonished.

"For many years I didn't tell anyone about this experience. I finally told Steve after we were married in the Salt Lake Temple—one of the rooms in the Salt Lake Temple was the closest to what I had seen, yet it was different. Before I went through the temple I did not know that there would be similarities to what I saw in the memory experience."

Dreams and Precognition Experiences

"There is another thing you might be interested in. I tend to dream about events, or I am warned about things before they happen."

"Can you remember any instances?" I asked Julie.

She laughed. "It's more like which one would you like to hear? They happen all the time."

"Do you tell people about your dreams?"

"I tell Steve every morning when they happen. Even my children will ask: 'Mom, have you had any dreams?'"

"Can you tell us about one where the circumstances are verifiable? By verifiable I mean that you told others of the dream, and then the events in the dream happened—and others witnessed the fulfillment of the dream."

"I'll tell you of one that was dramatic. Before I do, you should understand that I have different kinds of dreams. In one type of dream the events are symbolic, and in the other they are more realistic. Also, when the dreams are about something that's going to happen I know it by the feeling I get when I wake up. I have other dreams that are just dreams—they don't mean anything. In those non-meaningful dreams I don't get the same feeling as I do about the ones that are predictive in nature.

"When the dreams are symbolic, about 85% of the time they have to do with my own health, my children, or someone else close to me. They are about something we are going to have to go through, and I'm not going to be able to change anything—but I am prepared for it. I also know approximately how long the situation is going to last. In many instances, in the symbolic dreams, I don't know specifically which individual is going to be involved, I just know that it will be a grandparent, for example, or a child, but I don't know which one.

"One dream, which happened two years ago in November, an event happened that was sufficiently dramatic that I later recorded it on my computer. I dreamed that a lady came, and she seemed to be a lady with authority, and she put her arm around me. Then she explained to me that when someone's life is spared it is because that person still has a special mission to perform in this life. She repeated the message three times. As she delivered this message I saw men standing behind her who seemed to be Authorities. In my mind I remember thinking: *I cannot forget what I have been told. This is very important. These men are here to let me know that this was important and comes from someone having authority.*

"Knowing that the dream was meaningful, I was upset when I awoke—I knew that someone I loved would come close to dying. I also knew that he would make it through, because he still had a mission to perform. The decision for the individual to continue to live, I knew, would be made by 'General Authorities,' or someone in authority on the other side.

"Not knowing who it was, though, nor what the event would be, I was concerned. I woke Steve and told him about the dream. We were both frightened. I knew it was going to be someone in the family who was male, and I was afraid it might be Steve.

"The feeling of urgency stayed with me. We became so alarmed that we scheduled an early date to the temple to see if we could learn who it was. Sometimes when I get a dream of this nature I have repeats of the dream on succeeding nights for as long as three months. I didn't want to have to go through that ordeal.

"Within a couple of days we went to the temple, and we both prayed through most of the temple session to know who the dream was about. After the session we asked each other if the other individual knew who it was. Neither of us knew, but we both had the feeling that it wasn't Steve."

An Airplane Crash

"As we drove up to the house after the temple session, Sharee, my daughter, came running out shouting at us. She said that my brother, Ray, had been in an airplane crash. He had been life-flighted into the University of Utah Hospital.

"There were three of them in a small plane. They had been flying toward some property that he owns near Kamas, Utah, when the plane crashed. Ray was the most seriously injured.

"Ray's face took much of the impact and his head swelled enormously. One of his legs was nearly severed, and he had third degree burns where the engine, which came into the cabin, had burned him.

"They had crashed on a mountain in a group of Quakies, which softened the crash. It was in November, and cold. My brother's secretary, who was one of the three in the plane, was the least injured. She wandered around for a period until she found a farmhouse. The secretary reported that my brother was dead.

"They got help after some hours. When we got to the hospital they were sewing Ray together, and they didn't expect him to live. I told my sister-in-law and other relatives there that he would live, and I told them how I knew.

"Ray is about sixty years of age. He had nine pieces of steel put into his leg in order to attach the top and bottom parts of the leg. But he recovered and is today doing very well."

A Concept of Previous Knowledge and No Time

After Julie completed telling of the experiences I suggested that she respond to a few questions about each one. I began: "In the first experience, Julie, you said that you were teaching Allen. What were you teaching him?"

"I don't know. That's when there is a gap in my memory. I know that at the end I was telling him that where he was going was wonderful, and I assume therefore, that I was instructing him about where he was going and what he was to do there."

"And you felt that you knew those things yourself?"

"Yes."

"How did you know of them?"

"I had not been taught those kinds of things in detail. But I seemed to have a knowledge within me."

"Could it have been knowledge you had learned in church or from your parents?"

"No. I didn't learn it at home. And I had only become really active in church a couple of years before that. I had a general knowledge about the gospel, but not anything like what I seemed to be telling Allen. I don't remember specifically what it was, because the memory of what I said was taken from me, but I know that whatever it was the knowledge came from inside me."

"Why did you tell Allen there would be no time where he was going?"

"I don't know. As he walked away, I remember saying: 'You realize, Allen, there is no time there.' I was trying to point out that where he was going it would seem essentially no time and we would be with him again. The interesting thing about my comment is that I had no previous knowledge from this life of any such concept."

"What was Allen's reaction to all this?"

"He just listened very intently. He was very solemn, not the Allen that I remembered as a kid, but much more serious. As I talked, he listened with an extremely serious demeanor."

"When you first found yourself in the kitchen, did it seem real or more like a dream?"

"No, it was very real. It was just as real as everyday life."

"Tell me a little more about the light."

"I guess why it's so hard to talk about the light is . . . ," Julie paused to wipe away tears, "because it makes me homesick."

"Is that because you have known it before?"

"Yes. When I was in the light it felt natural—as if I were home."

Impact of Experiences on Her Life

"How have these experiences affected your life?"

"I absolutely know that there is a life after death, and I have no fear of death."

"Let me quiz you about that. Many folks who have had experiences such as yours say they have no fear of death. What about the pain of getting there, though? Do you have fear of that?"

"I've had a lot of illness, and pain associated with those illnesses, but my faith is I'm not going to worry about that. As far as death is concerned there is no fear. I'm as sure that there is life after death as I am of anything. Many other things I'm not sure about, but not life after death. I look forward to being able to go home to that light. This life isn't home—that's home!"

"Have the experiences changed your religious beliefs?"

"I have always known that the Church was true. I prayed a lot as a child; even all night long. The experiences, therefore, did not change my opinion about anything. They just gave further evidence of things that I already knew. There were certain ideas, though, which were brought into a different perspective by the experiences—the idea of where our real home is, for example. The experiences also gave me a desire to study more.

"There is one negative aspect of the experiences. I don't like the idea of being able to see the future, even dimly. In many instances the dreams of the future which I get are more traumatic than actually going through the events. For a long time I prayed that I wouldn't have the dreams."

Other Knowledge from the Experiences

"There were two personal bits of knowledge that I took away from the experience with Allen. The first bit of knowledge, which I got in the light, was of the lack of worry on the other side. We carry so many concerns and worries on this side—many that we are only partially conscious of—in the light there is none of that. There was no worry, no sorrow, no pain; all that was gone. It was like being in perfect understanding, perfect knowledge, perfect love, perfect acceptance.

"The second bit of knowledge was the feeling—still within me—of remembering the sensation: *This is reality. This is really how it is. The other experience, life on earth, is just something we have to go through, but this is truly reality.*

"From the memory experience I took away other bits of knowledge. First, of course, was the sure knowledge that I lived before. (Actually, the feelings while in the light during the experience with Allen also gave me that knowledge). The other bit of knowledge, though, was that things are very organized on the other side. People are given assignments, just as they are here in the Church, and there is the Priesthood. I knew, for example, that the three men at the front of the room in white had the authority to say when I was to come. People work very hard, indeed, on the other side."

Interview with Julie's Mother

After interviewing Julie, I talked to her mother, Verlie, on the telephone concerning Julie's experience. Her mother's memory of the event was slightly different. She recalls that during the night when Julie saw Allen, Verlie had been having a horrible dream that something terrible was going to happen. Terrified by the dream, she awakened, jumped out of bed, and went into the kitchen.

Julie entered the kitchen shortly thereafter and Verlie could tell that something was wrong. She asked Julie if it was her brother, Dale, and Julie responded: "No. It was Allen."

As Verlie remembers the incident it was only about two days when they got the telegram stating that Allen was missing in action. Then it was another week after that when they found Allen's body in Vietnam. She also remembers the timing of Allen's appearance to Julie as being coincident with when the military later said he was killed.

Chapter 5

AN EXTENSIVE EXPERIENCE

Elane Durham

It was at a local meeting of the International Association for Near Death Studies (IANDS), in Salt Lake City, that Carol and I first met Elane. We heard portions of her amazing story and arranged to interview her a few days later in our home. She visited us in October 1992.

Elane was born in June 1944, in Libertyville, Illinois, about seventy miles north of Chicago. She was raised primarily in the small town of Osceola, Indiana, as the oldest of four children.

Elane had a religious upbringing, and she attended church on a regular basis. On her father's side of the family many of her great-uncles and great-aunts were either ministers or married to ministers. Her mother's stepfather was also a minister. All of them belonged to a fundamental Christian faith. As a child, she was taught that unless her friends belonged to her church, they would not go to heaven.

As a young adult Elane had a curiosity about other faiths, and she looked into several religions, including the Methodists, the Presbyterians, the Catholics and the Jewish faith. She also had a brief exposure to The Church of Jesus Christ of Latter-day Saints, which she knew only as the Mormon church.

After Elane married in 1963 she moved to South Bend, Indiana, where she had her first child, a daughter. She subsequently had two other daughters. At the time of our interview she also had seven grandchildren.

62

A Terrible Illness and Prayers

Elane began to tell her story. "On October 22, 1976, I had a stroke, precipitated by a brain tumor, followed by a marvelous experience. I must tell you that this was the singular most important thing that has happened in my life.

"At the time I was attending the American Floral Arts School in Chicago, and I was just three days short of graduation. It seemed as if I had a cold coming on; a headache had plagued me for a couple of days, and I felt lethargic.

"My cousin was staying with me in a hotel, and she and some school friends went sight-seeing while I went back to the hotel room to rest. After having dinner in the hotel with a friend, things got hazy—I don't remember much. Apparently, I went back to the hotel room and got in bed. I remember looking at the clock, and it was 12:20 a.m. By 12:40 a.m. they had me in the hospital emergency room.

"My cousin, after returning home and retiring, had awakened me when she heard me cry out. She noticed blood on my lip where I had bitten it during a seizure. I was not aware that I was having seizures; I just felt tired, as if I were ill with a bad cold. A couple of seizures happened in the presence of my cousin, and she went next door in the hotel to get help. A classmate from school called the paramedics, and they arrived to witness me having another seizure. The paramedics took me—over my objections—to Mercy Hospital in Chicago.

"There were five seizures by the time I reached the hospital, and by 1:05 a.m. my heart had stopped for the second time. They revived me, but by this time I had lost my ability to speak, my eyesight was gone, and I had no sense of feeling. It was sort of a twilight state that I was in, and I didn't care about anything physical that was happening to me.

"As my physical senses deteriorated, my spiritual senses sharpened, and I became strangely aware of certain things concerning myself. The nurse who was attending me, I knew was having difficulty. From some spiritual sense I understood that she had never seen anyone die before; my physical emergency was troubling her. I knew that she was from the third floor, and that they were short-handed and had brought her in to help. I heard the doctor say to her: 'Look, if you can't handle this we'll get you out of here and get someone else who can handle it.'

"The nurse continued to struggle with her emotions and I became aware that she was offering a prayer. The prayer wasn't heard with my ears, but I could feel her prayer.

"By this time the medical people became concerned with what my religion was. My cousin was Catholic, and they assumed that I was too, so they sent for a Priest to give me last rites. I heard their discussion about getting a Priest. Cautioning them, the nurse said she was afraid I would hear them talking about my impending death. The doctor responded: 'She can't hear anything. She's out of it.'

"I next remember hearing the nurse greet the Priest with a sigh of relief. She exclaimed something on the order of: 'Oh my God, Father, I'm so glad you're here,' and he responded: 'What do we have here?' She proceeded to tell him that I had experienced eleven seizures that she knew of. Moving close, the Priest told me that the doctors were doing all that they could, and that I was a very sick girl. He said that he was going to pray because we needed God's help. He told me to move something if I could hear him; I don't know whether I was able to move or not.

"As he started to pray I could feel it. I recognized that it was much more than the last rites. He finished the last rites, per se, and continued with the prayer. It felt as if it were a power that washed over me in a series of . . . like megavolts of electricity. It was . . . I can't explain what it was like. There was a feeling of spiritual power.

"Then I felt a pressure on my chest. I didn't recognize it as a heart attack, but I heard them code me. The Priest later said that they quickly moved him out when that happened—and it would have been impossible for me to see him, yet I did."

Out of Her Body—An Incredible Light

"Suddenly I had vision. It was as if there were a part of me rising from somewhere in the vicinity of my head. I saw the Priest as I went past him. The nurse who had been praying was in my view, and I observed that she was a dark-haired girl. Noticing something on the bed, I realized that it was my body, and I knew that I didn't need it. I felt indifferent toward it.

"Almost instantly I was in a dense foggy area. There was no fear, and I knew I wasn't alone.

"Looking about me, I turned toward the right, and I saw a distant light that resembled a bright star. The light began to move toward me at an incredible rate of speed; at the same time, I had a sense of moving toward the light.

"As the light got closer to me I realized that it had a personality to it. Love and understanding were emanating from the light. It was the most immense amount of love that you could imagine. It was as though you were in the presence of the one person in your life who had loved you beyond anything, despite what you might have done, and that love was magnified many times. That's how it was, in a way.

"When I got close to the light, something on the side of my vision distracted me. I looked down and to the side and saw a host of people. Rays from the light were shining over the tops of the heads of the people, but they didn't seem to notice. They appeared to be shuffling around, and I could feel anger and confusion coming from them. It was as if they were all lost, and they were agonizing over the pain that they felt. They seemed to be earth-bound and unable to see the light that was over them.

"As I looked at the people I thought to myself: *You can go to the same place, all you have to do is look at the light.* At that point the light spoke to me—only not in language as here on earth. It spoke to me from everything that it was into everything that I was. I not only heard it, but I understood it with every fiber of my being. There was total communication between that being and my being.

"And he said to me . . . "

I interrupted Elane's narrative at this point and asked: "He?"

She continued: "It was a male kind of voice. And I understood that it was a man. He said: 'Through me you have eternal life.'

"In a split second a whole jumble of thoughts came together in my mind, and I knew that this was my Creator, my Savior. I understood that He had a part in the creation of the earth. Other thoughts tumbled through my mind, including thoughts of humility—because I wasn't sure that I belonged there."

"Did you see an individual?" I asked.

"No, but I knew He was there. He was part of the light, He was— How can I explain it? It was so much more powerful than seeing a figure. I was seeing Him with spiritual eyes, and that is so different from the way I saw things on earth that I can't begin to explain it."

A Life's Review

"Because of my religious upbringing I always tended to look at things as black or white, right or wrong; there were no in-betweens. Measured by that yardstick I frequently came up wanting in my own mind. In the presence of this marvelous being, therefore, I felt unworthy.

"I found myself reliving experiences where I had not behaved as I should have. In my mind, for example, my brother John was always a favorite of my Mom. If I did something wrong, and John got in trouble because of it, that was okay by me. It was his just reward for being Mom's choice—not that I was vindictive or didn't love him—it was more a sense of indifference. In the presence of the Light I relived incidents, such as those with my brother, that I had long forgotten.

"These were events from my life, not all of my life, but particular events, where I could feel the effects of my misbehavior. With John, for example, I could feel his sense of rejection when I did something that hurt him.

"As the events in my life proceeded, and I felt the distress of others, this being of love communicated the thought: *That's because of the society that you were raised in. You behaved in this way, in part, because of the way you were raised. And that is not enough to keep you from the presence of God. You did not turn your back on God.*

"Incidents appeared in my life where I had succeeded in a competitive environment and gotten ahead of someone else. I had not intentionally hurt other people, but my competitive success had the same effect as though I had. Their sense of rejection was evident to me, and I could feel their hurt also.

"I saw many of these events as though in a high-speed video, except one with my brother where I dropped a small block of wood on him. That series of pictures slowed, and I could sense his feelings of rejection and hurt. Moreover, I understood that he felt that *I* was the choice child of my mother.

"A feeling of the Savior's love was with me throughout this process. Once I realized that He loved me regardless of what I had done—I had not ever rejected God, I had always searched for Him—then my mind exploded with questions."

An Outpouring of Love

"A flood of questions entered my mind. I wanted to know why war and peace? why the deaths of babies? what was heaven all about? what was the correct Bible? what was the true church? and a million other questions.

"As these questions whirled in my mind He took me into Himself. I was surrounded and brought into the Light. It was a feeling that . . . similar to being hugged, only better. It was such an infusion of love.

"It's impossible to describe in words. I saw billions and billions of tiny sparkles, and I knew that I was one of them. Some were brighter than others, but all were surrounded by the love of God.

"While I was enveloped by the Light, I knew the answers to the questions that had formulated in my mind. Secrets from the beginning of time to infinity were clear to me. Myriads of things were understandable. I understood, for example, that when I left earth I would leave with whatever spiritual growth I had attained there, and I would take that spiritual growth with me into this new world."

A Teacher, and a Remembrance of Knowledge Long Forgotten

"As these feelings of love and knowledge enveloped me the light began to dissipate. Suddenly I found myself on a height taller than a mountain, overlooking a beautiful expanse of land with a massive body of water. In the sky above me there were two moon-like bodies. The atmosphere in the sky appeared to be a mixture of gray and white, and one of the moon-like bodies had a bluish tint to it. The other body seemed farther away, and it was pure white.

"I gazed at the pattern of the land below, and it seemed to be symbolic of how I fit in as part of a whole pattern in the universe. And I became conscious of a man standing next to me—a man who represented knowledge and authority; someone like Adam or Abraham. There was a sense that he had been there since the beginning of time.

"This superior being was there to guide me through the answers to my questions, and he began to teach me. One of my questions had been about war and peace. He told me that wars were not in God's plan, but because I had chosen to go *there*—and his hand went down in a pointing direction—I had subjected myself to an environment where wars could occur. Looking in the direction he was pointing, I could see the earth as a sphere off in the ... it's very hard to explain the way it was. I could see the valley, and at the same time I could see the earth off in space.

"The earth was a round sphere, but it looked as if it were in the middle of a dust storm. I could see the earth, but I could also see a lot of darkness, storm clouds, or something around it. The being with me let me know that the earth was the most dreaded place to go, but it was also the place to learn the fastest—because of the adversities. Earth was put here for us to learn, and we are here for that purpose.

"I immediately understood. It was part of the knowledge that was in me, and it was what he was telling me. Since I had chosen to come to earth, I understood that I had become susceptible to all of the vicissitudes of an earthly environment, including war. War wasn't part of God's plan, but he allowed it to occur as part of the teaching experience. In war we learn lessons of giving and receiving as well as the lessons of violence and destruction.

"In this manner I learned that there are analogous lessons regarding the rich and poor. For those who come to earth and gain physical wealth, they have a responsibility to use it wisely. And the poor person needs to learn how to receive in order to help the wealthy person learn how to give. Even the bum on the street teaches us important lessons.

"Similarly, for those who have special talents; they have a responsibility to develop and use their talents for the benefit of all. Those with wisdom and knowledge have a responsibility to teach others.

"I asked why little children had to die, and my teacher sort of chuckled. He said: 'You know they didn't have to be born. Suppose there is a pond of water and you drop a pebble into the water. The dropping pebble makes a ripple. Think of a child being born who immediately dies without drawing breath. That child is like the ripples in the water because of the number of lives that it touches. There are the parents, the grandparents, the doctors, and the nurses. And if a child lives for a few days, months, or years, think of the other beings that the life of that child touches.

"My teacher told me that death leaves behind a void that is hard for us to understand. But each day that we don't live, we get closer to immortality and to our ultimate destiny. Death and other adversities that we find in life, he said, should not be considered as adversities, but rather should be thought of as lessons learned. For those who become ill and disabled, they learn the lessons of receiving help from others and of endurance; and those who help the disadvantaged learn the lessons that service brings.

"As all this knowledge was re-awakened in me by my teacher I understood that there are only two things that we can take from the spiritual realm to earth; one is love, and the other is knowledge—at least that knowledge that is residual within us. And the same is true when we die and return to the spiritual realm. We only take with us love and knowledge—that additional knowledge that we've gained while in this life."

Questions about the Bible and the True Church— A View of the Future

"As a youth and young adult I had used the King James version of the Bible. In recent years a number of other versions of the Bible were produced, such as the American Standard Bible, the New World Bible, and others. Moreover, before the King James version was produced in England there were still other versions. I wondered which was the correct version, and I asked my teacher.

"In his response he didn't use the word *Bible* to describe it. He used the term, a *history of a people*. I don't remember the exact words, but that was the sense of it. At any rate, he told me that our Bible was only a small portion of the history of the people and the King James version was the most accurate. He said that more records had been found, and there were still more records to be found.

"A corollary question which I asked in conjunction with the question about the Bible was which church was true. As I told you earlier I had investigated a number of churches and I was still searching for the correct church.

"My instructor said that *The Church* was created in heaven, but that we, as individuals, had divided that church with our fears and with our groping for power and control. The word "pagan" wasn't used, but the sense of it was that humans had divided the original church in mankind's quest to rule.

"He let me know that when I found the church here on earth that believed in the history of the people (as described in the King James version of the Bible) and believed that there was additional history that had been found—and that there was still more to be revealed—I would recognize that church by the same spirit I felt there with him. He also told me that The

Church had Apostles and Prophets but that they weren't accepted any more today than they had been in ancient times when Christ was here.

"By this time in our discussion I knew that I was to return to earth. He told me that fifteen or twenty years in the future I would come upon a new people, and I would find them on my own. I would know I had reached that stage in my life because at that time Communism as I knew it would have been destroyed, and new governments would have been formed. There would also be massive changes in the government of the country where I lived.

"Concerning our government, I was able to see the variables which affected our future. If, for example, we became a caring people and helped others in need, then our government would flourish. On the other hand, if we continued in a selfish self-contained manner, then we would suffer accordingly."

Other Knowledge, and a View of a Premortal State

"Most of what my teacher told me was knowledge that I understood. It was as if he would say something and then I would think: *Of course, I know that*. He also let me know that some of what he told me I would forget when I returned to earth—I would not be allowed to remember it.

"In a global sense I knew that there were other galaxies and other worlds. There were other places to live, to learn lessons from. Earth was not the only place where lessons could be learned. In fact, I could have stayed where I was and continued to learn, but not as fast as if I returned to earth. The hardships and adversities of earth accelerate the learning experience, and those lessons help us to reach a more perfected state.

"My teacher let me know that children are the most important thing we can have. A major responsibility is to nurture and raise children, and to teach them right from wrong.

"While he was teaching me about the importance of children he asked me if I would like to see myself before I was born—before I came to earth. I told him I would, and it was as if I were looking in a bathroom mirror that was fogged over. I could see myself, but I couldn't distinguish how my hair was done or my facial characteristics. Seated in what seemed to be a waiting area, I observed that there were five beings around me. Two of them were in a teaching capacity and were strong spiritual beings, and three of them were lesser spiritual beings. They were guardian angels, or whatever, and the three lesser ones were there to learn—sort of angels in training.

"In this premortal environment I saw that I was making all the decisions for my life, the things that I chose to go through. These were things that I wanted to accomplish in order to learn various lessons. There were different choices available to me. I knew, for example, that I was going to be the oldest of the children in my family. There was a choice between three fathers and two mothers; I would have learned equal lessons from all of them. I knew that I would have a physical crisis and would be miraculously healed; and I would have a second health crisis which I would survive.

"My life on earth could be prolonged, I understood, by living so as to be in a helping capacity—helping others." Elane paused in her narrative and laughed: "That might not sound like such a good deal here and now, but over there it was just understood that helping others is a primary purpose.

"As I was making these different choices concerning my life one of the lesser spiritual beings remarked that the consequence of some of these choices would be that I would have a difficult life. He wondered if I were sure that was what I wanted to go through. One of the more advanced beings responded that I could advance faster by making such choices.

"We reached a point in the discussion where most of my questions were answered. My instructor made it clear that I must return to earth. I didn't want to return but he said I had to—my work on earth was not yet finished. He observed that if I *really* wanted to stay I could, but if I stayed I wouldn't learn my lessons as fast as if I went back. My instructions were that I should take back with me the love that I felt there and give it to others when I returned. By giving that love to others my own soul would grow.

"My teacher let me know that I wouldn't remember everything I had seen and heard when I returned, but sometime in the future I would again hear his voice through someone else's mouth. I would recognize it by the same spirit I felt while there in his presence. It would also be recognizable by the mile-markers along the pathway of life which identified particular events in time that he had told me about. And I would find a *people* who had much of what I was looking for.

A Beautiful Place—Visit by Deceased Relatives

"I was then enveloped by that same loving, golden light that I had felt before. Then the light kind of left and I found myself in a grassy area, with a hill to my left, and a river that ran by several hundred yards to my right. The colors were . . . they were beyond any earthly description. A vague idea can be obtained by looking at the rainbow hews seen through a crystal, only they were more brilliant. There were daisy-like flowers that ran through the grass. And the grass—each blade had a life force of its own. The trees had a personality of their own.

"I should tell you that I was dressed in a long white flowing gown. The whiteness in the gown was different from any white I had seen before; there were depth and iridescence associated with it. It was an *alive* white, as were all the other colors. It was a pure white, and it was as if you could see into its depth and glowing beauty. My hair was long, unlike what it was in life.

"I ran across the grass, and my feet didn't touch the ground. I could feel the air around me—not that there was a lot of wind—just a refreshing feeling of the air.

"There was a sound in the air that completely defies description. It was as if there were a multitude of voices, and a multitude of instruments, blended and playing soft music. The twittering of birds and other beautiful sounds were all melodically instrumented into the music which wafted through the air. The sounds just flowed into me in a soft, soft manner."

I interrupted Elane's description of the music to ask: "If you were to characterize the music, would it be similar to modern day rock music?"

"Oh my, no."

"Country music?"

"No."

"Jazz."

"No—It was more . . ." Elane laughed, "it was a Bach and Beethoven type of thing."

"Did you normally listen to Bach or Beethoven?"

"No. Sometimes I did, but I was more inclined toward rock and roll. I considered Bach and Beethoven to be old-folks music."

"Okay, you were looking at a hill and a valley with a river running by it, and beautiful music filled the air. What happened next?"

"In the distance by the river there were six or seven people standing by some trees, and I could tell that they were waiting for me. It was as if they knew I was coming; one of them looked up and said: 'There she is!' A man leaning against a tree motioned with his arm and said: 'Hurry, Elane, everyone's waiting.'

"Running toward them, I felt the air against me, but my feet didn't touch the ground. Power and energy were coming off of everything. I realized that everything there had a life and personality to it.

"Two women broke away from the group and began running toward me. When they got within about twenty feet, I recognized one as my grandmother. She had been dead since I was about nine years old. The man against the tree was my mother's step-dad, and he had been dead since I was sixteen or seventeen. The lady immediately behind my grandmother was Aunt Virginia, my husband's aunt, who had died the previous February.

"All of them were dressed in white, a white which radiated light. Their hair and faces were not the same as on earth, but I recognized them quickly. They were about thirty years of age in appearance, much younger than when I had seen them last. Aunt Virginia was badly crippled when I knew her in life with one leg shorter than the other. Here, she was completely restored to normal function.

"As I saw my relatives and felt of their joy, I had the thought: *Man, if my kids could only see this; if they could only see Aunt Virginia now.* I no sooner had the thought, than: WHAM. It was a heavy duty body slam, and I was back in my body at the hospital. I was on the gurney in the emergency room, and I could see the defibrillator poised above me for a second jolt."

Back in Her Body

"I was frustrated and upset. Where I had just come from I was without pain, and I could go anywhere as quickly as I could think of it. And I could get answers to my questions as soon as I formulated them in my mind. Having enjoyed the freedom of a butterfly, I suddenly was back in the cocoon. I wanted my freedom back.

"Even as I thought of how wonderful it was on the other side, though, I also remembered what my teacher had said about love, and about giving to others. I also remembered that my work on earth was not yet finished.

"For some time I continued to go in and out of my body because of the continuing physical emergency. At one point I found myself in a room near the ceiling while I watched two doctors discuss my case. One of the doctors had a clip-board with papers on it, and he said to the other doctor: 'What are we going to do about this? There were several people hurt in a car accident, and we don't know how many will need the ICU room. Would it be possible to move Elane into a private room?' The second doctor said that he thought I would be stable enough to do that, but they would need a private nurse for me.

"For a short while their conversation centered around the fact that there was no one there to authorize a private nurse. They said they would put a Nun in with me until my family got there. Then the one doctor showed a comment on the clip board sheet to the other doctor and asked: 'What should we do with this?' The other doctor examined it and said: 'Oh, we've got to get rid of that. If something were to happen to her and the family got wind of it they could sue the hell out of us.' What they subsequently did was erase off of my hospital record a comment that I had died that night. One of the sheets that wasn't erased was later sent to my physician in Indiana, and it showed that my heart had stopped and I had died.

"Later I awakened in my room and found a Nun seated reading a book; later, still, there was a second Nun. In both cases they told me I was very sick and shouldn't try to talk. They buzzed for a nurse, and she gave me a shot that put me to sleep.

"When I next awakened there was a nurse moving around near my bed. I was so exhilarated by my experience that I wanted to talk about it. What I didn't realize was that my speech was hampered by a stroke I had suffered from the many seizures. A nurse told me my husband was waiting. When he came in I tried to tell him about my experience, but it was difficult to make the words work right. A neurosurgeon stuck his head in the door and my husband asked him: 'What is this? My wife says she hears voices, somebody calling her.' The neurosurgeon responded: 'Oh, trauma victims go through this kind of thing. Don't worry about it, she'll get over it.'

"Once I had stabilized sufficiently that my life was not in danger they began an extensive series of tests. They ultimately found, through a pneumoencephalogram, that I had a brain tumor. It was small and slow growing, and it was fairly deep in the brain, so I decided, against my physician's wishes, not to have it removed. They would try and control the seizures with medication.

"Nearly two years later the seizures returned with force, and I had to have the operation. It was a soft fibrous tumor, and they removed it. That was fourteen years ago."

Finding "The People"

"For many years after the experience I felt quite ecumenical. I didn't find any one church that gave me the same spiritual feeling I had enjoyed in the presence of those marvelous beings. The prediction that I would find a people puzzled me, but nothing came of it.

"After my experience I remembered the comment from my teacher that there were other scriptures available. The Dead Sea Scrolls attracted me. Thinking that they might represent what I was looking for, I sent for them. There was also an advertisement on The Book of Mormon, and I sent for it. Neither book caused me to do anything, principally because of short-term memory problems caused by the brain tumor. I wondered about the Mormon Church—I had heard and enjoyed the Tabernacle Choir—but I couldn't find it in telephone books. There was no 'Mormon Church' listed.

"About two years ago I was visiting with a neighbor. Standing in her front yard, I happened to notice a handicapped man, on a bike, delivering sales flyers.

"As I looked at him I got a special spiritual feeling about the man. I thought to ask him if he might like to mow my lawn. Assuming that he would be delivering another sales flyer in a week, I decided that I would ask him, then, if he wanted to do it.

"Before the week was up this man (his name was Irv) came to my front door and asked if I wanted to have my lawn mowed. I hired him and he began working on my yard. On one occasion he asked me if I went to any particular church. I told him that I sometimes went with my friend, but I wasn't tied to a specific church. He asked me if I wanted to go to church with him on Sunday, and I told him we were committed to go to my friend's church that day. Irv then asked if he could drop by and visit after church on Sunday.

"I agreed to his visit, and on Sunday Irv came by. He brought a Book of Mormon, which he gave me.

"Irv and his wife became friends with me. They helped me through a difficult period in my life. I attended church with them and finally found out that the Mormon Church was, in fact, called The Church of Jesus Christ of Latter-day Saints.

"The family aspect of the LDS Church was attractive to me, and I began to listen to the missionaries. One of the first things they did was to ask me what I believed. I said: 'If I told you there were more than one heaven, what would you think?' They nudged each other and asked me what I meant by more than one heaven. They were even more interested when I told them that there were three heavens, and that there were different levels in each of the three.

"The missionaries kept smiling at each other. I told them that there were living beings on other places besides earth, and I asked them if they could believe that. Many worlds had been created in addition to earth, I said, and I asked them if they could believe that Christ had a hand in the creation of the earth. I made the point that Adam and others of us were also involved in the creation of the earth. I told them that angels did not have wings. These were all things that I had learned from my teacher in the spiritual realm, and I still remembered them vividly. 'Red Book Magazine' had previously written a story about my near-death experience, and I showed the missionaries the article.

"The missionary Elders were quiet through most of this discussion, except for their continued glances at each other. When I was through they pulled out a flip chart and showed me the three heavens. They let me know that the Church believed in life on other worlds. They told me many other things, and as I listened to those young Elders it was as if I were hearing an echo of the spiritual being I had met on a high place in a different world. An enormous sense of déjà vu hit me as I listened to them.

"I attended several church meetings, and I went to a baptismal service. In each of them I felt of the spirit that I had previously felt in the presence of my teacher during my NDE. Praying about it, I received an answer, and I was baptized on July 5, 1991.

"When I found *the people*, I didn't want to turn loose of what I had found. The spirit was recognizable with what I had previously known, and it was throughout the church. That was a major factor—feeling and following the spirit—in my decision to move to Utah."

Interview with Her Missionary

Some time after interviewing Elane, I had the opportunity of chatting with Elder Wayne Peck, who was one of the missionaries who first taught Elane. He confirmed Elane's account of what happened when they met her. He said she was the most open and had the deepest questions of anyone they had taught. She immediately understood the gospel as they explained it to her. It was as if she had heard it before.

Chapter 6

A COURAGEOUS MAN

Bill

It was a cold winter evening, in November 1992, when I drove up to Bill's house. He was waiting, in his wheelchair, with a cheerful greeting as I entered. Despite his obvious disability Bill had a muscular appearance, and he had remarkable mobility with his chair. He seated me in a large overstuffed chair, and he moved his chair so that I could easily use the recorder to tape his remarks.

Bill informed me that he was born on April 7, 1950, in Salt Lake City, Utah. He was the oldest of three brothers, and the family traveled extensively when the children were growing up—their father was an electrical engineer. Bill had a broad education; by the time he was sixteen years old the family had been around the world five times. They had lived in Australia, Saudi Arabia, Puerto Rico, Jamaica, and Venezuela.

As a young man Bill spent time in the Marine Corps, with two tours of duty in Vietnam, and then he finished his schooling at Westminster College in Salt Lake City. Fifteen years were spent working for the police department in Salt Lake City.

His immediate family was of a Protestant faith while he was growing up, and many of his aunts and uncles belonged to The Church of Jesus Christ of Latter-day Saints. Bill was exposed, therefore, to a variety of religious beliefs from his different relatives. As an adult Bill had been married and had three children.

A Nasty Accident

Bill began to tell his story: "Over the 24th of July holiday in 1991, my brother Bob and I decided to go to Saint Anthony, Idaho, and ride our ATVs [All Terrain Vehicles] in the sand dunes near Saint Anthony. I had been an ATV enthusiast for a number of years, and we looked forward to a pleasant holiday of outdoor sport.

"We left Salt Lake early in the morning, and by early afternoon we had set up our camp in the sand dunes of Saint Anthony. We ate lunch—Bob's son was there with a friend, and we fed them—then Bob and I took our vehicles on a survey of the area. When we were about two or three miles from the camp site, I suggested that we return so as not to worry the kids."

"Were your vehicles three-wheeled or four-wheeled?" I asked.

"They were four-wheeled. We had started the machines up to return to camp, and we had ridden about two hundred yards—I'm not sure what happened, the speed was only about twenty miles-an-hour—and I remember being thrown over my machine. I hit on my head; I had a helmet on, but it was a tremendous blow when I landed. The pain was instantaneous and severe, and I blacked out.

"I was unconscious for less than a minute. When I came to I was face down in the sand, and I couldn't move any portion of my body. My brother, Bob, came running back, but all I could do was rotate my head. My arms and legs wouldn't move.

"When Bob came up I asked him what happened, and he said that he didn't know. I asked him where my machine was, and he said: 'It's on top of you.' I couldn't feel anything.

"Bob was able to remove the machine from me. I told him to go for help, but before he left I asked him to pile sand around my head to immobilize it. Because of the extent of my paralysis I was fairly sure that my neck was broken. I also told Bob that the paramedics should be informed that they would have to fly me out.

"Bob started for our campsite. About half way there he encountered a group of people, and he sent them for help so that he could return to me. The paramedics arrived within about forty-five minutes, and a helicopter arrived within about another forty-five minutes."

Medical Complications

"The helicopter transported me to the Eastern Idaho Medical Center in Idaho Falls. They gave me a CAT Scan, took x-rays, and performed other tests. The doctor came in and told me that my spinal cord was severed and I would be paralyzed for the rest of my life. My back was broken at T-4/T-5, about nipple level. I also had a closed head injury, and my neck was injured. My ribs were all broken in the left rib cage, and there were nine fractures on the right side. I had traumatic pancreatitis and many other problems.

"The accident happened about three in the afternoon. By one o'clock in the morning they had flown me to the University Medical Center in Salt Lake City. They had to get me to the medical center in Utah because both of my lungs were collapsing from the injuries, and they suspected that I might have torn the aorta of my heart.

"In Idaho, before they flew me to the University of Utah Medical Center, the doctor told me they might have to get a heart team together to operate on my heart. I asked him what would happen if they didn't operate, and he said that in that instance I would die. I wondered if death would come quickly or be drawn out, and he said it would be rather quick. A major concern I had was about my spinal cord injury, and, when I asked him about it, the doctor told me that I would never walk again. I was overwhelmed by the magnitude and suddenness of my injuries.

"Athletic and outdoor sports had always been an important part of my life. At the time of my accident I was training for a triathelon that was going to be held in Park City. I played football in high school and college, I skied from the time I was a small child, I enjoyed ATVs—in short, I was oriented toward sports and the outdoors—and the prospect of a life of paralysis was devastating. It seemed to me, at the time, to be a fate worse than death, so I told the doctor that I would not have the heart surgery that he thought I might need. I also told my brother, Bob, not to let them operate on me, just let me go.

"At the University Medical Center they did a number of other tests. By that time I had gotten Adult Respiratory Distress Syndrome (ARDS), which is usually fatal, and my heart was erratic. They put an external pacemaker on me to keep my heart beating regularly as well as other equipment to keep me alive. Then I developed pneumonia, and I got a staph infection in the blood. I was on a ventilator and I had tubes attached to various parts of my body; by this time I was comatose and the medical prediction was that I would not live."

Healing Hands

"Bob called a couple of my relatives who were LDS and asked if they would come and give me a blessing. My cousin, and Bob's brother-in-law, who were both active in the church, came to the University hospital and gave me a blessing. Medically, when they gave me the blessing, I was in a coma and could not hear what they were saying. The fact is, however, I could almost repeat verbatim what they said. I have, since, lost some memory of their words, but at the time I was totally aware of what they were saying.

"I still remember them laying their hands on my forehead and asking that I be given peace to accept whatever was the Lord's will. There was no specific request that I be allowed to live or that I be healed; rather it was that I would be granted peace and acceptance.

"As the blessing proceeded I felt hands on me—hands from those giving the blessing, but also other hands as well. The peculiar thing was that it was almost multi-dimensional—I could feel their hands, and I was looking at the scene as if from the perspective of a balcony. And . . . and there was this tremendous feeling of peace and well being that came into my body.

"From this elevated position I first saw my cousin and Bob's brother-in-law with their hands on my head. Then, as I looked at the scene, I saw other less distinguishable people around me; and I had the feeling that their hands on me were *healing* hands.

"Next, it was as if I shifted perspective from a balcony position to a position directly above my body. Looking down, I saw me, my body, with the people around it. Being somewhat quizzical, and trying to figure out what was happening, I looked, and . . . and I found that they were praying over me. It still wasn't clear why they were doing this, but I was filled with an awesome peace and calmness.

"It was strange, I could feel this warm peace in my body, yet I was looking at myself from above. The most fascinating aspect of the scene was that physically I only saw two people in the room besides me—my cousin and Bob's brother-in-law, who were giving the blessing.

Surrounding the bed, though, were all these other people with their hands on me; I could feel their hands on me. I couldn't distinguish them clearly, but I felt . . . I had a sense that they were relatives that had gone before me.

Through an Archway

"I can't tell you if my other experience was chronologically next, or how close it was to the experience with the blessing. I can pin the time down for the experience with the blessing because my cousin told me of the time—it was the afternoon of the day following the accident—but I can't do that with the next experience. All I know was that it was sometime during the four-and-one-half week period that I was comatose.

"The experience began when I found myself in a beautiful meadow; it was . . . I can't describe it. The meadow was incredibly beautiful, and I was walking along a path. The colors were vivid, and there was every color imaginable. It was just . . . I've tried to describe it to other people, and I couldn't—its beauty was beyond description.

"As I walked along the path in the meadow I came to a stone archway. It seemed almost as if I were called, or drawn, to the archway. I walked through it and entered a courtyard where I saw my father. He was dressed all in white, and he was bathed in sort of an iridescent white light.

"We approached each other, and I remember telling him that I was feeling lost and confused. I realized at that point that I was either in the process of dying, or I had already died. My confusion centered on my earthly life. I was feeling a great loss because of my children, and I was sharing that feeling with my father. Additionally, I wasn't sure that I wanted to live in the paralyzed state that the doctors said I would live in.

"My father said to me: 'You aren't going to be lost or confused any longer. Everything will be fine. It's not time for you to be here, now, but when it is I will be here.' Then he embraced me—there was an enormous outpouring of peace—and he took me back to the archway. As I entered the archway, I had the feeling that everything would be okay. That's the last thing I remember until I came out of the coma.

"When I came out of the coma, my youngest brother, Tom, was there, and my mother. They asked me if I knew where I was and what had happened. I remember telling them that I had been with Dad, in response to which they looked at me strangely."

Recovery

"When I regained consciousness, I became aware of the magnitude of physical problems that were still with me. During the little more than a month that I was comatose I lost 65 pounds. My paralysis was from the nipples down, and there were other complications. I had traumatic pancreatitis, pulmonary problems, and the head injury. These various problems kept me in the hospital for eight-and-one-half months, and for about half of that period I was totally immobile in a TLSO (a fibre-glass cast which immobilized my back and isolated it from my neck.) No food could be given to me by mouth for five months because of the damage to my pancreas. I was on the ventilator for the four-and-one-half months that I was in a coma, and I breathed oxygen for a short period after that.

"They transferred me to Seattle for my rehab., and I stayed there until March 1992, when I returned to Utah. They were unable to do any surgery on my back because of the location of the injury. I was in a back brace for about six months."

At this point in the interview, I commented to Bill that he looked remarkably well for the extent of his injuries, and for the relatively short time that had elapsed since his rehabilitation in Seattle. His comment was: "I've been doing really well. Actually, I had sort of a miraculous recovery. All of the doctors at the University Hospital referred to me as the miracle baby—there were at least seven different times when the doctors called my mother and told her that I wouldn't make it beyond the next few hours. They also told my family that because of the level of my injuries, if I did live, I would never be independent; I would always need help."

"And do you need help?" I asked Bill.

"No, I live alone and care for myself. I drive my own car, and I work every day at an industrial concern."

"You are kidding!" I responded. "What do you do at your work?"

"I am a salesman. I sell commercial laundry equipment," Bill said, and it was obvious that he was proud of that accomplishment—and legitimately so. In light of the relatively recent traumatic accident and rehabilitation ordeals he had borne, his recovery and achievements truly warranted feelings of pride. He also told me that he worked out three days a week in a special gymnasium. One of his goals, within the next couple of months, was to be fitted with leg braces. With the aid of the braces and crutches he hoped that he would be able to increase his mobility in a walking program.

Bill's house, as I saw it, was the picture of neatness. Certain areas had been modified to make them accessible by wheelchair. He did all of his own cooking, and he took care of his other needs. He performed his own dressing and personal hygiene, for example, and this he did despite being paralyzed from the chest level down. Medical personnel had continuously told him that he could do none of these things without significant help from others. Bill said that he had set for himself a goal to overcome obstacles that stood in the way of his independence.

Analysis of Bill's Experience

I began to ask Bill questions about what had happened to him: "Was there anything about your accident that you remember as particularly unusual?"

"There was the terrible surge of pain when I hit, then I remember thinking: *So this is what it's like to die. It is not so bad.* Everything happened so quickly that I didn't find it that unpleasant."

"When you had your first out-of-body experience and were looking down on yourself, and you saw these other people you thought were your relatives, can you tell me a little more about them?"

"I could definitely feel their hands on me. Later I talked to my cousin about them. I said: 'I could clearly hear your voice and that of Lance during the blessing, and I could see you guys, but who were all those other people holding their hands on me?' He responded: 'Bill, there was no one else there,' to which I said: 'Oh yes there was.'"

"Could you tell how they were dressed?" I asked.

"I could distinguish shapes, in, maybe, an off-white or gray color, but they were not as clear as those giving the blessing, or as my Dad was in the later experience. During the blessing I could feel a surge of warmth or energy going through me. It went from my head to my toes, and I had this enormous feeling of well-being. It's interesting that when the blessing was taking place I could feel things in my body, the warmth and the pressure of hands, despite the fact that I was paralyzed. Those were the only feelings I have been able to have in my body since the accident."

After I had interviewed Bill, in a separate meeting, I met Bill's cousin who had participated in the blessing. He had a written record of the incident, and he gave me a copy of the write-up. A significant difference from what Bill remembered was that the cousin said there were three individuals who helped with the blessing (two acting as mouth). Besides those individuals, Bill's mother, another lady, and another man were present in the room when the blessing was pronounced. However, Bill can only remember seeing the two individuals who gave voice to the blessing—plus the other spirit individuals who were his deceased relatives with the healing hands.

"Concerning the experience with your Dad, you mentioned that you went through the archway into a courtyard. What do you mean by a courtyard?"

"That was the impression that I had. I had gone from the meadow through the archway into this area that resembled a garden courtyard. My Dad was clearly visible, and . . .and I can remember seeing three other people who were in the background. They were not really clear, and I didn't have any contact with them. I sensed their presence, and then my Dad approached me and all my attention was focused on him."

"How old was your Dad when he died?"

"He was fifty-six years old."

"Did he look fifty-six years old when you saw him?"

"He really didn't have an age. He didn't look old, and he didn't look young—it was just my Dad."

"You said he was dressed in white . . ."

"It was more that he was bathed in white, an iridescent white."

"When you spoke to your father and he spoke to you, what kind of communication was it?"

"His lips may not have moved when we were communicating—but it was a clear message from him."

"You said that you felt him when he embraced you . . ."

"Perhaps it wasn't an embrace in the physical sense. I knew that I was embraced by him, though, and there was a tremendous amount of love and peace which flowed from him to me. I sensed that everything would be okay."

"Why do you keep using the word *peace*?"

"Because that, more than anything else, is the thing that I felt. And it continued after the experience. When visitors came to the hospital, for instance, many expressed the fact that there was an aura of peace about me. My cousin remarked that coming to see me was like recharging his batteries. Others made similar comments."

"Could the experiences have been dreams, or hallucinations?"

"I'm positive that they were not dreams or hallucinations. They were so different from anything I had ever experienced, and they were very real."

"How real is very real?"

"As real as you and me sitting here."

"How have the experiences changed you, if they have?"

"They have given me the ability to cope with what I previously thought was a fate worse than death. The other point is that when I was on my journey, if you will, I found that things I had previously valued highly, material things, really had no value. Feelings of love, on the other hand, persisted both there and here. The accident has also brought my family closer—in a more supportive way."

"Is there any message you would like to leave for others?"

"I think the message might be distilled from some of the things I learned. I was not prepared for what happened to me. When I think back on the time that I took to go on the trip to Idaho, for example, when I fussed with my jeep, the trailer, my camping equipment, and my ATV, as though they were the most important things in my life. The real issues in my life, on the other hand—the relationship with my children, the relationships with other people who were close to me—did not assume the importance that they should have. Material things no longer have the attraction for me that they once did. Love and relationships with my family and others close to me are now the most important things in my life."

Chapter 7

TWO WOMEN WHO SAW
THE LIGHT

Louise

The snow was stacked four feet deep in our front yard, in February 1993, when Louise drove up. She was a diminutive dark-haired young woman with a lovely smile. She greeted Carol and me with enthusiasm.

Louise was born in Logan, Utah, in February 1957, and she was one of five children. She was raised in Logan and attended school there. Attending college at Utah State and the University of Utah, she obtained a Bachelor's degree in Sociology. Louise had been married but was unmarried at the time of our interview. She was employed in the fields of sociology and law enforcement.

A Premonition and an Accident

Louise began her story: "At the time, in the late summer of 1981, I was married, and we were living in Rock Springs, Wyoming. We were moving back to Utah so that my husband could go to school. For about a month before we moved, we both had a feeling that something bad was going to happen to one of us. We did not talk about it to each other because it made us feel uncomfortable. We didn't know whom it would happen to or what it would be, we just knew it would be something bad.

"The day came to move, and we loaded a truck we had borrowed from my uncle. We drove to Logan and unloaded the truck without difficulty.

86

I was tired and wanted to wait until the next day before we returned the truck, but my husband insisted that we should return it to my uncle in Clarkston that night.

"My husband left ten or fifteen minutes before me in the truck, and I followed in the car. There is a little place called Amalga, and there is a house next to a bend in the road at Amalga. I came around the bend and saw a small dog alongside the road. He ran into the street and was barking. Another car was coming and I tried to keep going, but the dog did something that startled me, and I went off to the right side of the road. In trying to correct and get the car back on the road I hit the lip of the road. This flipped my car sideways into the path of the other car.

"The last thing that I consciously remember thinking was: *Oh my, they are going to hit the car.* Some time later I woke up on the road. In between when they hit and when I woke up I had my experience—when it started."

Two Men in White

"I found myself coming out of a dark tunnel toward a bright white light. There were two men, all in white, standing there. One, I could see clearly, and the other was standing behind a mist, an opaque mist.

"I wanted to keep going to where the second man was, but I couldn't move beyond the first man. Before this incident, I should explain, my husband and I had many questions about things, especially about children, and these questions came into my mind as I stood there with this being in white. I don't remember all the questions, but I do remember that we communicated without talking. It was as if words were exchanged through our minds, and many of the questions I had were being answered.

"While this was happening, the second man came out of the mist toward me, and I knew when he came forward that I couldn't go beyond the mist. I had to stay where I was.

"My happiness was extreme—it was the greatest peace and contentment that I had ever felt. The experience was unique; I had never felt that way before, nor have I felt that way since. It was pure bliss.

"I knew I was going to have to go back, but before that happened there was a voice that came from the other side of the barrier. One of the main questions that my husband and I had was whether or not we could have children, and if so, when? The voice said: *Just be patient—your time will come to have children.*"

A Visitor from the Other Side

"Then I remember going back, and I woke up on the road with paramedics attending to me. When I first woke up, and for some time after that, my body and soul were separate. I heard somebody's voice talking to the paramedics say: 'Oh my back hurts,' and I remember thinking: *What on earth is going on—who is that whose voice is talking to the paramedics?*

"It took me about a day to figure out that it was I talking; and it was about three days before I stopped, off-and-on, being separate from my body. It was as though I could see a shell, my body, separate from *me*.

"During this period in the hospital I was visited by someone from the other side. I had a very dear friend who was killed, with her husband, in a plane wreck when she was nineteen. In the first forty-eight hours while I was in the hospital she came and stayed with me. I couldn't talk to her, but I could see her. She left a little bit before my body and spirit came back together."

Questions About Louise's Experience

Louise finished her story and sat quietly. I suggested that I ask her some questions about the experience, and she agreed. "Tell me about the bright light that you saw when you first left your body."

"It was just an extremely brilliant white light. It came, like from all over, and it focused on me. I've never seen anything like it."

"Were you in the light, or looking at it?"

"There was a sort of funnel toward me; I was looking into the light, but the light was coming to me. The farther out I looked, the more widespread the light was."

"Can you describe the mist that you saw?"

"It was a type of soft fog, and it was very definite along a wall-like line. The fog-wall came down to what I was standing on, and I couldn't see the end of it either up or sideways. I remember looking over my left shoulder and seeing stars behind me. It was as if I were in the clouds and the earth was below me. The second man was standing on the other side of the fog-wall, and I could see him less clearly than the first man—until he came through the mist. I couldn't see anyone else, but I knew there were other people behind the mist, and that's where I wanted to go."

"Could you describe the two men you saw?"

"It's been so long ago . . . there wasn't anything of particular note about them, they . . ."

"How do you know they were men?"

"I just knew it; it was obvious. They were dressed in white and they blended into the white light."

"Why did you use the word *peace* in describing how you felt?"

"I don't know how else to explain it. It was just an extremely calm, happy feeling—something I had never felt before. There was an intense peace, and I didn't want to leave it. I wanted to stay there very much, but it was like my husband was pulling me back. It was for *him* that I came back."

"When you first saw the two men, you said that *we* had questions. What did you mean by *we*?"

"My husband and I. We had a few questions about the Church. The main question we had, though, was about children, because we both wanted to have them. To that point we had not been able to have any, and we did not have a medical reason why not. Later we did get a medical reason why my husband could not father children."

"What church did you have questions about?"

"The LDS Church. We were studying and looking for some answers to different questions. The environment we were living in made it difficult to sustain a religious experience. We lived in Rock Springs during the boom, and the ward, there, was not as strong as the wards we had come from. Because we didn't have children some of the members didn't treat us kindly, and we were struggling with that issue."

"So both of your backgrounds were LDS?"

"Yes."

"Could your experience have been a dream or a hallucination?"

"Not to me."

"How did it seem?"

"Real. In a lot of ways it was more real to me than the rest of my life."

"When you came back, you said that you heard yourself. Where was the real you during this period?"

"I was inside my body, but it was as if I were standing in a shell—and the shell was talking. I was separated, and yet I was inside my body. It was as though I were in a space suit, my body, and it was talking while I was in it. It's hard to explain . . . I was sort of in a facsimile of me, and it was talking."

"You distinguished between what you called the spirit and the body. Can you explain that distinction?"

"The body was the physical body, and the spiritual was the mind and everything else. It was like . . . I don't know quite how to describe it. It was as if the essence of *me* were a totally separate being from the physical part of me. And the physical part of me was the shell. It was the essence of me that was functioning during much of the experience. When I was in the emergency room, for example, the essence of me was talking and joking, and I didn't feel any pain. The physical part of me was reacting differently, though.

"In talking to family members afterwards, it was amazing to me what they saw coming from the physical part of me as compared to what I remember coming from the essence of me. From their description, my physical person didn't move much or do anything. I just lay there and let the doctors work on me. Yet the essence of me was talking to all the people working on me, telling jokes—and I couldn't understand why they didn't laugh. I was in a good mood, and I could see the humor in my situation, but they didn't share in my humor. It was only later that I realized they didn't hear what the essence of me was saying."

"You mentioned that your friend visited you. How did you know it was your friend?"

"When she was alive we were so close we knew what each other's thoughts were. It was she; I just knew it. She moved like my friend, and she looked like my friend, with the same long blonde hair. She was always bubbly during life, and the spirit in my room had the same cheery, bright attitude. Her clothing was very light in color. When she first appeared, the hospital room was dark, but there was a brightness around her."

"Did she say anything?"

"No, she was there for comfort. She was just there."

"Has your experience changed your perspective at all?"

"Well, I definitely know that there is something on the other side, and I didn't know that before. Also, it is the place that I want to go back to when I die. When I have a hard time about things in life, this experience is the one thing that I hang onto as something that I know for sure."

"Are there any messages you would like to leave others?"

"Just that there is something on the other side, and I know that for sure. I'm looking forward to having that peace again."

Joyce

Carol and I drove up to Joyce's home on a cold winter afternoon in February 1993. She greeted us warmly, and she seated us near her as she arranged herself on a special chair designed to minimize problems associated with recent back surgery. Despite her obvious discomfort her eyes sparkled with anticipation and with the joy of life.

Joyce explained that she was born in Salt Lake City, Utah, in 1946. She was raised in a family of five children in the Salt Lake area. Joyce had previously been married, and she proudly showed us a picture of her son and his wife.

A Difficult Birth—A Strange Experience

Joyce began her story: "My son was born in December 1970, and he weighed nine-pounds-three-ounces; the birth was carried out as an emergency C-Section. My body was shocked from the operation, and my intestines stopped functioning properly. I had a bowel blockage a few days after the operation. All together I was in the hospital for thirty-two days.

"They took me off all oral food and water. I couldn't even suck on damp things. My tongue got so dry that they finally let me suck on lemon tasting cotton swabs.

"At one point they told my husband that I wouldn't make it through the night. My temperature was high, and they kept packing ice around me. I was asleep, and then—it seems so strange to talk about it—I found myself standing in a hallway. I think I had on my hospital gown, and I don't remember my feet touching the ground.

"It was dark all around me except for that light. There was a light that was the brightest thing I had ever seen in my life. Longing to go to that light, I didn't recognize anything else that might have been going on.

"There was a tunnel that went down and off to the right, and that's where the light was coming from. I felt that if I walked down the tunnel and around the corner I could . . . I had to go to that light.

"Momentarily standing still, I heard a voice to my left. I think it was a man's voice, but I'm not sure. The voice said: 'It's not your time, you have to go back. You have a husband to take care of and a baby to raise.'

"Then the thought came to me: *I've got a baby. I've got a son.*

"The next thing I knew I was awake, I was in the hospital bed, I was hungry, and I felt better. My doctor came to see me, and I told him that I had had a really weird dream. His response was: 'We lost you last night.' He let me know that he didn't think it was a dream.

"At the time I had never heard of near-death experiences. I thought it was some kind of realistic dream. After the experience I read about others having similar things happen, and I realized that I wasn't alone in what I saw. Now I know that there is another side, and I'm not afraid to die. I'm not anxious to go—I want to live, but I know that death is just another side of life.

"My experience made me appreciate something about every day—it doesn't matter if it's ugly weather, or if I'm not feeling well, or whatever—I find something beautiful about the day." As Joyce explained how she felt about each day, and even though she was obviously feeling the results of a recent surgery, her eyes reflected her joy of living and talking to us at that moment.

Analysis of Joyce's Experience

I began to ask Joyce some questions concerning her experience. "Can you explain what the light looked like?"

"It's hard to describe. How do you see a light that bright?"

"Was it similar to the sun?"

"If the sun were there . . . it would be like the sun was shining right into the room. Yet . . . it didn't seem that the light hurt my eyes. But I'll never forget it."

"Why will you never forget it?"

"It was drawing me. I *had* to go to that light—I wanted to go, but it was like I was stopped, and something wouldn't let me go on. Then the voice mentioned my son, and I thought: *I've got a baby.*

"My baby is the one that brought me back, I know he was."

"Tell me more about the voice."

"I'm pretty sure it was a man's voice, and it was off to the left behind me."

"Did you look to see?"

"No. I didn't turn; I don't think I was supposed to know who it was. There was a lot of love in the voice."

"What do you mean a lot of love?"

"It was a gentle voice, it was kind. And the love I felt was unconditional. It was wonderful. It was beyond any love I had ever felt in this life. The voice wasn't demanding when it told me to go back, but when it spoke I knew that was what I had to do."

"Did you hear it?"

"I don't know whether I heard it with my ears, or if I heard it in my mind."

"You mentioned that you first thought your experience was a dream. Did it seem as though it were a dream?"

"No, it seemed like it really happened, but at the time I figured that was the only thing it could be."

"What was your religious background?"

"I wasn't raised in a religious environment. I'm LDS now, and I don't go to church all the time, but I do believe that God answers prayers. This experience changed my views on religion, and I now believe that God hears every prayer. I'm a big believer in prayer, and I worship God every day."

"Has the experience affected you in other ways?"

"Yes, it has made me appreciate life. Another thing . . . the voice said: 'You have a baby to raise.' I took that seriously, and I felt all those years that my primary goal was to raise my son. And, I assumed, when that was done I would be taken. My son is now my best friend. I've enjoyed every moment with him—he's a wonderful person."

"Do you have any messages you would like to leave others?"

"Yes; don't ever think that this life is all there is. I feel sorry for those who think that there is nothing else. There is so much more!"

"How do you know that?"

"It was the feeling I had while in the light—the peace that I felt."

"Why did you use the word *peace?*"

"That's how I felt; I felt serene, I felt loved. I know that death is only a word, and the spirit lives on. We are only a shell of our real selves."

Chapter 8

CHILDREN'S EXPERIENCES

Eileen Pitcher and Jennifer

Carol and I visited Eileen in her motel room, where she, her husband, and her children were staying prior to returning to their home after an extended stay in Egypt for her husband's work. Eileen smiled, invited us in, and seated us next to the window where we could watch the February snowfall.

Eileen's even features were accented by large brown eyes, a dazzling smile, and a warm personality. She informed us that she was born in 1952 in California. She had brothers, and Eileen and her brothers were raised by her mother who was divorced. They grew up in Utah, where their grandparents lived, and they were active in The Church of Jesus Christ of Latter-day Saints.

Jeff, Eileen's husband, was employed in the international arena, and she informed us that he was a wonderful man. Both Eileen and Jeff had previous marriages, and they had seven children between them. Eileen was introduced to Jeff by her brother, and they later married.

Jennifer, the first of Eileen's and Jeff's children, was born in 1981. Eileen said that Jennifer was an active child who appeared to live each minute to the fullest, even as a small child.

Eileen told Carol and me that, for many years, she had often had spiritual warnings concerning events in her life. These warnings usually involved relatives or someone close to her. The spiritual communications, in some instances, were so dramatic, and the later actual events so sure, that her family had come to rely on them. Her husband and children understood that when the warnings came they should pay attention.

A Spiritual Warning and a Reassurance

Eileen began her story: "In about 1985 I began to have feelings that something bad was going to happen. It was a panic type feeling; it persisted for months, and it seemed to center around Jennifer. I told my husband about it, and I had him put dead bolts on the door. As the year progressed the feelings became even more pronounced.

"Finally, the feelings got so strong that neighbors, and others of my friends, noticed that something was wrong. I would call them frequently, for example, and ask if my children were there, and I would urge them to check and see if everything was all right. It became almost an obsession, as if I had to know where the children were for each moment of time. Some of my neighbors began to tell me that I needed to settle down and be less obsessive about the children's welfare.

"My husband and I were getting ready to go on a vacation, the first one where I had agreed to leave the children, but I didn't feel good about it. I told my husband about my bad feelings, but he said we needed to go.

"On the day before we were to leave, I was driving to a doctor's appointment, and as I passed through an underpass this strange electrical feeling went through my body. Simultaneous with the electrical feeling the Spirit told me that there was going to be an accident, it would be one of my children, and the child would be okay.

"I asked the Spirit which child would be injured and the answer was: 'Jennifer.' I asked: 'Will she live?' and the Spirit responded, 'Yes.' I asked, again: 'Do you promise that she will live?' and the answer was: 'Yes, I promise.' I then asked, 'Will I be able to raise all of my children to adulthood?' and the Spirit told me yes. At that point I insisted on getting a further commitment by saying: 'Are you sure—do you promise me?' and I could feel someone right there in the car with me—no face, no body, just a presence—and the Spirit again told me: 'Yes, I promise.'

"Our communication was not vocal. It was a mental communication on a spirit-to-spirit level. When I got the final reassurance from the Spirit that Jennifer would live, the tears flowed from my eyes. I continued my trip to the doctor happy in the knowledge that my daughter would live.

"When I got home I told Jeff that we couldn't leave on the trip until he completed the fence in our back yard to protect our children. I insisted that my feelings were still there about the accident, and I wanted to take every precaution. I told him I thought Jennifer was going to be run over, and I wanted the fence completed so she couldn't get out of the back yard.

"Jeff went to one of our neighbors, who was a doctor, and asked for his help in finishing the fence. He told Dave, the neighbor, about my feelings concerning Jennifer, and Dave agreed to help.

"During the morning breakfast, before the children went out to play, I looked at them and said: 'If any of you get hit by a car, *do not die,* because Mom and Dad and the doctors will help you. Promise me that you won't die.' The children looked at me and said: 'Okay, Mom, we won't die.'"

A Terrible Accident

"Jennifer was five years old at the time, and she went over to the neighbor's house to play after promising that she wouldn't go into the street. Jeff and Dave were working on the fence in the back yard, and I was scrubbing the floor trying to get ready for our departure at six. At two-thirty in the afternoon, while I was working on the floor, I had this overwhelming feeling that I should call again to my girlfriend's house, where Jennifer was playing.

"My girlfriend said: 'She's fine, Eileen. I just fed her a hot dog, and they're playing in the cul-de-sac. Nothing's going to happen.'

"I hung up the phone, and I had that electrical feeling again—then the phone rang. My girlfriend was on the phone, and she said: 'Jennifer's been run over.' I said: 'I knew it.'

"Calling to Jeff in the back yard, I told him that Jennifer had been run over. Jeff and Dave, the doctor, ran to my neighbor's and found Jennifer. I got there shortly after them. They were holding my bloodied child in their arms. Her stomach had been mashed flat, and she was all scratched up. She looked at me and said: 'I'm okay Mommy, I didn't die.'

"A one-ton truck with dual wheels on the back had run over her. The driver had been smoking marijuana. Jennifer was on a hot-cycle when the truck ran over her. The driver said he felt something that seemed to be a child's toy, so he stepped on the accelerator to get over it, stopping when he heard a muffled scream. Then he got out and saw a child with the truck's rear wheels on her. He got back in the truck and pulled it off her. Then he picked her up and set her on the grass, thinking she was dead.

"While he was searching for help Jennifer jumped up and started yelling at the truck driver. He was shocked that she was still alive; he picked her up and brought her to my neighbor where my husband and Dave found them.

"Jeff and Dave rushed her to the hospital where they examined her. Her stomach was crushed flat, and they told us that it was unlikely she could live. She was still conscious, and she kept asking for water. She had learned about blessings in Primary, and when I asked her if she wanted her father to give her a blessing she said yes.

"The policeman who was there and Jeff gave Jennifer a blessing. In the blessing she was told that her mission in life had not yet been completed, and she would live to complete it. She was also told that she would touch many lives, and she was promised that her face, which was badly damaged, would not sustain any scars.

"They transferred her to the McKay Dee Hospital in Ogden where they had better facilities. My husband rode in the ambulance with her, and my girlfriend drove me in her car. When we got to the hospital nine physicians examined her. By then her face had swollen and turned purple, and her eye was bulging out. They said she was probably hemorrhaging and her brain was swelling. One of the doctors told us that she couldn't live through the night.

"I began to doubt myself and my husband's blessing. I turned to him and said: 'You promised she would live!' At that point I remembered what the Spirit had told me the day before, and I offered a silent prayer.

"They did a CAT scan and X-rays, and they found no broken bones. The doctors still didn't offer much hope. They said an aneurysm could be the cause of her death. She was in intensive care for eight days."

A Visit by a Great-grandfather

"While she was in intensive care, and in her greatest pain, she kept calling for her Grandpa Lemmon. We asked her why she called for Grandpa Lemmon whom she had never met. We asked her if she meant her other living grandfather. She insisted it was Grandpa Lemmon—who was actually her great-grandfather on my husband's side—who had died many years earlier.

"During this difficult and painful period for Jennifer I urged her to fight and stay alive, and she kept reassuring me that she wasn't going to die. She said that Jeff and I should go on our trip since she was going to be okay. The hospital physicians still felt that Jennifer would not live, and they had us talk to a psychologist to prepare us for what they thought was inevitable.

"As time progressed, the hospital staff began to talk of a miracle. They observed that it had to be a miracle that she was still alive. They had no explanation as to why she was still with us.

"Jennifer was taken to therapy each day and treated for her injuries. The therapist, whom we got to know, asked who Grandpa Lemmon was. He said that Jennifer kept asking about Grandpa Lemmon. Explaining that he was her great-grandfather, we told the therapist that Jennifer had never met him. We had no idea why she continued to talk about him; we thought she was mixed up over her grandfathers, and we told the therapist that.

"After eight days they released Jennifer because she was so anxious to return home. We did not talk about the accident to ourselves or to Jennifer because it was too painful for us. Jennifer healed well, with no scars on her face, and we resumed life.

"Two years later, when Jennifer was seven, we went to a family reunion in Idaho. Great-grandmother Lemmon was still alive and would be at the reunion, and this would be the first opportunity for Jennifer to meet her. In Great-grandmother's house she had one wall devoted to pictures of relatives—grandchildren, great-grandchildren, children, spouses, and others. Great-grandfather Lemmon was active in athletics during his life, having been a professional ball player when he was young, and his wife had pictures of him on the wall amongst all the others.

"When we arrived my son took Jennifer to the wall of pictures, and she pointed to one of them and said: 'There's Grandpa Lemmon. That's how he looked when he came to me while I was under the truck; only, he was all dressed in white.' We were astonished, and we queried her further about the incident. We asked her if he said anything to her, and she said: 'Yes, he told me that he loved me and everything would be okay, and to tell Grandma that he loved her.'

"The picture that she had selected was taken when Great-grandpa Lemmon was thirty-five years of age. He was in coveralls with the farm as backdrop. I showed her some other pictures when he was older, but she said he didn't look like that. When Great-grandmother Lemmon came in and heard Jennifer, she cried and cried. She told us that she had seen him too, and he looked as he did when he was young."

A Conversation with Jennifer

Shortly after I finished interviewing Eileen, the door opened and a lovely girl with short curly blond hair entered the room. She was a typical eleven-year-old with the bouncy energy of youth. She asked her mother if she could go swimming in the motel pool. Eileen asked her to join us for a moment. She sat next to me, while I positioned the tape recorder, and she displayed the complete trust only possible from the very young.

Our conversation was as follows: "What is your name?"

"Jennifer."

"How old are you, Jennifer?"

"Eleven."

"What grade are you in school?"

"Fourth."

"What other country did you just return from?"

"Egypt."

"How did you like Egypt?"

"It was okay, but I like it here."

"And you will have some new friends, won't you?"

"Yes."

"Jennifer, once, a long time ago you had a truck run over you, didn't you?"

"Yes."

"Can you tell me what happened?"

"I was riding my bike, outside, and this truck was parked over there. I saw it, and no one was in it, so I went over to the other side of the street on the bike. The truck started to go when I was trying to get up the hill. I couldn't get up the hill, and he ran over me."

"Do you remember any of what happened when he ran over you?"

"He stopped on top of me, and he got out of the truck."

"Did you see anybody or hear anything when you were under the truck?"

"Yes, I saw my grandpa," said Jennifer in a matter-of-fact tone.

"What did your grandpa say, and what did he look like?"

"He was in a white robe, and he told me I would be okay and that they would take me to the hospital."

"Did you feel that he was telling you the truth?"

"Yes."

"Had you ever seen your grandpa before?"

"No."

"How did you know it was your grandpa?"

"I don't know, but . . . like a year later we went to my grandma's house. My brother picked me up and asked me which one I saw, and I pointed to my grandpa."

With Eileen's urging Jennifer then showed the scar on her stomach where the truck had run over her. It was an obvious scar, but it had healed nicely. There was no sign of scarring on her face. She was a beautiful eleven-year-old full of the joy of life. She quickly left us and reappeared in her swimming suit. She and her friend bounded from the room toward the swimming pool.

Rocky and Berta

Carol and I visited Rocky and his mother, Berta, on a bright spring day in 1993. Berta was a youthful appearing petite lady with an energetic manner. Rocky and several beautiful children were in and out during our visit, and it was obvious that love and respect were shared by the mother and children.

Berta was born in Kansas in 1950, and her parents moved to New Mexico where she grew up. There were four children in Berta's family, and her father died when she was five years old. She had a loving step-father who helped raise her until she was in the eighth grade, when he died.

Schooling for Berta was accomplished in New Mexico. She completed high school and attended college for one year. Upon reaching the age of twenty-one, Berta and her mother moved to Colorado and opened a wig and clothing business.

In 1978 Berta married her present husband, and in 1984 they moved to Utah. At the time of our visit, they had eight children; three of them were adopted.

Berta was raised Methodist, and her husband was raised Baptist. Neither of them, as they were raising their children, was actively involved with their particular faiths. In 1983 Berta began reading from the Bible and telling the children Bible stories, but church attendance was sporadic.

After visiting with Berta and her delightful children, and absorbing what she had to tell us of her background, Carol and I asked her to tell of the events leading up to the experience. She began the story.

A Bad Fall and a Prayer

"In November 1983, we moved to Oklahoma City where my husband had been transferred for his work. In May 1984, my son, who had turned four years old that February, came in the house soaking wet from a mud-puddle he and his friends had been playing in. I told him to go upstairs and change his clothes.

"His friends were waiting at the front door. My neighbor and I were sitting near a window, and I saw a flash go by the window, but I dismissed it from my mind when I looked over and saw nothing. The neighbor and I continued visiting until the little children came in and asked for Rocky.

"The children went up to Rocky's room when I directed them there, but they returned shortly saying that Rocky wasn't in the bedroom. Instantly I knew that the flash I had seen was my son, so I ran out the door and found Rocky, unconscious, under his window. He had fallen twenty feet from the second floor bedroom to the concrete below and landed on his head. He told me later that he leaned against the screen on the window and it gave way.

"We got the ambulance to take him to the hospital, and at the hospital they contacted the best pediatric surgeon in the area. Because Rocky's brain was swelling so badly, the surgeon told us he would have to operate immediately. To allow for the swelling the surgeon had to open a hole in Rocky's skull about the size of a grapefruit.

"After the operation we waited for three days while he was in intensive care. Tubes were hooked to him in many places, and he was breathing with the aid of a breathing machine.

"Prayer and waiting were my primary activities. There was a chapel in the basement of the hospital, which was a Catholic institution, and I frequented it when I wasn't with Rocky. On one occasion when I was praying, I recalled a passage from the Bible where it said, in effect: *He's not mine, he is your son, you gave him to me;* and I felt like that. My prayer reflected that passage and I asked Heavenly Father if Rocky would remain in a coma or if I would get him back. The pain concerning my son was intense and I was sobbing as I prayed—I asked for a sign. I knew that

Rocky didn't belong to me, he was just lent to me from God, but I needed an answer.

"After completing my prayer I entered the elevator and came back upstairs. Waiting for a moment in a small waiting-room on my son's floor, I attempted to regain my composure. While I was sitting on a chair in the room, my crying ceased, and I felt all the pain leave me. A wonderful feeling of peace came over me. Then a voice . . . a voice with peace and love spoke to me and said, very casually: 'He will be fine.'

"Wondering who was speaking to me, I rose and looked up and down the halls to see who was there. No one was present. There was just that marvelous feeling—I wondered whether it was Jesus or an angel that spoke to me. Entering Rocky's room, my husband who was in the room, said: 'Rocky, give me your hand.' At that moment, for the first time since the accident, Rocky moved—he gave me his hand.

"I took that as the sign I had asked for. Rocky's recovery was still difficult, though. For the next two weeks it was obvious his brain had sustained severe injury. His eyes would roll wildly, and he appeared frightened. We attempted to get 'yes' and 'no' answers from him with hand signals."

Recovery, and a Story of a Visit to Heaven

"After two weeks he was released to go home, with frequent trips to the therapist. When we left the hospital one side was partially paralyzed, but he could walk with a limp. Words did not come for over a month, then Rocky began to speak again, one word at a time.

"Since I was with Rocky most of the time to aid in his recovery, I was present when he began to talk. He kept trying to tell me something. Before the words came he would point. Often he would point up and then he would point at himself. Thinking that he was trying to tell me of his fall I would respond: 'Yes, Rocky, you fell out the window.' That didn't satisfy him, and one day as I was sitting next to him he said: 'Me, heaven!'

"I was startled by his answer, and I asked him: 'What?' He repeated: 'Me, heaven!' at the same time making the motion upward, and then pointing at himself. I asked him if he went to heaven, and he shook his head yes. Musing over what he had said, I dropped the subject.

"As the weeks stretched into months for Rocky's recovery a strange phenomenon occurred. Simple words concerning his everyday activities continued to give him difficulty, but he started quoting things from the Bible. I was not that expert with the Bible, but I would search out what he had been saying. To my surprise, the passages he quoted were accurate replications of similar passages from the King James version of the Bible.

"During this period of Rocky's recovery, he told me that he had seen my father. Dad had been dead since I was five years old, and I didn't remember him myself. There weren't many pictures of my father, and I didn't speak much of him since I was so young when he died. Rocky insisted, though, that he had seen his grandfather. I asked him what grandfather looked like, and he answered: 'He looks like me,' meaning that his grandfather looked like himself. Rocky is the only dark-eyed, dark-skinned, dark-haired, child that we have. He is similar in complexion and features to what my father's pictures show.

"Through the following months, Rocky told me that Jesus had taken him by the hand and taken him to heaven. When I asked him what it was like there, he said that there were homes there, too, only they were kind of cloud-like. People had families, he said, and they live in homes like here.

"Jesus visited Rocky and gave him an apple. Heavenly Father also visited him. Rocky's frequent reference to Heavenly Father and Jesus caused me to ask: 'How do you know the difference between Heavenly Father and Jesus?' He responded: 'Heavenly Father has light hair and Jesus has dark hair.' Explaining how they communicated he said: 'They talk to you but they don't move their mouths.'

"These vignettes continued to come from my son for some months. It was as if he had an inner knowledge of some distant place—a place that I had not taught him about. Once, for example, he told me that Jesus and Heavenly Father had power. I looked up passages in the Bible, such as Mark 12:24, where it referred to God's power, and I wondered how a five-year-old could know that. I certainly didn't teach it to him.

"With time, a rather complete picture emerged of Rocky's visit to another world where Jesus and Heavenly Father dwelled. So, I asked him why he came back. He cried and said: 'I'm sorry, Mom, I liked heaven. It was wonderful there and I didn't want to come home. But Jesus said I had to come back. He told me that my mother needed me.'

"Wondering about this further I asked Rocky: 'How did you get back?' 'Jesus has powers,' he said, and then he put his hand to his lips and motioned outward. When Rocky did that the thought came to me: *It's no more said than it is done.*

"These revelations from a five-year-old child astonished me. Seeking help from clergy and hospital personal, I asked about some of the things Rocky was saying. No one seemed able to help, yet I knew in my heart that I had heard a voice—and that Rocky was telling me of factual events that had happened to him. For years, because of the many doubters, I put it aside. Then I started reading books of people who had gone through near-death experiences. I discovered that their experiences were similar to what Rocky had told me. The discovery that others had shared similar experiences was most comforting.

"Once, after having read some books on the subject, I was explaining to others in the room that Rocky did not remember leaving his body. Rocky happened to be standing nearby, and he looked at me in a stunned way and said: 'I do too remember leaving my body, Mom. When the doctors were working on me, I floated up near the ceiling and I could see them doing something on the side of my head where I got hurt. That's when Jesus came and took my hand.

"As the years have passed Rocky has forgotten much of what he told me. Key elements of what happened to him are retained in his memory, but the details are lost.

"Rocky's recovery has been truly miraculous. There is some residual damage, and recent psychological tests have confirmed that damage—his slowness of speech, for example. Rocky should be able to lead a normal life, though, and we are grateful for that."

A Tragic Accident

"In October 1989, Rocky, his brother, Sage, and his sixteen-year-old brother, Shane, were in a car wreck. Shane had driven to the spa to pick them up from a swimming lesson, and on the way back the car got out of control and struck a pole. Shane was killed instantly.

"Rocky was in the back seat, and he ran the two blocks to home. Running to the accident I found that the police and paramedics were there trying to extract the boys from the car. Shane appeared gone, and Sage was critically injured.

"Watching this scene in agony, the thought came to me: *It's okay. I know he is gone, but Rocky came back to tell me that the soul has a place in heaven.*

"It all seems to me, now, like a puzzle that fell into place." Berta struggled with her emotions as she attempted to continue. "Survival from the loss of one of my children would have been almost impossible if I hadn't known it was okay. Rocky taught me that there was a beautiful place where Heavenly Father and Jesus took care of people like my son."

Questions of Berta

Berta agreed to answer questions I had. I began: "You say you only went to church infrequently. How did Rocky know the scriptures?"

"I have no idea; especially for a four-year-old. When I searched the scriptures out, I found them to be almost word for word."

"Was it from the New Testament, the Old Testament, or both?"

"It was mostly from the New Testament."

"Do you remember the specific scriptures, now?"

"Unfortunately, no. I have never been one to know the scriptural details. Frequently he would cover several scriptures, particularly when he was trying to explain something to me."

"Can you remember some of the subjects you discussed?"

"One subject that surprised me was that Jesus told Rocky it was okay for him to come back, because we are all going to be together as families in heaven. And then Jesus said: 'I promise you.'

"Frequently when Rocky told me something, like the comment about families, in his own words, then he would say something from the scriptures. To be taught by your four- and five-year-old son was unnerving."

"Had you taught Rocky that you would be together as a family when you went to heaven?"

"No. It's not something I was raised with. Rocky knew that my father had died, and I said that he was in heaven, but I didn't talk about being together as a family."

"Are there other subjects you discussed with Rocky?"

"Once I asked him: 'You saw God?' and he said: 'He prefers that we call him *Heavenly Father.*'"

A Visit With Rocky

Rocky, who had been running in and out during our interview with Berta, came over and sat when Berta called him. His dark hair, smiling eyes, and pleasant demeanor were the characteristics of a healthy boy. I began the interview.

"Tell me your name."

"Rocky."

"How old are you?"

"I'm thirteen."

"What grade are you in school?"

"I'm in the sixth."

"Do you like school?"

"Yes, it's okay." -

"And you like sports?"

"Yeah."

"Do you remember back when you got hurt?"

"Yes, kind of."

"Can you tell me what happened?"

"I remember being in my room, on the window-sill. I was leaning against the screen, it popped out, and I fell to the ground."

"Do you remember hitting the ground?"

"No. I remember looking down on my body while the doctors worked on me."

"Is there anything else you remember?"

"I remember Jesus and heaven."

"Do you remember anything about Jesus or heaven?"

"No. That's all I remember."

"Can you recall what happened during your recovery?"

"I remember I had to learn everything all over again—I forgot everything I knew."

"Did you tell other people about what happened to you?"

"I think I did, but I don't remember."

"Okay, thanks Rocky." That ended my interview with a charming thirteen-year-old.

Chapter 9

A MAN WITH A MISSION

Jack

He came to our house in late February 1993. He was a tall, young looking man with even features, penetrating brown eyes, a neatly trimmed short dark beard, and a ready smile. Between calls on his engineering job, Jack said that he had some time to talk about his experience.

I shall call my new-found friend *Jack*. Jack was born in Toronto, Canada, in 1953. He was one of five children, with two older sisters and two younger brothers. He was raised in Toronto and southern Canada until he was 18 years old. Several different high schools in Toronto accounted for Jack's intermediate education, and then he went to the University of Toronto where he majored in engineering. He started in civil engineering, and then he changed to chemical engineering, and he received his degree in that field in 1977.

Jack was recently married, a year-and-a-half ago, to a lady who was a Las Vegas dancer for many years. Shortly after his marriage he moved from Canada and took an engineering sales job in Salt Lake City.

For reasons that will become apparent as you read this story, most names have been changed or eliminated. Jack informed me that he was fluent in Arabic and French; he spoke English with a slight Canadian accent. He was obviously a very capable individual. Speaking quickly and with assurance, Jack knew his subject intimately. His experience was among the strangest and most interesting of the numerous near-death experiences I had heard in my research with various people over the years.

As I listened to Jack's story, it became evident that he had lived a more adventuresome life, up through his graduation in college and a few years after that, than most of the population does in an entire lifetime. The thing that impressed me most during the interview, though, was Jack's complete assurance that he had been led and protected in these many adventures by the Lord.

An Experience that Changed His Life

Jack began to tell his story. "When I was between four and five years old, I had a friend who lived down the street from me—I'll call him Bob. Bob was one year older than me, and he tended to be a trouble maker. I went to his house one day, and he was looking through a book in his basement. There was a cartoon picture of a man lying down with a golf ball between his upper lip and his nose, and another man with a golf club ready to hit the ball.

"Bob decided that this would be a good thing to try, and I would be the one to have the golf ball under my nose. He didn't have a golf club so he got his baseball bat. I lay down with the golf ball on my lip, and he took a good hard swing with the bat. He hit me in the forehead just above my right eye.

"The next thing I remember was that I was standing, behind Bob, watching my body walk down the yard with blood streaming out of the head. I saw myself walk through the yard. I came back into my body for a moment at the fence—to go through the fence and yell at him that I would never play with him again—and then I went out of my body again.

"My mother found my body about five hours later. I was cold and had no vital signs. My mother is an occupational therapist and she knew, medically, that I seemed to be dead. She carried my body home, and she called my dad and a doctor that lived near us.

"During the time that I was out of my body I met, in heaven, three beings who stood in front of and around me. It was all very gray, and there was a pale light in the middle of where I was standing. The one being facing me, who had a beard and looked quite young, wasn't speaking so much from his mouth as he was speaking from his heart to my heart. I couldn't see the other two beings as well as I could see the one speaking to me. He said such deep things to me—things that had to do with my future life.

"He told me that for the rest of my life I would find myself helping people. From now on in my life, he said I would be different from others, and I would have the protection of beings from the other world. He said that I would do great things for God.

"I came back into my body in my parent's bedroom, and I regained consciousness watching the doctor look into my face. I forget much that happened after that, except that my mother, after the experience, began calling me *Thee* instead of *You.*" Jack chuckled as he thought of his mother. "To this day she still does it. It shocked her because I just came back to life on the bed, and it affected her greatly. My father drove across town rapidly when he heard of the accident. When he got there, I had returned to life.

"From that incident on, I felt a real closeness of Christ in my life. I felt power in my prayers, I loved to read the Word, and I always had God close to me. The United Methodist Church was our primary church when I was young, and after that experience I . . . I felt completely different from my friends.

"The need, for example, to love my enemies. . . . My mother told me: 'Don't go back and play with your friend Bobbie.' My response to her was that Jesus said we should love our enemies. Later in life—it's funny—Bobbie became a criminal and served time in prison. I saw him some years later and he had been arrested in the United States for statutory rape, and he boasted about it. He turned out to be a bad egg."

A Strange Sign in the Sky—A View of Hell

"In my youth, as I was growing up, I had many spiritual experiences. One very strange one occurred when I was between eight and ten years old.

"I had my own separate bedroom far from the rest of the family. One night I remember looking out across the fields and seeing something that looked as if it were an enormous pair of dividers. It was like lightning, and it was walking across the fields.

"As I watched this strange apparition, someone spoke to me and said: 'That is the sign of Satan walking the earth. He shall return and measure out the earth, and this shall be his rule—controlling the earth.'

"Often thereafter, in my youth, I would be wakened from sleep by a finger pushing on my back, or by a large black human shape in my room. I learned not to be afraid of them, and I also learned how to appropriate the power of Christ to command them to leave.

"In 1964 when I was eleven years old we moved to London, Ontario. In the period that we lived there from 1964 to 1967 some of my friends were involved with Ouija Boards, seances, and hypnotism. No one was able to hypnotize me, but I could hypnotize others. Often, in the seances, we had evil spirits that would come, and I was always able to send them away.

"Later we moved back to Toronto, from 1967 to 1972, and I went through high school with no unusual incidents. Then I went to college at the University of Toronto to study engineering.

"Ever since I had my early near-death experience I have been on a spiritual quest—more than a quest, a mission. From that time on I've known and recognized the Lord's hand in my life. I have had God's guidance, and I have felt the special presence of Christ in my life.

"Because of these feelings, when I was in the university, I took a year off from school. I was frustrated with the system. It was the mid-70s, my eldest sister was a Communist, and I had a strong feeling that I should go out west. So I moved to the west coast of Canada where my other sister was living.

"In the summer of 1974 I had been working at Esso Chemical in Sarnia, Ontario, and I became aware of a calling that I had. I had been doing some long-distance running, and I spent much of my day in the Bible and in prayer. I studied the lives of Elijah and Elisha and I came to believe that what they did was commonplace for someone who had faith in Christ. This knowledge prepared me for some events that happened shortly after that.

"After my work term was complete, I dropped out of school and moved to British Columbia to 'find myself.' During this period I became involved with a woman who was a teacher of Tarot. She was from Alaska and was deeply involved in black magic.

"On a particular occasion I was sitting in the living room of a house with this woman. We put a candle on the table, and she started an incantation. During the incantation an Eskimo appeared that we could see through. He was playing a flat drum.

"While she was doing the seance, I went out of my body with the woman, and we descended into hell together. We went down this huge red shaft. We could see people as silhouettes on different levels. As we passed the people I could feel their agony; they seemed to be hopelessly trapped in their levels. Stark terror gripped me as I felt of their despair.

"Returning from the shaft, through some transition I didn't understand, we came to an immense area that I recognized as the earth. Enormous numbers of people were leaving the earth to a place where a giant bearded angel was holding a door open for them. I understood these people to be the dead who had died in the love and grace of God, and He was calling them up from the earth. The people were illuminated, and they were passing through the door into heaven.

"The next thing I knew we were no longer in the hell-heaven scene, but instead were back in an earthly environment near the house we had left. It was a wooded area, and it was a very real physical environment. I could touch and smell the trees.

"I literally walked back into my body, and that was the end of that particular incident. It was a bizarre experience, and it seemed to have symbolic significance.

"Some time after this experience, I was present in another seance at my house with the same woman and two of her friends. During the evening they asked me to reveal whom I associated with in a previous life, and who it was that I emulated most in that same previous life. I told them Jesus Christ and they were terrified. Leaving the house, and walking into the woods, I felt the power of Christ on me. Speaking with a loud voice, I called on Him to cast Satan out of my house. The people who had been involved in the seance left—they ran out of the house.

"During this strange part of my life, when I was trying to find myself, I met many different people. Because of some spiritual gifts that I seemed to have I became well known among a cadre of unusual folks. Among others, during this period, I met a man named Moses David who was the head of a cult called The Children of God. The cult was actually a front for a massive drug ring throughout Canada, and Moses David wanted me to get involved."

A Dangerous Assignment

"A person I met when I came to the west was an officer in the Royal Canadian Mounted Police (RCMP). He was aware of some people I associated with, and we became friends. It turned out that he was an undercover agent for the government, and he recruited me to be a *deep sleeper*. I took up work as a deep sleeper doing narcotics investigations.

It was on a little island on the west coast called Protection Island. While I was doing this work my cover was blown.

"I had rented a house, and since it was a large house, I had sub-rented portions of the house to others. One of the young men that I sub-rented to was a felon from the east. This young felon got into a fight with my undercover friend with the RCMP. It was Christmas time, 1974, and the RCMP officer broke the young man's jaw, upon which the young felon called a colleague to come and *hit* (kill) the RCMP officer. Somehow they found out through their channels that I had been feeding information to the police about all the drug dealers on the island.

"There were hundreds of pounds of cocaine going through the island, also other drugs. The drug trade tied into many people that were in the human resources part of the government. It tied into police officers, and even into members of the navy—a nearby navy base was being used in the trade.

"The young man who had his jaw broken brought a friend to the house one evening. The friend of the young felon went to sleep early, while I was out, and when I returned I found him sleeping on the couch with a sheet covering him. I could see a gun in his hand under the sheet. I got discreetly out of the house, and I made it to the mainland without getting shot. They realized, of course, that I had discovered their plans.

"Later, in Vancouver, another couple of hit-men tried to get me. It was March 10, 1975, late at night, and they were after me. I got to a region in downtown Vancouver near St. Joseph's Hospital. The drug ring was led by The Children of God group whose head, Moses David, I had met earlier. They were distributing drugs across the country with the aid of local crisis centers and local officials. My RCMP friend and I had cracked the whole thing, and the drug runners decided that they would get rid of us.

"These two hit-men cornered me in front of St. Joseph's Hospital. They were both standing in front of me with their guns drawn and pointed at me. It was right next to a hotel called The Century Hotel. I looked at the sign on the hotel and saw the word *Century* and I heard my grandfather's voice in my heart saying: *Jack; the first hundred years will be the hardest.*

"A tremendous feeling of peace enveloped me, just as if an angel had touched me. Walking straight toward the two men, I passed them and they were powerless—they couldn't shoot. They couldn't do anything. As I walked past them, I felt led by a spirit. One of the men followed me until I came to a little storefront church near an Italian restaurant.

"The church was a charismatic Pentecostal type, which I entered, and I sat in a front pew. This fellow who had the contract on me came in and sat down also. The church people were just at the beginning of their prayer meeting. A woman stood up to address the congregation. Then this young hit-man stood up and confessed that he had a contract on me and was going to kill me that night.

"The congregation listened as the hit-man confessed to the whole thing. He told how he and his friend had been trying to get me all day, and I had been evading them. He was 'saved' that night, but I wasn't—or so they said—because later he 'spoke in tongues,' but I didn't. I didn't do what the little Pentecostal group expected of me, but I knew that the Lord's hand had been on me.

"What came out of that experience was that The Children of God were forced to leave North America. Moses David was up for a possible indictment on criminal charges with relation to the drugs, so he sent an epistle to all of his groups across the country, and they left. They went to Europe and Asia, many to Thailand.

"My perspective of this whole affair was that God used me to liberate a lot of young people from the power that this fellow had. He had perverted the gospel to the point where he taught people that salvation was through sexual perversion. He was distributing drugs all over North America."

Working with the Muslims

Jack next told me of an intermittent period from 1976 to 1983 when he devoted much of his time to teaching Christianity to the followers of Muhammad. He worked, during this period, out of a mission in Toronto, in Paris, and in Algeria, North Africa. His life was in danger on numerous occasions as he attempted to carry out what he believed was a calling from Christ. Nine of his associates in the work were assassinated. Jack believes that his life was preserved by heavenly intervention so that he might be able to continue to carry out his mission. Many followers of Muhammad did embrace Christianity as a direct result of Jack's work. He became fluent in both the Arabic and French languages during this period.

Questions about Jack's Experiences

Jack agreed to have me ask him some questions. I started with: "This almost seems trite, but I usually ask it of people I interview; how have these experiences affected your life?"

"I've had a very different life. I don't live day-to-day with the goal of how much money I'm keeping in the bank, or how many sales I'm making on my job. What is most important to me is my relationship with other people. That is the central focus of my life."

"Concerning your out-of-body experiences, why did you call what you saw *heaven?*"

"During the experience where the giant was at the door, there was a bright, bright light, and I saw that it was heaven."

"Tell me about the bright light."

"It wasn't a light, so much, which I saw, it was a light that I felt. I could see the people in it, and I could sense their tremendous elation as they went through the door up into the light. And there was a sound from them, just . . . it was like singing. It was a beautiful sound."

"What did *you* feel?"

"I felt wonderful inside. I was excited, and I felt *alive.* It seemed to be life itself."

"You said there were many people there . . .?"

"Millions, I think. The numbers were incredible."

"What were the people doing?"

"They were flying. Moving around the door, they continued into what resembled an enormous field. They appeared to be suspended, not walking."

"Did they have wings?"

"No. There were no wings. They were just basked in this light. Some of them were turned to me, and their faces . . . it was as though they could see me also. Their faces were friendly. I felt so welcome there."

"What did the field look like?"

"It was flat, and it seemed to extend out in every direction. It was strange, the whole experience seemed so symbolic, and yet there I was. This enormous bearded person, who was letting the people through the gate, was an angel, or . . . something I didn't understand."

"Was this large bearded person bathed in light?"

"He was separate from the light, this side of the door; the light was on the other side. To hold the door open for the people, it seemed to take much force."

"How were the people dressed?"

"It's hard to describe, except that they were clothed in white."

"Did you see other colors in the field?"

"No. It wasn't . . . well, yes and no. I think that my whole ability—my senses were in a different plane or dimension. I felt color, I felt light; it was a complete experience. I can't describe it as though it were a city street or a farm field here; it was so different."

"Did you want to come back?"

"When I was there, no. There was this tremendous longing inside me to go where the people were going, and to be with them. Indeed, whenever I have problems with . . . I'm a diabetic and sometimes I get in trouble with that. Also, in 1979, I had malaria. During an especially bad bout with malaria, when I was in the hospital with a very high temperature, I had a repeat of part of the experience.

"Again I saw hordes of people, and this time it was like a parade of people, and there was love flowing through and from them. I was above, watching them, and feeling this great love. I experienced a repeat of the longing to be with them that I felt previously."

"You mentioned that you heard something that sounded like singing coming from the people. What was the music like?"

"I can't say that it was like rock, or classical, or marching music. It was extremely pleasant, and it was as if a deep tone permeated my body. It was something that spoke to me in the language of love."

"In these experiences, did you see Christ?"

"The first person I saw, when I was a child, I believe was Christ."

"What did he look like?"

"He had a thin, fine-featured face, and he was wearing a beard. His hair was long behind him. He was wearing a straight robe that was gray in color, against a background that was gray."

"Why did you come here to tell me your story?"

"I really felt led when I saw the little advertisement. Often I am led by the Spirit, and I respond to those promptings. Advertisements don't usually attract me, but my wife and I were trying to sell a camera. *The Happy Ads* caught my attention, so I picked them up and glanced through them. I saw your ad and I sensed that I should call you. My story has never been written down or published, and I felt that I should see you."

"Are you familiar with the near-death literature?"

"Not really. I've heard of some stories, but I've not read any books on the subject. I've rarely told my story. I don't like to push it on people who might feel uncomfortable."

Chapter 10

A LESSON IN PAIN

DeLynn

DeLynn had stopped off at the University of Utah Medical Center for a brief check-up when I first met him in March 1993. He smiled and shook hands as we sat in the hall to conduct our interview.

Having read a little of DeLynn's experience before meeting him, I knew that he had severe chronic health problems. When he joined me, therefore, I was unprepared for the vigorous, lively man who shook my hand with aggressive good nature. He was shorter than the average man, but his youthful appearance and energetic nature dispelled my preconception.

DeLynn was born in October 1951 at the Utah Valley Hospital in Provo, Utah. Upon his birth the medical people observed that there was something wrong with his body. He was secreting excessive salt, and he was having severe intestinal and pulmonary problems. These problems ultimately led to a diagnosis of cystic fibrosis.

During much of his youth DeLynn was raised in the Orem, Utah area where his family found a physician who could properly treat DeLynn's disease. Until the age of five or six, DeLynn was not able to eat normal foods; he grew up on liver, rice water and fruit. His diet allowed no milk, no greases or fats, and no whole grains. This restricted diet was largely the cause of his short stature.

DeLynn was the oldest of four brothers and one sister. All of the children were adopted so the genetic origin of his disease was unknown. He and his brothers and sister were raised in a typical Mormon atmosphere.

Both of DeLynn's parents had obtained higher degrees. DeLynn's father had a doctorate in chemistry, and DeLynn's mother had a master's

117

degree. Because of their educational status they actively sought information concerning DeLynn's symptoms in medical journals—at that time, cystic fibrosis was not well understood. It was not discovered as a genetic disease until 1945, and most of the research was in the eastern part of the United States. DeLynn was ten years old before they identified his problem as cystic fibrosis.

After attending high school in Orem, DeLynn went to Brigham Young University where he obtained a Bachelor of Science degree. His education was interrupted by a two-year mission for The Church of Jesus Christ of Latter-day Saints to the Florida South Spanish Mission, which included Puerto Rico.

During his youth, and later, DeLynn and his parents learned how to minimize problems with the disease. Diet was a prime control factor, and he learned to avoid excessive sun or heat. However, DeLynn believes that there was another factor that contributed to the long-term control of his disease. I will let him tell his story from this point.

A Father's Blessing

"By the time I was five years old my parents had faced many crises with my health. Neither they nor the medical community knew what the real cause was of my recurrent health problems. My parents were concerned about my long-term survival; consequently, one day my father sat me down on the sewing stool in our home and gave me a blessing. In the blessing he promised that if I remained faithful to the Lord, as a little boy, and later as a responsible adult, I would receive all of the blessings of a normal person. He told me that I would be able to go on a mission for the Church, I would be married, and I would live a normal life.

"Had my father known how serious my disease was, he might not have promised all the things that he did. As it was, since he was largely ignorant of the real implications of my illness, the blessing he gave was unrestricted. Subsequently all of the promises in the blessing were fulfilled. I still remember the promises as he gave them. The blessing has had an enormous impact on my life.

"Concerning the promise of marriage, I met a returned sister missionary in the Salt Lake City Mission Home where we were both teaching classes. This young sister was a superb teacher and I was impressed and attracted to her. At the time, we were both dating and engaged to separate fiancés. We were each having trouble with our respective relationships. We used to get together and commiserate over our respective problems. It took me about three years to get my head together and ask my friend to marry me. We were married in July 1977 and have since adopted our two boys, who are now eleven and seven."

Health Crises

"After we were married, I fell ill with pneumonia and other difficulties related to cystic fibrosis, but nothing life-threatening until January of 1985. For one week I couldn't pass anything, and I felt very ill. I was not sure what the trouble was. It turned out that I had a blocked bowel—common with cystic fibrosis—and it was a serious blockage. It got bad enough that I couldn't even stand up.

"My wife took me to the Utah Valley Regional Medical Center after I collapsed on the morning of January 10. The doctor examined me and said that he had to operate immediately or I would die. I doubted that my illness was that serious. He again assured me, with the utmost urgency, that there must be an immediate operation or they could not save me.

"They operated right then, and they found two liters of black sewer water in a gangrenous bowel. They removed the diseased portion of the bowel—and my appendix burst. I was in very serious condition, but I recovered. That was the first major operation that I had.

"Because of the severity of the disease I had in my bowel, and because of scar tissue from the first operation, one-and-one-half years later the bowel became blocked again. I returned to the same hospital and the same doctor, and he operated again. Two days after that operation it abscessed, and they had to operate a third time.

"The third operation was on my hospital bed. They could not put me under anesthesia because that would have killed me."

"Did they use a local anesthetic?" I asked DeLynn.

"They used no anesthetic at all. My surgeon instructed one of the three nurses to lie on my legs and hold me so that I wouldn't move. The other nurse was instructed to hold my hand and tell me when to breathe in order to keep me from hyperventilating. The third nurse was the surgeon's operating assistant.

"After disinfecting the area, the surgeon retrieved a pair of surgical scissors which he plunged into the abscessed area in order to reopen the incision. There was a crunching feeling throughout my body as he slowly cut through the abdominal wall. I was writhing in pain. Finally he stopped cutting and pinched open the abscess. The scene was so gruesome that the nurse lying on my legs passed out. After cleaning out the infected area, he sewed me up with rough, catgut thread. When he tied the knot, the thread broke, upon which he ordered a larger needle and thicker thread. Needless to say, the entire process was extremely painful and emotionally traumatic.

"After that series of operations I recovered and resumed life. In November of 1988 I was admitted to the Utah Valley Hospital with a moderately high temperature, pneumonia, and a severe sinus headache. They let me go home for Thanksgiving dinner; however I felt so bad and my teeth were hurting so much that I couldn't eat. I went back to the hospital. The next day I went to my dentist and had him take X-rays, thinking that I might need root canal work on my teeth.

"My dentist said that I had the worst case of sinusitis he had seen. He urged me to see an Ear, Nose and Throat Specialist. I returned to the hospital and they had an ENT specialist examine me. Upon completing the examination he explained that I must have an emergency operation.

"Three hours later I was on the operating table. They asked me to count backwards from ten as they administered the anesthetic. Before I lost consciousness I remember thinking: *I wonder if I'm going to wake up from this one?*

"When I awakened, my wife, as usual, was waiting for me. She reassured me that I had behaved well and the doctors were pleased. Unlike other operations, however, I noticed that I had many wires attached to me. I was wearing an oxygen mask and there was an urgency about the people as they attended to my needs.

"I asked my wife: 'What's going on?' and she said: 'It was a difficult operation and you bled a lot. They had to give you two units of blood.'

"They put me in the Intermediate Care section of the hospital and for four days I was in and out of consciousness. Blood continued to be lost down my throat, requiring that I receive three more units. This worried me because of the fear of contracting AIDS.

"I remained in IMC until Tuesday, November 29, when they put me in a private room. My doctor came into the room to remove the nose packing that had been tightly packed into my sinuses to minimize bleeding. As he was pulling the packing out of my sinuses through my nostrils, it seemed as if there would never be an end to the packing. The pain was excruciating. I was crying from the intense pain, but he just kept pulling and pulling. My mother left the room because she could not bear to see me suffer such pain.

"When the doctor left I just wanted to go to sleep and forget the pain. I was totally exhausted, both physically and emotionally."

A Trip in a Tunnel

"In the early morning hours of Wednesday, November 30, I woke up to the realization that I was no longer in my body. In fact, I was being drawn down a tunnel. Had it not been for the books I had read about near-death experiences, I would have probably been ignorant of where I was."

I interrupted DeLynn's narration and asked: "You had read books about the near-death experience, then, before you went through this?"

"Yes. For some reason I had a fascination with the subject."

"Okay, so you were in the tunnel. What happened next?"

"I found myself being drawn toward a bright light that was down the tunnel. The tunnel was about seventy-five yards long, and as I was drawn toward the light, I finally realized where I was and I said to myself: *Whoa, stop!* I had to consciously say, stop. My movement wasn't by walking, it was more like floating. But it wasn't floating, either. It was a different process than anything I had experienced in mortal life.

"As I told myself to stop, I stopped moving. I was about half-way down the tunnel with the light at the end I was moving toward. Turning around and looking at the opposite end, I saw my family sitting there. My wife was there with our two boys sitting on her lap. I thought to myself: *This is really strange.*

"Before I had this experience, and knowing how serious my disease was, I told myself that if I ever went through a near-death experience, I would ask a set of questions. My first question was: *If I came into this world naked, how do I leave the world?* I looked down and saw that I was dressed in a white garment, tailored like a jump suit. The material had a thick weave to it, yet it had the softest feel of any material I had ever felt. It was softer than silk and it glowed. The color of the material was the whitest white I had ever seen. The suit covered most of my body. Starting with a snug, but comfortable neckline, it had full sleeves to my wrists, and full legs to my ankles. A curious part of the suit was that it had no openings such as those we need as humans. I wondered briefly about this aspect of the clothing, but then I focused my attention on other questions.

"One amazing aspect of my experience attracted my early attention. Because I had suffered from cystic fibrosis since youth I was not aware that breathing could be a pleasant exercise. I soon noticed, in the tunnel, that I was breathing and it didn't hurt. I could actually fill my lungs and it didn't burn, it didn't sting, it didn't tickle! How exhilarating it was for someone who had never breathed without difficulty. Filling my lungs was such a pleasure that I stayed in the same place for a moment simply enjoying it.

"Not only were my lungs responding without pain, I next noticed that I had no pain throughout my body. Pain had been a constant companion throughout my life; I had learned to accept it as normal. I learned there, however, that pain was not normal. For the first time I realized how intense my pain had been. It was a wonderful feeling—to be without pain—one that I sometimes have to force myself to forget when I am having painful sieges in the hospital.

"A second question that I had puzzled over was: *If I am a spirit when I die, do I really have substance to me?*

"To find out whether I had substance, I rubbed my hands together and I felt my face with my hands. In both cases I found that I had form and substance. I could feel myself. Looking at my hands, I saw that they looked like my hands normally did, except there was a glow to them. My feet weren't visible, I'm not sure why, but I knew that I didn't have shoes or socks on. These discoveries excited me. I remember thinking: *Wow! This is great.*

"Another issue that I had wondered about from reading the near-death literature was the physical characteristics of the tunnel. When that thought entered my mind I found myself at the side of the tunnel. My tunnel was about as wide as this hallway (about 30 feet), and it resembled a half-circle. The texture of the tunnel, which I felt, was rough and undulating. The side of the tunnel was cool. Indeed, it had temperature, texture and form.

"One of my anxieties about death was that of fear. To my delight I found that the emotion of fear was nonexistent. There was absolutely no worry, no concern, no fear. My primary emotion was a feeling of security. I was alone, and yet I knew that I wasn't alone. There was something else there that was encompassing me. I felt warm and serene—fear couldn't exist in that environment. It was a wonderful feeling."

A Familiar Voice

"At this point in my experience I became aware of a voice talking to me. My surroundings, and my analysis of them, had so interested me that I had not paid attention to the voice at first. It was a soft, fatherly voice that kept repeating my name. Facing the light, and then turning 90 degrees to my left and looking up at a slight angle, I looked to see where the voice was coming from. There was no one that I could see—but the voice persisted, not in my ears, but in my mind. I finally responded by asking the voice: *What?*

"The voice didn't immediately respond. I wondered how I could hear with my mind and not my ears, and I learned that it wasn't necessary for me to understand the process just then. My mind next thought the questions: *Why am I here? Why me? I'm a good guy—why did I die?*

"The voice answered: *You are here because you have earned the right to be here based on what you did on earth. The pain you have suffered qualifies you to be here. You have suffered as much pain in 37 years as a normal person might have suffered in 87 years.*

"I asked: *It's pain that gets me here?* and the answer was yes.

"This still puzzled me so I asked: *But why was it necessary for me to suffer so? I was a worthy member of the Church; I kept all the commandments. Why me?*

"Then I received a most startling answer. He said to me: *You chose your disease and the amount of pain you would be willing to suffer before this life—when you were in a premortal state. It was your choice.*

"While I was hearing this voice, I became aware that it was a familiar voice—it was one that I knew. It was a voice that I had not heard during my mortal lifetime. When it was speaking to me, though, there was no question but that I knew who it was. There was enormous love for me in the voice."

"You said, DeLynn, that you knew who the voice was. Who was it?" I asked.

"It was my Father in Heaven."

"It was not Jesus Christ?"

"No."

"And you felt love in the voice?"

"We don't have a word that would describe what I felt from Him toward me. The closest word we have is *love*, but it doesn't begin to describe the feeling. There is no appropriate description in mortal tongue that can explain the feeling—you have to feel it."

A Premortal Choice

"When He told me that it was my choice, in a premortal environment, to suffer when I came to earth, I was both astonished and incredulous. He must have understood my incredulity, because I was immediately transported to my premortal existence. There was a room that I was viewing from above and to the side, but at the same time I was sitting in it. In a sense I was both an observer and a participant. About thirty people were in the room, both men and women, and we were all dressed in the white jump-suit type of garment.

"An instructor was in the front of the room, and he was teaching about accountability and responsibility—and about pain. He was instructing us about things we had to know in order to come to earth and get our bodies. Then he said, and I'll never forget this: *You can learn lessons one of two ways. You can move through life slowly, and have certain experiences, or there are ways that you can learn the lessons very quickly through pain and disease.* He wrote on the board the words: *Cystic Fibrosis*, and he turned and asked for volunteers. I was a volunteer; I saw me raise my hand and offer to take the challenge.

"The instructor looked at me and agreed to accept me. That was the end of the scene, and it changed forever my perspective of the disease that I previously felt was a plague on my life. No longer did I consider myself a victim. Rather, I was a privileged participant, by choice, in an eternal plan. That plan, if I measured up to the potential of my choice, would allow me to advance in mortal life in the fastest way possible. True, I would not be able to control the inevitable slow deterioration of my mortal body, but I could control how I chose to handle my illness emotionally and psychologically. The specific choice of cystic fibrosis was to help me learn dignity in suffering. My understanding in the eternal sense was complete—I knew that I was a powerful, spiritual being that chose to have a short, but marvelous, mortal existence."

A View of Gethsemane

"While I was marveling at this new-found knowledge, or rather, from the reawakened knowledge that I previously had, I was again transported to another era. This time I found myself looking on a different scene—the scene was the Garden of Gethsemane. Looking down from above, I saw Christ undergoing his ordeal of pain with dignified endurance."

"When you were transported to these different scenes in time, DeLynn, did you ask to see them?"

"No, they were completely automatic. The first one seemed to be in response to my astonishment when the voice told me that I chose the disease, cystic fibrosis, in a premortal life. I suspect that the second scene, in Gethsemane, was to teach me more about the value of a dignified endurance of pain."

"Did you feel anything when you saw Christ suffering?"

"I felt bad that he had to go through it, and I felt empathy for him. I also realized why he was doing it; I understood that it was his choice, just as cystic fibrosis had been my choice."

A Familiar Home

"When the scene in Gethsemane closed, I found myself back in the tunnel. At this point I realized that I had come *home.* Everything was familiar—especially God's love. His voice was a familiar voice of unlimited and unconditional love.

"The knowledge I was obtaining, too, was knowledge that I had held before. The events in my experience merely reawakened in me a dormant part of my memory, and it was wonderful. I no longer felt picked on because of my pain and illness. I understood the choices I had made and the reasons for them. And I understood the tremendous love that God had for me to allow me to make those choices—and to suffer pain.

"The realization that this was all by my choice had an enormous rejuvenating effect on me. I was no longer a victim of chance, or worse yet, of some punishment for wrong doing. In the broadest sense I now saw myself as a master of my own destiny—if I lived up to the possibilities of my choices. Instead of looking at cystic fibrosis as a severe disability, I was now able to look on it as my truest mentor.

"It was astonishing, the speed with which I was learning. Knowledge that had somehow slumbered deep in my soul was released, and I was extremely exhilarated by this reawakened knowledge. Light and knowledge were flowing into me from every direction. I could feel it. Every part of my body was reverberating with the light gushing in. Even my fingertips were receptors of light and knowledge. It was as if I were drinking from a fully engaged fire hydrant. I was excited with the thought of going further into this wonderful world of knowledge and love. So I turned, expecting to travel toward the light at the end of the tunnel."

A Decision to Return

"The light was overwhelming. It was at the end of the tunnel, and it lighted the inside of the tunnel. It was pure white and it was the brightest bright I had ever seen. I was drawn to it, and I turned to move in that direction.

"As I turned, I heard my youngest son, who was three at the time, ask: 'Daddy, what are you doing?'

"I asked: 'What?' and he repeated: 'What are you doing?'

"I answered: 'I don't know. What am I doing?'

"The Voice then said: 'What do you want to do?'

"Evidently I was going to have to make another choice, and that choice would involve returning to my family or staying where I was.

"Speaking to the Voice, I asked: 'If I choose to go back to my family, can I go back, and what will be the consequences?'

"The Voice responded: 'You may return, but you may lose your reward.' My reward flashed before me, and I saw that eternal happiness would be mine if I chose to stay.

"The Voice also told me that there were no guarantees if I returned. He said that if I chose to go back to earth I would have greater pain than I had ever felt in life to that point. Puzzling over the risks of returning, I then asked: 'What gives me the right to go back?'

"The Voice said: 'You have learned accountability and responsibility. If you choose to go back you have the obligation to teach those principles to your family and your employees.'

"I wondered about that charge and asked: 'What do my employees have to do with it?' He didn't answer the question. I later learned that my employees were included so that I would, in time, overcome my fear of telling others about this entire experience. They, too, were part of my 'family.'

"When I finished asking questions about returning or staying, I again analyzed the risks and rewards of staying or returning. After I was satisfied that I understood the options, I said: 'I choose to return.'

"The Voice asked me: 'Are you sure?'

"My response was: 'Yes, I'm sure.

"He asked, again: 'Are you sure?'

"My answer, this time, was: 'Yes, I think so.'

"A third time the Voice asked: 'Are you sure?'

"This time it hit me. My answer must be certain—I must not lie to myself or try to conceal my real intent from Him. I looked again at my family. I thought about it, and I said: 'Yes, I choose to return.'

"The next thing I knew, I was back in my hospital room. The pajamas I was wearing and the bed linens were soaked. The doctors and nurses seemed concerned, and one of the nurses asked me what happened. Not wanting to tell her about the experience, I said that I must have choked. She responded: 'You did more than that!'"

Out-of-Body in the Hospital Room

"The night nurse came into my room, to stay the rest of the night with me. I asked her to watch and make sure that I didn't go to sleep—I was afraid to sleep. The experience I had just been through was so traumatic I was afraid to repeat it.

"Settling in a chair behind me, the nurse talked to me for a while. Her chair was far enough behind me that I couldn't see her without twisting to an awkward position in the bed. Suddenly, however, I could see her. Finding myself sitting up in my bed, I waved my arms at her to see what she would do. I was amazed that she didn't see me.

"During this brief period, I was acutely aware of many small events happening around me. It was about 2:00 a.m., and the clock in the room was ticking loudly. I was conscious of people in the hall outside my room and of the light in the hall. It was an increased sensitivity of my complete surroundings. Sounds were much clearer than they normally were.

"Wondering what was going on, I turned my head and saw my body lying in the bed. The real *me*, my spirit self, was partially removed from my body. I was sitting out of my body from the waist up.

"Thinking to myself: *Here I go again*, I wondered what to do. I offered a little prayer in which I said: *Lord, I don't want to leave*. The impression came to me: *Well, then, lie back down in your body*. I lay down—I felt no transition—it was as if I just woke up.

"Without moving a muscle I said to the night nurse: 'You can't just sit there and knit. You've got to help me stay awake.' She responded: 'How do you know I'm knitting? You can't see me.' I told her that I knew everything that was happening in the room.

"The nurse commented that I had scared her enough that night. Six months after the event I asked the same nurse what her experience with me was during this period. She said that when she first came back into the room and found me, I was cold and gray, my mouth was open, my eyes were glassed over, there was no pulse, and my skin was clammy. That's when they called for the crash-cart and the doctor to resuscitate me."

Questions About DeLynn's Experience

In order to better understand some of the events in DeLynn's experience I received his permission to ask questions. I began: "When you first moved into the tunnel you mentioned that breathing was pleasant for you. Were you breathing air, or what?"

"I don't think it was air, but I have no idea what it was. The pleasantness and reality of my breathing, though, is still vividly clear in my memory."

"When you found yourself in a premortal environment, what did the room look like?"

"It was a rectangular room, everything was white, and we were sitting in desk-type chairs. I was assimilating the teacher's instruction as fast as he gave it to us. Notes were unnecessary. I simply absorbed everything I was told instantaneously."

"Did the information you were getting seem as if it were new information?"

"The procedures we were being taught were new, but the principles guiding those procedures, I already knew. The *how to* portions of the earthly experience were new. I remember thinking about it and wondering if I were ready to pay the price, and then deciding that, yes, I was willing to pay the price."

"So, when you saw yourself in the premortal environment, you could actually remember how you felt in that earlier time?"

"Yes. I knew my thoughts from the premortal experience. I could see myself sitting in the room, yet I knew what I had been thinking and feeling when I was in that room. I can remember thinking: *Be careful about that choice—you don't even know what pain is.*"

"So it was as if you were two different people, yet you had the feelings of both?"

"Yes. They were simultaneous feelings."

"When your son talked to you in the tunnel he asked you what you were doing. Have you asked him about the experience?"

"Yes. He is unaware of having talked to me."

"But you are convinced that he did talk to you?"

"Absolutely. He never opened his mouth, but I heard him call my name, and I recognized his voice."

"You mentioned the tunnel as a short one. You didn't feel that you traveled a long distance?"

"No, it was about the length of a football field. There was a drawing power, like a magnet in the center of my chest that drew me into the tunnel and toward the light. I didn't travel far."

"When you returned to your body, did you feel pain again?"

"Most certainly. There was no pain associated with returning to my body. I didn't feel that process; I just woke up. The pain associated with my operation was severe and instantaneous, though. Of course I've had other pain related to my disease since then."

"What was your recovery like?"

"I was out of the hospital within the next few days. My energy was up, and I felt invigorated. That didn't take away the pain, however, I just dealt with it better. The experience has helped me over time to deal with pain better."

"Have you had greater pain than before?"

"I thought when the doctor used scissors—to slice into me without an anesthetic—that I couldn't experience worse pain. This past winter, the winter of 1992-1993, I was in the hospital over ninety days. They almost lost me twice. Again, I had a blocked bowel in which they used barium while X-raying my bowels. I was unsuccessful in cleansing my bowels of the barium, and it set up like rocks in my intestine. Passing those rocks almost killed me. I became allergic to most of the pain killers they were giving me, and I had to pass the barium rocks over a period of four days without pain killer. The pain was so bad that if it hadn't been for my Dad, I don't think I would have made it."

"What did your Dad have to do with it?"

"My father died in March 1992. He came back and gave me a blessing, and that relieved me of the pain."

"What do you mean, your father came back and blessed you?"

"My father and I were very close. He was the one that gave me the blessing when I was five years old. When he died, I became aware of it before the doctor called. The same voice that I heard in the tunnel told me, during the night, that my father had died (Dad died early Monday morning). My father came to me at 1:30 a.m., Tuesday morning, and told me several things, including why he had to go, what I should be doing, and what my mother should do regarding our genealogy. Then Dad said that he would be with me when I had medical emergencies.

"In August 1992, when I was in so much pain from the barium (morphine shots administered every two hours were not helping), one night at three in the morning, I cried out: *Lord, what did I do wrong?* I also cried: *Dad, you promised you would be here!* Suddenly my father was at my bed and I felt him put his hands on my head. Within a few seconds, there was a feeling as if someone were pouring something warm over my body. It cascaded from my head to my toes, and the pain left. My father smiled and then he left. The next day I began passing the stones."

"You said that your choice was to come back to earth despite the knowledge that you would be subjected to greater pain. Do you know why you made that choice?"

"I wanted to be with my family—I would do anything to be with my boys and my wife."

"Did you have a feeling for any mission you might have?"

"Yes. My purpose for being, now, is to teach people accountability and responsibility; to teach them that they are agents with freedom to choose; and to let them know that there is a Father in Heaven who loves them beyond all description."

"Because of this experience, have your feelings about life or death changed?"

"Absolutely. Life has greater meaning, since I no longer look at myself as an unfortunate victim of disease. Nor am I the victim of other circumstances caused by family, parents, neighbors, and others—or of 'accidents.' Instead, I make the choices that decide my fate. That is a wonderfully liberating feeling."

"Has the experience changed your religious perspective?"

"Yes. It is still my knowledge that The Church of Jesus Christ of Latter-day Saints is the Church of God. Nothing I saw or heard during the experience contradicted what I had previously learned in the Church. My priorities have changed, however. I am more people oriented than I was before. I used to be program oriented, but now I know that people are far more important than programs. My experience taught me that the Lord has boundless love for *all* people, whether or not they are members of The Church."

"Is there any message you would like to leave for others?"

"Yes. Despite what the world teaches, there is a loving Father in Heaven who loves *every* person. That love, which I have experienced, is indescribable. We are literally the children of God, and He knows each one of us by name. He is willing to bless us with any righteous desires that we have. All we need to do is ask—and be willing to pay the price."

Chapter 11

TWO WHO TRIED SUICIDE

Karen

She was a shy, blonde, lady with a graceful, feminine manner. Her appearance illustrated the fact that she had been a model at one time. She spoke in gentle tones as she visited with Carol and me in late March 1993.

Karen told us that she was born in the state of Washington, in April 1956. She was raised in Washington until the age of nine. Her parents were divorced, so Karen spent part of her youth traveling between her mother and father. When she was nearly eleven, she moved on a semi-permanent basis to be with her mother in a southern state, where she spent the remainder of her youth and early adulthood.

There were eight siblings, including Karen, in the two families of her mother and father. Both of her parents were loved and enjoyed by Karen. Her father was a devout Mormon, and her mother was remarried to a Catholic man, so Karen was exposed to both religions. She graduated from high school and finished two years of college.

Travel and illness were frequent companions of Karen during her adult life. She moved to Salt Lake City about five years ago.

Karen's Suicide Attempt

The story, as told by Karen, begins: "In 1976, I was going through a divorce, and my best friend and I went to Los Angeles, California. My friend and I shared an apartment in Burbank.

"A therapist I was seeing, because of depression, had prescribed some tranquilizers to get me through this trying time. Everything that had happened to me was overwhelming, and I was unable to cope. The divorce, the move, the work, the depression—they were too much.

"One night as I was lying in bed, asleep, I was awakened by a male voice saying: 'I'm going to get you. Sooner or later, I'm going to get you.' The event frightened me and I sat up, wide awake. I told my roommate, and she said it was just a dream, and not to worry about it.

"About a week later, everything seemed so hopeless that I took the bottle of tranquilizers. My full intention was to kill me. It seemed the best way to handle my problems, just go to sleep.

"It didn't work out the way I wanted, though, because I fell out of bed and woke my roommate. She called the ambulance at about one o'clock in the morning. At the hospital, I found out later, they pumped my stomach and put charcoal in it. They didn't think I was going to make it. My heart had stopped, and they used defibrillator paddles to restart it.

"During this period I became aware that I was conscious, but I was enveloped in total darkness. It was pitch-black all around, yet there was a feeling of movement. My conscious self assured me that I was in the form of a spiritual body.

"A male voice spoke to me, a different voice than the one I heard a week before. This voice said: 'You have a choice. You can stay here, or you can go back. If you stay here, your punishment will be just as it is, right now. You will not have a body, you will not be able to see, touch, or have other sensations. You will only have this darkness and your thoughts, for eternity.'

"Terrified because of the experience, and because of what I had heard, I understood that this would be my private hell. There would be no contact with other life or with the sensations of life, for eternity. Yet I would remain conscious with my thoughts in total blackness.

"Frantically scared, I knew immediately that I had made a terrible mistake. Telling the voice that I had made a mistake, I asked to go back, to return to life. The voice said, 'All right, you may return.'

"Suddenly I felt myself being pulled back. It's hard to explain. There was total darkness, yet I had the feeling of movement as I was pulled back.

"Next, I found myself in the hospital room, in an elevated position, looking down. I could see the doctor, I could see my roommate, I could see my body in the bed. My roommate was crying, and the doctor was explaining something to her. It was clear that they thought I was gone.

"While I was watching this scene, I felt myself slowly descending. Then, suddenly, I was sucked into my body. It was fast.

"My next conscious act was to open my eyes and see my doctor looking down on me. Surprise and a relieved smile showed on his face. He asked me if I could squeeze his hand. With great effort I was able to do a feeble squeeze, and I knew that I was back by the grace of God."

Questions About the Suicide Experience

Karen agreed that I could ask some questions. I began: "You said, Karen, that there was total darkness where you were. Did you have any physical sensations while you were there?"

"None at all except for the feeling of motion when I left and when I arrived at the dark place. The sensations that I felt were in thought form only. I was so frightened of the concept of being stuck in total darkness. It was horrifying to me, and it still is today."

"You said that this would have been your hell. Is that what the voice told you?"

"No. He didn't tell me that, it was an inner knowledge."

"What is your feeling, now, about suicide?"

"I know beyond a shadow of a doubt that if you do commit suicide, there is a hell for that. There might be different types of hell for other people, but for me that darkness—with just my thoughts to keep me company—would have been absolute agony."

"Under the same circumstances, would you try it again?"

"Absolutely not. It's kind of ironic now, because I am a cancer survivor, and I've had to fight very hard to stay here on earth. Life is now very precious to me."

"Why is life so precious to you?"

"Because I am here for a reason, and we all have lessons to learn. Life is a gift from God."

"How do you know that?"

"From the suicide attempt, and from past experiences that I have gone through."

A Devastating Experience

"In 1988, after marrying again, I had a heart-breaking experience. My husband, whom I loved dearly, left me for another woman. I was pregnant, which we had planned, and I was at a loss with regard to what I should do next. My life seemed over. Abortion is against my belief, and I had a moral dilemma, yet I could see no alternatives. So I decided to terminate the pregnancy.

"After the procedure, my sister and I were sitting in the waiting room, and I started to hemorrhage. They took me back into the room where they had done the procedure. I just kept bleeding. The physician was unable to stop the bleeding, and it was excruciating.

"It became very scary, and I began to pray. I prayed: *God, forgive me for what I have done. Please take the soul of the child that I destroyed to heaven—please forgive me. And please don't let the child feel the pain that I am feeling.* Through all this, I knew that I was going to die. Then a strange thing happened. In the corner of the room, up near the ceiling, I saw a black dot. The dot sort of opened up, slowly, until it was about two feet in diameter. It remained for perhaps one minute after I prayed, then it slowly diminished in size and disappeared. I was astonished, and I couldn't explain it, but I knew, somehow, that the black dot or hole was a passageway.

"Finally, a nurse said: 'Doctor, I think we are losing her. She is going into shock.' They called for an ambulance which took me to a hospital where my lost blood was replaced, and I recovered."

Cancer

"Four years ago, in May, they discovered that I had cancer of the colon. It was discovered when I went in for a checkup, I felt tired all the time. They found a metastasized mass the size of my fist.

"The surgery was at a hospital in Salt Lake City. It took five hours, and my life was again threatened. It was very serious.

"My boyfriend, who was Catholic, gave me comfort during this period. After the operation, the doctors told my boyfriend that they didn't expect me to live. My boyfriend, who was upset, tried to help me. When I awakened, he asked me to tell him what I would choose if I could have anything in the world. I told him that I just wanted to be Catholic; then I drifted off.

"For some time I had been searching for something, but I wasn't sure what. I lived across the street from a Catholic church, and I would go inside and kneel at one of the altars and pray. I found out later that the altar I prayed at was for hopeless causes. Anyway, my boyfriend talked to a Priest, and he told the Priest that I would probably die, but my last request was to be Catholic before I passed away.

"The following day a Priest visited me in the hospital. He asked me some questions about my desire to be Catholic. I assured him that was what I wanted to do. The Priest further explained that he could give me a blessing: The Blessing of the Sick. They used to call it The Last Rites, but they changed the name because of the connotation.

"I became Catholic and had the blessing. I received my first Communion and Host on my death bed. It was very peaceful. Suddenly I felt as though I were immersed in a stream of water, rushing over me from my head to my toes. The feeling was continuous for about a minute—as if someone had laid me in a stream. It was the most intense experience, of the type, that I had ever had. The spiritual feeling stayed with me. I knew I could go through anything.

"When this feeling of peace enveloped me, I noticed the Priest grabbing the end of the bed. He said: 'Something marvelous has happened,' and he seemed elated. Then he said: 'You know that you are cured of cancer.' And I knew it.

"The Priest told me to do what the doctors told me to do. He said that I should subject myself to chemotherapy, or whatever else the doctors said, but I should understand that something profound had happened to me. Peace continued to be with me, so I knew, with great joy, that he was telling the truth.

"The first doctor that I had seen, a month after the operation, told me in front of my boyfriend that it was hopeless. He said that I could start on chemotherapy, but it was a waste of time. I was going to die in a matter of days, he said. Another lady doctor said that I should prepare for a funeral. Ultimately, I found another doctor who felt there was a chance, so I started the grueling ritual of chemotherapy.

"Since the operation I have been in and out of the hospital three or four times, not because of cancer, but because of scar tissue and complications from the first operation. My present doctor says there is no sign of cancer, and there is a 98% chance that it will not return. He says it is a miracle."

Spiritual Guides

"After becoming Catholic, I prayed and meditated throughout the time that I was having chemotherapy. Prayer and meditation reinforced my faith and gave me the strength to endure the pain. About a-year-and-a-half ago, while I was praying and meditating, something profound happened. It was during meditation, and I knew someone was visiting me. When I shut my eyes I could see the being. It was a guide, or spiritual being, who was there to help me.

"The first spiritual being to visit me was Mary, the mother of Jesus. My initial reaction to the visit was: *Why me? Who am I to be worthy of a visit by Mary?* She told me that she came in response to my faith and prayers. Because of my prayers I was able to talk to her mentally. She also said that I had been forgiven for the things I previously did that were so wrong. My purpose now, she let me know, was to concentrate on living life, and she told me that I had a special task to do. It took me a while, but I finally came to terms with the idea of a spirit person visiting me.

"Other spirit beings visited me, and their purpose was to help me during this very difficult time in my life. They helped me to know that everything would be okay. One of the guides, in a loving way, asked me: 'Are you ready to do the things you are supposed to do?' In the visits I came to know that the Lord loves me very much. The peace that I felt when I received the blessing was again mine."

Further Questions About Karen's Experiences

"In your operation for cancer, you said that you returned to the hospital several times. Did you have other operations?"

"Yes. My intestine became twisted, from scar tissue induced by the first operation, and I had to have it removed. This second operation became a crisis when it got infected, and I almost died again."

"Based upon your experiences to date, including your first out-of-body experience, have they changed your outlook on life?"

"Most definitely."

"How?"

"I know that God and Jesus are always with me—they are with all of us. To have contact with God and Jesus we must pray and meditate daily, and have faith.

"There is no question in my mind that there is life after death. I am certain that there are heavens and hells. For us to be with Him, all he asks is that we do the best that we can and follow Christ's teachings."

"Did you always feel that there was a life after death, and that there were heavens and hells?"

"No. But after my experiences there was no question in my mind. It's a certainty within me that can't be taken away."

"Could your first experience have been a dream, or a hallucination?"

"No. It was real."

"You said that you finally came to terms with the idea of being visited by spirits. What did you mean by that?"

"My imperfection bothered me. I'm just an average schmoe, far from perfect, and it didn't seem reasonable that I should be so privileged. It became clear, though, during the visits that the Lord loves us all, regardless of what we did. We are all special in His sight. If anything, He cares about a sinner even more, in some ways, because He wants the sinner to return to his fold."

"Why are you telling me this story?"

"I'm not proud of what I did. But I feel that by telling my story I will be able to help other people. Also, I work with a cancer survivor's group, for example, and I try to help where I am needed."

"Are there any messages you would like to leave others?"

"Just that we have a purpose here, there is a life after death, and there is a God who loves all of us—a forgiving God. The love that God feels for us, we should try to replicate in our feelings for others. Our purpose in being here is to learn what life presents us with and to overcome obstacles. Life is a training ground. As situations present themselves we should try to do the best we can, that's all He asks of us."

Dallas

He was a short, but rugged looking man, with a neat beard and a sparkling sense of humor, when I visited him at his home in the spring of 1993. Dallas was born in Beacon, New York in 1939. He was one of the twin boys his mother had, and he had two stepsisters from a later marriage of his mother.

Dallas went to high school in Toledo, New York, and he joined the navy from 1958 to 1962. From the navy, he moved to Houston, Texas where he spent most of his life. In Texas, Dallas found employment in the oil fields, and this led to an extensive career in construction.

After moving to Texas, Dallas married a lady he described as a beautiful redhead. With three children and three grandchildren, Dallas was a vibrant looking grandfather when I visited him.

Taking a job as an oil field supervisor in Wyoming, Dallas moved to that area during the oil boom of the '80s. This area of the country attracted him, so he moved to Utah when the oil boom ended.

When Dallas was being raised, his mother was attracted to the Episcopalian faith which she attended with the children; some neighbor children occasionally took Dallas to Catholic masses. As an adult Dallas investigated many religions including Jewish, Baptist, Pentecostal, and Methodist. He joined The Church of Jesus Christ of Latter-day Saints in 1968, after a dream and a spiritual experience.

Dallas finished telling me of his youth and early adult life, and I asked him to tell the circumstance that led to his out-of-body experience. He began.

Despair and a Suicide Attempt

"In 1973, after ten years of marriage, my wife and I broke up. The breakup was in part due to conflict with her mother, but I was devastated. In addition, I had serious health problems. I struggled along for five years or so, but life was not good. Just before Valentine's day, and after my fortieth birthday in 1979, I decided that life was not worth living.

"To commit suicide I decided to use a rifle. Carefully disconnecting the phone so that it would not interrupt my concentration, I got my twenty-two rifle and loaded it with a hollow-point bullet.

"Gathering my courage, I braced the butt of the rifle against some furniture, put the point on my chest just opposite my heart, and pushed the trigger with my thumb. Penetrating my chest, the bullet broke two ribs, tore into my heart as it disintegrated, passed through my diaphragm, and penetrated my kidneys and my liver.

"It was about 6:00 p.m., and I was in my home in the master bedroom. As soon as the gun fired, I was overcome with enormous pain in my chest. The pain was so bad that . . . I would never do that again, no matter what the reason."

Out-of-Body to a Marvelous Place

"Suddenly I felt myself slipping out of my body. Everything went black; then I felt myself traveling through a tunnel of light. When I was nearly to the end of the tunnel, it became very bright and beautiful. There was a garden, and the beauty was indescribable. I've been to many art museums around the world, and it was more beautiful than anything displayed in any museum.

"Standing in the garden was the Lord Jesus Christ. The feeling I had was beyond description. As wonderful as the garden had been, it was no longer my center of attention. My whole being focused on this magnificent personage standing before me."

Interrupting Dallas's narration, I asked him to describe Christ. He struggled as he attempted to put into words what he had seen.

"The robe he was clothed in was white beyond any description, with a beautiful sash in the middle—it was gorgeous. His hair was long and it was a golden-brown color, and he had a beard. Actually, in terms of describing Christ himself, the closest I can come to it is the print of a painting I saw in Deseret Book Store some years later.

"The painting is entitled *The Second Coming*, and the original painting was done by the artist Harry Anderson. I purchased a print that I hang in my bedroom, because it is the best representation of what I remember seeing when I stood at Christ's feet. When I first saw the picture it brought back the memory of my experience, and I stood in front of the picture crying. As good as that painting is, though, it is a poor representation of the magnificent being I saw before me."

A Conversation with the Lord

"The Lord called me by name and told me that I had done a foolish thing, and it was not my time to be there. He said that there was a lot of work on the earth that I must do for Him. There were certain things I must accomplish with my family before I would be allowed to return to the Lord.

If I did what He asked, He said that my life would be great—not great in an earthly sense, but great in a spiritual sense, and I would be richly rewarded on the other side."

"The feelings I had when in His presence were overwhelming. It was an experience that . . ." Dallas paused in his description.

"How did you know it was Christ?" I asked.

Dallas chuckled, and then said with emphasis: "Because you can *feel* it. When He said: 'I have work for you to do,' and when He was talking to me, I just knew who it was. There was no doubt. I knew it was He as well as I knew who I was.

"The Lord then said that I had to go back, but I told Him I didn't want to go back. He made it clear that it wasn't up to me; there was this work that I had to do, so I must return."

"When you spoke with the Lord, Dallas, how did you converse?"

"Actually, I don't think I ever spoke. It was more mind-to-mind conversation than it was vocal words. He was able to read my mind and know what I was saying, and I knew what He was saying . . . I could hear His voice, but it was more in my mind than my ears. We had telepathic communication going between us; it was so neat!"

"What were some of the things the Lord asked you to do?"

"Some of what He said I have forgotten, but I remember Him telling me that I had to do things with the Church and with my family."

"He did tell you to do things with the Church and your family?"

"Yes. Taking the initiative, I asked Him about the Church. I don't know why I asked Him about the Church, but I did. The response was: 'You are where you need to be for what you have to do. You are in the right place.' That's what He said."

"What else did the Lord tell you?"

"That my health would be restored. At the time of my suicide attempt, in addition to the massive physical injuries from the gunshot wound, I had previously been diagnosed as having asbestosis and lung cancer. The asbestosis was from work I had done as an insulator on construction projects. The Lord said that all of these health problems would be cured."

"Are there other things you remember about being in the presence of the Lord?"

"I will never forget the feeling of being totally enveloped in warmth, it was . . . it was sort of like walking into a heavy fog, so heavy you couldn't see through it, that was everywhere. Only instead of fog, it was a feeling of warmth, of love, of compassion—it was a tangible feeling, almost physical in nature. This wonderful feeling enveloped me.

"When I first saw the Lord and that feeling encompassed me I cried uncontrollably. The feeling took over my whole body, every part of my body was affected. It completely shrouded me with an unbelievable joy. The scriptures speak of the love of the disciples for Christ, and I now know how they felt."

"So the Lord then told you that you had to go back?"

"Yes. It's interesting how He did it. At the time I was not an active member of the Church and I didn't understand some of the things I saw. When we were finished talking, the Lord raised His right arm to the square and commanded me to return to my body."

"How much time elapsed between the time you left your body and when you returned?"

"I have no idea. I cannot comprehend how time worked there."

"Did you, by any chance, have a review of your life while you were in His presence?"

"No. Only those things happened that I told you about."

Physical Recovery

"Finding myself on the floor of the bedroom, I felt this tremendous pain and burning sensation in my chest. Because I had lost so much blood and was so weak, I couldn't sit up, even though I tried. So I lay there all night bleeding onto the carpet (they later had to replace the carpet).

"In the morning I found enough strength to struggle into the kitchen and get a glass of milk from the refrigerator. In the process of struggling to get there I ruined all the carpet in the house by leaking blood all over.

"After drinking the milk I blacked out and collapsed again. Lying on the floor I kept drifting in and out of consciousness. Late in the afternoon, twenty-seven hours after I shot myself, I awakened and watched the room get light. It just lit up. There was no one present that I could see, but I felt a presence and heard a voice. The voice told me to reconnect the phone and call my neighbor.

"The voice kept urging that I fix the phone, but I felt so weak I could hardly move. The voice said: 'I told you that you would not die. There is work for you to do.' In my weakened condition I said: 'But Lord, I've lost so much blood that I can't stand up without passing out.' The voice then said: 'You can, now. I command you to do it.'

"Instantly, I was able to stand, reconnect the phone and call my neighbor. Upon arriving, the neighbor looked at me and commented: 'You stupid idiot, what have you done?' While he called the ambulance, I went in and took a shower to remove all the blood from me. Dressing myself, I went to the hospital in clean clothes.

"We got to the Veteran's Hospital in Houston about ten o'clock at night, and they operated on me an hour or so later. They later told me that I spent seven-and-one-half hours on the operating table. One-third of my blood had been lost before I got help, and they replaced it with thirty-six pints.

"Later, when some of the operating team members visited me during my recovery, I asked them what they thought when my heart stopped twice on the operating table. They asked how I knew that, and they wanted to know who told me.

"No one told me. Twice, during the surgery, I felt my heart stop, just as it did when I had my experience. During the surgery, when it stopped, I felt a hand on my shoulder, and the greatest feeling of warmth came over me. Then the voice said: 'I told you I wouldn't let you die. Everything will be okay.' That happened twice.

"The chief surgeon visited me sometime later, and I told him what had happened during the surgery. He said: 'I believe that you did have an unusual experience. Your heart was so badly damaged when we sewed it up we figured you only had about thirty minutes to live. There had to be a higher power—using better medicine than we had—otherwise you would be dead.

"In addition to sewing up the heart with about fourteen stitches, they had to repair the diaphragm, and they removed bullet fragments from throughout my body. Four small fragments are still lodged in the heart muscle, and they show up whenever I have an X-ray.

"A few years after my suicide attempt I had chest X-rays specifically to look at the state of my lungs. They found that the cancer signs had all disappeared. Previously my left lung was seriously affected. The later X-rays showed it to be clear, and the doctors thought the two sets of X-rays (before and after) were from different patients."

Chapter 12

A MAN AND A BOY

Chuck

It was a warm spring evening in 1993 when I visited Chuck at his home in Salt Lake City. His two dogs, a Dalmatian and a mixed breed, greeted me with wagging tails and friendly sniffs. Chuck was equally friendly, and he showed me some of the pictures and other mementos he had accumulated over the years. His deep voice assured an easy taping session.

Chuck was born in Salt Lake City in 1943. He was raised, with one sister, in the Salt Lake City region. His schooling was primarily in Utah, including college at the University of Utah.

Religious background provided by his family was from the LDS Church, and Chuck served a mission to Denmark for that church in 1963 and 1964. Previously having been married, he had three children when I met him.

When he returned from his mission, Chuck became attracted to police work as a career. His natural aptitude equipped him well for starting in this field.

After attending the Police Academy in Salt Lake City, he joined the police force. As a result of exposing some drug-related crimes while still in the Academy, he was transferred directly to undercover work. He served only about a month in uniform before he started the undercover work. Chuck now tells his own story.

A Dangerous Assignment and a Shooting

"Police work commenced for me in 1965, after finishing at the Academy. The Academy schooling was carried out, in those days, at the Metropolitan Hall of Justice. While I was working for the Salt Lake City Police Department as a reserve officer, I was living in Bountiful, a few miles north of Salt Lake.

"To allow me to do undercover work we set up a story where I was supposedly kicked off the force for improper behavior. This provided the cover I needed so that I could work in undercover narcotics. In addition, I had a retail store in Bountiful that provided additional income—and helped provide cover. The undercover work was in Salt Lake City, and for a while I was lent to the Food and Drug Administration of the federal government to help them in some narcotics work. Later, the FDA was supplanted by the Federal Bureau of Narcotics, and that was later replaced by the DEA.

"In 1968 I had made some substantial busts. As with most undercover police work, there comes the time when you must testify in court. When the cases get large, and you have to testify, your cover is blown. As the result of these cases I was exposed, so I was reassigned to uniform police work.

"A reserve officer, at that time, put in a minimum of fourteen hours a month. The work shifts were fairly flexible, starting on Friday or Saturday evenings, and allowing us to work the required time. It was a good arrangement and I enjoyed the work. We often helped indigent people and others who needed assistance, and the variety of assignments made the work interesting.

"Knowing that my cover had been blown, I took normal precautions, but it was difficult to protect against all circumstances. A fellow, I'll call him Jim, was introduced to me through a mutual acquaintance. He, and another friend of his came over to my apartment one evening, supposedly for friendly chit-chat. What I didn't know at the time was that Jim, who needed money, had been paid $5,000 to hit (kill) me.

"The hit was set up to look like an accident. Jim and his friend were in the apartment, and Jim had a .38 revolver that he was fooling around with. He was pretending to practice quick drawing, with the wall as his target. Under the guise of its being an accident, as I came out of the kitchen, Jim drew on me. The gun fired—he shot me point blank from about six feet. Striking me in the right chest, the bullet entered just beyond the middle of my chest, at about nipple level.

"The bullet went completely through me on a downward angle. The doctor later found it under the skin on my back, just above the waist. At the time, though, I was not aware that I had been shot by a gun loaded with live ammunition. Looking down at my shirt I saw the hole in it, but I assumed it was caused by a wad from a blank cartridge. I thought it had been a joke, and I remember being angry that he didn't take the wad out so that it wouldn't ruin my $25 shirt."

Out-of-Body

"While I stood there looking at my shirt, I gradually sank to the floor. As I sank to the floor I saw Jim crossing himself, and saying things like: 'Please don't die!' He apparently realized the enormity of what he had done, and I finally did also.

"It felt, at first, as if a gust of wind hit me in the face. Then a crushing feeling came over me in my chest, and I went down on my knees—praying. Realizing what had happened and that I might die I was praying that my father, who had died a month earlier, would come and get me.

"When I fell to the floor, there was this big crushing feeling—and it was black, it was murky, it was empty, it was a void. Breathing hurt fiercely, and I knew if I exhaled too far I wouldn't be alive anymore. If I could continue to breathe in a shallow manner, I felt that I could stay alive.

"Next, I remember seeing my body on the floor. The strange thing about it was that it didn't seem out of the ordinary. My face was facing the floor, yet I could see my entire body lying there. It seemed perfectly normal to be standing there looking at my body.

"Jim's friend went over to the phone, and he said: 'I can't remember the damned phone number for the police department.' To help him, I told him the phone number, but he didn't pay any attention to me. In the meantime, Jim was fretting over my body, saying things like: 'Please don't die; I didn't mean to do it.'

"After watching this scene for a short while, everything went blank. It's not clear to me how long I was out, but again, I found myself looking at my body on the floor. As I watched myself, my friend Charles, from the Bountiful Police Department, came in.

"Charles grabbed my wrist and held it with his thumb. He was trying to take my pulse. I said to him: 'Charles, you can't use your thumb to get a pulse.' It seemed important to tell him that, but he apparently couldn't hear me. He ignored what I was saying and continued to feel my pulse with his thumb.

"Suddenly I felt an enormous pain in my chest and my back. The pain was as if someone had taken a branding iron and used it on me. No longer could I see my body lying there. Instead, I could see Charles's knee in front of my face.

"Seeing from the corner of my eyes, his thumb on my wrist, I again told him that he couldn't get a proper pulse using his thumb. This time he heard me, and it appeared to shock him to hear me talking.

"As I lay there with Charles trying to help me, I was fearful of dying. Then it struck me—I had been dead."

Recovery

"The ambulance arrived and they put me on a stretcher. Not wanting to shock the apartment residents, and being slightly embarrassed, I asked the paramedics to cover my face when they carried me out. In the ambulance I asked them not to run the siren. They reminded me that I had been shot and it was their job to handle the equipment. They ran the siren.

"Upon reaching the hospital they took me to the X-ray table, and they asked me to hold my breath while they took the X-ray. In order to breathe I had been taking air like a rabbit, and they had the guts to tell me to hold my breath!

"Then another medical technician came in and said he needed to draw some blood. I told him to put his beaker under the hole where I had been shot. The strange thing, though, was that I did not bleed very much. The bullet had passed clear through me without severing any major arteries. My main physical problem was just in getting enough air. And I hurt like the blazes.

"Charles came to my room sometime later with the doctor. They had the X-ray and Charles said: 'You're lucky to be alive.' They showed me the bullet in the picture, and they could feel it under the skin on my back.

"They removed the bullet, and I stayed in the hospital from Tuesday night to Thursday afternoon. Then they released me."

A Beloved Father

"Thirty days to the day before my accident, my father was killed. There was a mining accident where he worked in Wyoming, and he was crushed. A skip-hoist that he was working on moved when it shouldn't have, and the bucket crushed him.

"That was tough on me. My Dad was the finest man I ever met. Amongst his peers he was loved and respected, and I loved him dearly.

"Anyway, after I was released from the hospital I needed some attention. My mother offered to help me, so I went to her house in my old bedroom for about a week.

"One night as I was lying in bed I was saying my prayers, and I was offering thanks for having a second chance. Suddenly my Dad was there in the room. I felt him; I knew it was he.

"The experience was intense, but the message was simple. I asked if he were my Dad, and he replied yes. We communicated on a pure level, and it was as if a million things were said between us. It was so clear, similar to a computer dumping its contents into me. And while he was there I felt warmth, as if I had a fresh start in life.

"My Dad was such a good man—I wasn't so sure about myself—and I asked him if I had been allowed to live because of him. Had he pulled strings with someone up there to keep me alive?

"He answered: 'No. There's a reason you lived. You have something that you have to do.' I asked him what it was, and he said: 'You will know.'

"That was the end of the experience, and I've been banging my head for twenty-four years trying to find out what it is that I am supposed to do."

Chuck was retrospective for a moment as he thought back on his experiences. Intruding on his thoughts, I asked: "Are there other experiences that we should discuss?"

"There are several other instances when my life was in jeopardy, but they weren't out-of-body experiences."

"Tell me about them."

Life-Threatening Situations

"Once when I was helping a fellow police officer, someone driving by shot me in the chest and my badge deflected the bullet. On another occasion, my back was broken in an automobile accident which nearly killed me. Perhaps the worst, though, was when a doctor told me that I had a brain tumor from which I couldn't recover."

"What were the circumstances of the brain tumor?"

"In 1983, because of some serious problems with the State social service agencies over adopted children, I spent enormous sums of money and lost my business. During that period I started drinking heavily. The drinking made the problems worse, so I vowed to quit—and quit I did. Alcoholics Anonymous helped, and with my new sobriety I was able to get a job with G.T.E.

"After some months on the new job I noticed that I frequently was dizzy. The people at A.A. told me that the dizziness was related to my previous drinking. They called it the 'dry drunks.' For a period, therefore, I assumed that my previous heavy drinking was the cause of my distress. The dizziness didn't stop, though; in fact it got worse. My vision began to get blurry, and I had awful headaches.

"When the problems got so bad that I couldn't function, I went to the University of Utah Medical Center where they subjected me to a three-day battery of tests. When they finished, early on a Friday, the doctor called me in and told me that I had an inoperable brain tumor. According to his reckoning I had about two years to live. He was very matter-of-fact about the whole situation."

"What did they do about the brain tumor, if anything?"

"They talked about several possibilities: a hospice program, another program on coping with cancer, and an experimental drug program using Interferon. Ultimately I was selected to participate in their experimental drug program.

"Interferon, the drug, was administered intravenously, and after every administration I had a difficult time getting around. The treatment was for six months, once a week, and the side effects were bad.

"After the six-month period they subjected me to another battery of tests for three days. The test results weren't available right away—not for four days. It was getting close to the weekend, and I was anxious to know the results. Finally, the doctor saw me. He reported, again in a matter-of-fact manner: 'Well, the cancer is gone. We don't know whether it shrank, was dissolved by the Interferon, or what, but it is no longer there.'

"I asked the doctor what my prognosis was. His response was: 'You're somewhat overweight, but otherwise you are fine.' My initial reaction to his pronouncement was to get depressed. I was completely prepared to die. Now I would have to face the everyday problems of living, again. Bills would come due, I would have to get myself a steady income again, problems with the family would have to be resolved. In short, I would have to learn to live again."

"Have any of the previous symptoms of the cancer returned?"

"No, and it has been about nine years."

"You mentioned the car wreck that broke your back, when was that, and what happened there?"

"It was a couple of years before my treatment for cancer. When the doctors first checked me for the brain tumor, they thought the symptoms might have been related to the injuries from the automobile accident, but it turned out the tumor was unrelated."

"What were some of the things that happened in the car wreck?"

"My head hit the steering wheel. There was a fracture of my skull, fractures in both my neck and back, and there was severe damage to both of my eyes. For one-and-one-half years I was legally blind."

"How was your sight restored?"

"They did laser surgery to repair damage to the optic nerve of one of the eyes, and they worked on the other one. I can see well now."

"Are there any permanent problems from the fractured vertebrae?"

"I'm stiff occasionally, but otherwise I do fine."

"What were the circumstances behind your being shot in the badge?"

"It was November 1975, and I was assisting another officer who had stopped to help someone stuck in the road. While I was standing on the ice by the side of the road a car went by and we heard a thump. I thought the car had hit a rock that popped up and hit me in the chest. Monty, the officer I was helping, looked at my badge and noticed something stuck in it. On looking at it closely we saw that there was a bullet stuck in it. We were never able to find out who did it."

Chuck went into the other room, retrieved the badge, and showed it to me. It was a large police officer's badge with the bullet lodged between two pieces of metal. It had obviously prevented serious injury or death. After examining it, I asked him: 'What was your reaction to this shooting?'

"My reaction was to get out of police work. I figured the odds were against me." Chuck laughed as he explained how he felt. Then he showed me the scar where the bullet had penetrated his chest in the previous shooting.

Final Thoughts

During the entire period that I was interviewing Chuck it was apparent that he had a terrific sense of humor. Finding amusement in some of life's most difficult problems that had afflicted him, his eyes sparkled as he told me of them. I was not surprised, therefore, when I asked him if there were any messages he would like to leave others and he told me, in effect, that we shouldn't take ourselves too seriously. As with others who have had an NDE, Chuck also felt that we should be involved in helping others, but he qualified his feelings by saying: "When we help others we shouldn't put on sackcloth about it."

Chuck proudly showed me a picture of his adopted son before I left.

Mike

He had just finished a busy day at work when I visited him at his home in Salt Lake City on an early spring evening in 1993. Although obviously tired from his work, Mike extended a cheerful hand, and he seemed anxious to tell his story.

Mike was born in Salt Lake City, Utah, in 1962, and he had two older brothers and two older sisters. His intermediate education was at Granger High School, and he worked for a while after graduation. Then he attended Salt Lake Trade Tech for three years. In 1985 Mike married his sister's best friend; at the time of my visit he and his wife had three children.

Although Mike was raised in an LDS neighborhood, as a child, neither he nor his parents attended church regularly. He grew up, therefore, with minimum formal religious teaching.

Prayer, a Hunting Trip, and a Fall

Mike began to tell his story: "The first experience that brought me closer to God was when I was about six years old. A little kitten that I had got its neck broken through my accidental closing of a door. It really hurt my feelings, and I prayed, and prayed. . . . I prayed that it would wake up, but it didn't.

"Feeling terrible, I put it in a box and gave it a burial with a little cross over its grave. My prayer, then, was that Heavenly Father would take it into heaven. I had a spiritual experience that helped me to understand my prayer was answered. From then on, I knew that there was a God.

"The next experience I had with the Lord happened when I was about nine years old. A seventeen-year-old neighbor boy, who was friendly to me, invited me to go on a hunting trip with him to Price, Utah. It was just to be a weekend trip, and my parents gave permission for me to go. Two adults were to go with the two boys.

"On Saturday morning we hiked up to a ridge in the mountains above Price. There was a cliff, and we climbed the back side of it until we reached the summit. Sitting on the top, we rested and had lunch. After lunch the two adults went exploring and told us to stay. In an hour we got impatient, and the other boy left.

"It was a cold fall day, and the afternoon was getting late. I shouted to see if anyone would answer. There was no response, so I decided to go back the way I came. Our vehicles were just below the ridge.

"Leaving the ridge in the direction I thought would take me down, I soon found myself on the edge of the cliff. A small draw appeared to offer a way to get down, so I started to climb down it. Jumping off a large rock, I landed on a crevice that became a dead end. I couldn't go forward, and the rock I had jumped off was too high for me to climb back up.

"Stretching to reach the top of the rock, I grabbed something and lifted—it gave way and I fell. My fall down the cliff was about 250 feet. There was no feel when I landed; I don't remember the fall or when I landed."

Out-of-Body and a Visit to the Stars

"The next thing I knew I was standing looking at myself on the ground. It was dark outside and starting to snow, when I fell, and it was a strange scene as I tried to contemplate what had happened to me. The really peculiar thing was that while I could see my body lying on the ground, I . . . the real *I*, was standing with my feet about six inches off the ground.

"There was a sense of floating, and the realization came that I must be dead. As part of my discovery that I was dead, I leaned close to my body and reached out to touch it. My hand, and it was a hand, went right through my body lying on the ground. It was a shock.

"Suddenly I felt myself being drawn into the sky. The stars went by until there were no more; then I entered a tunnel of light and my speed seemed to accelerate. Eventually I came to a black void—there was no light at all. Wondering what was happening, I put my hand in front of my face, but I could see nothing.

"While I was in this black void, there was a noise in the background. The noise was from the whispering of many others in the void, and I could feel their presence. I kept asking: 'Who is there? Who is there?' but I got no response. Whispering noises continued, so I put my hand out to see what was there, and I touched something. Whatever it was that I touched let out an awful noise. It sounded as if it were a snarl or roar from some wild cat. I was very frightened by the noise.

"At the same time that I was in the black void, I could hear the people that I had gone hunting with calling me. It was very strange. I knew I had left the earth, yet I could hear them calling my name."

A Place of Light and a View of the Future

"Coming out of nowhere, while I was puzzling the whole situation, a giant cone of light appeared. It was off in the distance, and I started going toward it. During this whole period I continued to hear my friends calling me, but since I didn't know where they were I kept moving to the light.

"Something in the light seemed more important to me than anything else. The light was more important than my friends calling me. I was drawn to it.

"When I reached the edge of the light, I could see the shape of a human in it. A man in the light reached out his hand, and I reached to touch him. Upon touching him, I knew immediately who He was. The confusion that I had felt, and every fear, left me.

"This wonderful Being called me by a name, not my earthly name, but some other name. I knew He was addressing me, but it was not a name that I had been called while on earth. I have since forgotten it.

"The Being urged me to enter the light, and He said: 'Come, I want to show you something.' He took me up, and we went to another place, a different world bathed in light. Located in a large field was an enormous and beautiful gate. It had jewels on it and it was of a shining golden color. My guide pointed at it and said: 'That is the gate to heaven.'

"Next, the Being said: 'It is not your time, yet, to be here. You must go back.'

"I knew it was the Lord I was with, and I begged to stay with Him. He again told me that I had to return. So I asked Him why. His startling declaration was: 'I'll show you why.'

"Five figures appeared before me in a bright light. The Lord let me know that one of the figures was I, as an adult; a second adult figure was my wife, and three smaller figures were my children. I was told by the Lord that one of my future children would perform significant service for Him, and I had to go back so that His purposes could be fulfilled.

"That was the end of the experience. The Lord took me by the hand and brought me back."

Rescue and Recovery

"When I regained consciousness, it was morning. It was hard to walk, but I scooted down the hill. While I was resting before trying to get to where the car had been, I heard people calling for me. Yelling as loud as I could, I listened for them. They heard me and told me to stay where I was.

"The Search and Rescue team had been looking for me, and they were above me on the mountain. They had to go around from up above and come at me from below. When they got to me they put me on a stretcher and took me to the hospital in Price.

"After the initial examination in Price, they flew me to the University of Utah Medical Center in Salt Lake City. At the Medical Center, they found that my arm was broken in several places, my nose was broken, and worst of all, I had a head fracture. They had to operate on my head and arm.

"All together I was in the hospital for three months. I don't remember everything about it, but I got better."

Questions About Mike's Experience

Mike agreed that I could ask him some questions. I began: "How did you feel when you first found yourself looking at your physical body?"

"At first, before I went into the black void, I wasn't afraid or anything. Mostly, I was interested in finding out what had happened.

That's when I reached down to touch my body and my hand went right through it."

"How did you feel when you were in the black void?"

"I was scared. There was this multitude of whispering beings around me, and they confused and frightened me. Then when I reached out and touched that thing . . . or whatever it was, the snarl was scary."

"The cone of light that you saw, can you describe it more fully?"

"That's the thing . . . it wasn't there, and then it was. It was sort of in the middle of my vision. Above the cone it was black, and below the cone it was black. It just appeared and I felt drawn to it."

"Can you describe the figure that was in the light?"

"The figure was a man; he was in a white robe, he was transparent, and he was very bright. Instantly, upon His touching my hand, I knew it was the Lord. I was filled with peace, I felt calm, and there was an assurance that the peace would stay with me. There was an overpowering love coming from Him to me—I could feel it. The warmth I felt . . . There is no experience in life that can duplicate what I experienced there in His presence."

"How did you know it was the Lord?"

"There were the love and the comfort that He gave. He was radiantly beautiful, dressed in a white robe, and He had long brown hair. His dress and appearance were that of the Lord—He showed me the nail prints in his hands."

"Where were the nail prints?"

"They were on his wrists."

"Was there anything else about the Lord that was unusual?"

"There was the music, and there were angels. When I was in His presence, I heard this wonderful music. It was beautiful."

"Describe it."

"I can't."

"What kind of music do you listen to here?"

"Country-western."

"Was it like country-western?"

"No. There were a multitude singing something like hymns, or humming. The sound was unbelievable . . . it is hard to explain."

"What do you mean, a multitude?"

"There were angels, thousands of angels, dressed in white robes and singing. They were kneeling down with their arms outstretched, and they were singing."

"When you were told to go back, why didn't you want to go?"

"I'm not sure. As far as me missing my mom, or my friends, or my dad, that didn't seem to matter. Nothing could replace the feeling that I had when I was with Him, and I didn't want to leave."

"When you went with Him to another place, what was it like?"

"We first went up, then down to the ground where the beautiful gate was. There was a large wall that the gate was mounted on, and He let me know that heaven was beyond the gate. I was then shown myself and my family."

"How did it feel to be looking at yourself, as a child, but seeing yourself as an adult?"

"It excited me. That vision, or whatever it was, convinced me that I should go back. I was enthralled with the idea that one of my children would provide a special service to Him."

"Could you recognize the features on your children or your wife?"

"No. The faces weren't that clear. They were shapes that seemed to be about twenty feet away. It was bright where they were, and they were shadowy figures."

"Could you see anything that looked like landscape?"

"Yes. Rocks and other things were there. All around the gate there was a large field."

"Were there colors?"

"Mostly the colors were associated with the gate. It sparkled with many jewels and with the golden material that it was made of."

"After the scene with your future family, then you returned?"

"Yes. Taking me by the hand, He told me that He would take me back. We returned and I could see my body lying there. He had me lie down, and I sort of floated into my body."

"Could the whole experience have been a dream or a hallucination?"

"I know it was not a dream or a hallucination."

"How do you know?"

"When I first came out of my body, the first thing I thought of was that it must be a dream. That was when I reached down with my hand and it went through my body; then I noticed that my spirit body was standing above the ground. I looked around and could see the forest, the trees, and it was starting to snow. It was too real to be a dream. I can still picture it as a vivid experience."

"Have you told this story to many people?"

"No. Just my wife."

"Have you read much about stories like this?"

"I've never read any stories, but I have seen some things like this on TV. The television stories that I saw were a year or two ago."

"Are you associated with any organized religion?"

"I'm just a believer. When I do go to church it's to the Christian Fellowship Church."

"Are there any messages you would like to leave for others?"

"My message to others is that when they see the Lord they will know who He is. There will be no question about whom it is when they see Him—if there is the slightest doubt then it is not the Lord. Doubt will flee when He appears; He will know you and you will know Him."

Chapter 13

DIVERSE EXPERIENCES

Lavor Allen

Lavor and his wife, Thelma, were waiting at their home as I drove up on a spring day in 1993. They expressed interest in my research work concerning people who had gone through a near-death experience, and they asked to see the book *Glimpses of Eternity*. After discussing the subject for a moment, Lavor began to tell me of his background.

He was born in Logan, Utah, in April 1912, and he was one of eight children. When Lavor was seven years old, his mother contracted influenza during a severe outbreak in World War I, and she died. His father never remarried, and Lavor was frequently alone during his youth.

Attending schools in Utah, Lavor completed Junior High School, and then he took a job. Both of Lavor's parents belonged to The Church of Jesus Christ of Latter-day Saints, and Lavor maintained activity in that church throughout his life.

He married young, and he and his wife, Ruth, raised two girls and a boy. After many years of marriage Lavor's wife died, and three years later Lavor married again, to Thelma. While he was raising his children Lavor worked as a carpenter. At the time of our visit, he was retired.

Heart Failure

Lavor began his story: "In 1968, when I came home from work one day, I was working in the back yard on a swing that needed to be taken apart. When I was about two-thirds finished with the swing, I started feeling strange.

160

"Going into the house to lie down, I told my wife that I felt funny. My lungs seemed full of fluid. When my wife and I listened we could hear my chest splashing. It was like a canvas bag half-full of water.

"Lying down on the bed to rest, my chest continued to make noises. As my wife heard the noise, I heard her say she would call the doctor—then everything went black.

"I found out later that the doctor agreed to come, but in the meantime he told my wife, after she told him I was unconscious, to keep talking to me. He said she should keep saying: 'Lavor, come back,' repeatedly. If she didn't do that, he said that she would lose me. So she kept calling me back until help came. They later diagnosed my illness as heart failure."

Visit to Another World

"My first conscious moment was when all pain left me, and I felt as though I were leaving my body. Looking down, I saw my body lying on the bed beneath me. For a time I just floated around in the room observing things.

"Then I became aware that I was moving, and I entered an area with beautiful grounds. It was outdoors, and everything seemed white—or a pretty color. There was a shine about everything, as if bushes and flowers had been waxed.

"A trail went through the grounds, and I followed it, not walking, but sort of floating over it. Ahead of me on the trail I saw a couple of people. Getting close to the couple, I saw that it was my dad and my mother, both of whom had died. My mother had died when I was just a child.

"It seemed as though I said: 'I'm here to meet you.' My dad responded: 'You've got more work back there. Now, be sure and go back.'

"There was something else he told me concerning an uncle of mine, named Percy. It's not clear in my memory what he said about Percy, I just remember that Dad said something about him. He also told me, again, that there were some things that I had to do.

"Despite his telling me to go back, I hesitated. I didn't want to come back.

"Finding myself back in my room, I was hit by immense pain. It was the most painful thing I've had to endure in my life. Leaving my body was a wonderfully peaceful experience, returning to it was extremely painful.

The doctor was there, and he was treating me. Instructing my wife to get me to the hospital, he told her to hurry or she would lose me.

"They put me on a blanket in a station wagon, and they rushed me to the LDS Hospital in Salt Lake City. It was some time before I realized what had happened to me. In the hospital they drained a great deal of fluid from my lungs. They kept me for a little over a week, and then I recuperated at home for many months after that. After a couple of years I recovered some of my normal abilities, but I was unable to go back to work.

Questions About Lavor's Experience

I began to ask questions. "What did you think when you first saw your body lying beneath you?"

"It seemed strange. At first I thought it might be someone else lying there, yet I knew it wasn't."

"Did you learn how your spirit body was dressed or how it looked?"

"No I didn't."

"How did it feel when you were out of your body?"

"As though I were floating on a cloud. There was no pain, and I was relieved of all troubles from this earth. It was a wonderful feeling, to be without pain or responsibilities."

"Can you describe in more detail what you saw in the garden?"

"Flowers were there, and they were beautiful. The colors were so bright that the flowers almost seemed artificial. Light was everywhere, and I remember a light blue color."

"When you were on the path, you say you floated?"

"Yes; yet I was in the upright position."

"How did your father and mother look?"

"They were dressed in white, and my mother's red hair showed. In terms of age, they looked as I remembered them."

"What did you say to them?"

"The only thing I said was that I was there to meet them, and when Dad told me that I should go back, I told him I didn't want to."

"How did communication take place between you and your father?"

"It was not voice, it was . . . how should I say it? . . . It wasn't through sound—and yet it was."

"Why didn't you want to come back?"

"Because of the beauty that was there, and because of the feelings I had with my parents."

"Apparently you decided to return, despite not wanting to. Why was that?"

"Communication with my father was so strong that I decided he knew what he was talking about. So I came back."

"Did you tell others of this experience?"

"Not for some time; then I told my wife, Ruth. My children have only heard part of my story."

"Had you read anything of near-death experiences?"

"Not before it happened to me. Afterwards, someone gave me a book that described similar experiences."

"Did the experience seem as if it were a dream or a hallucination?"

"No. It seemed real."

"Has it changed your life?"

"Yes. If my work is still not finished, then I would like to do whatever I'm supposed to do. Wondering about Percy, for example, has bothered me. It would be nice to know what I'm supposed to do about him."

"Who was Uncle Percy?"

"He was my Aunt Nettie's husband, and he was dead at the time of my experience. Aunt Nettie was my Dad's sister."

"Do you have any feelings about death?"

"Death itself has no fear for me. I do fear the possibility of a long period of incapacity before death."

"Are there any messages you would like others to have, based on your experience?"

"We should live the best life we can, because we're never sure when we'll be called home. Accomplishing what we were assigned to do must be important, because I was sent back to finish up my work."

Barbara

Carol and I visited Barbara at her home on a spring day in 1993. Upon entering her house we noticed a profusion of growing plants, and Carol and Barbara discussed their mutual attraction to plants—and the difficulty of keeping them dusted. Barbara was a cheerful lady with dark hair and an earnest manner. Her teen-age daughter, Candace, was present to hear her mother's story.

Barbara was born in 1952 in Murray, Utah, and she had two younger brothers and an older sister. She was raised and went to school in Utah, and she had never been out of Utah. Marrying her high school sweetheart, they had two daughters, Camille and Candace. After a divorce and nine years of being single, she married her present husband.

Religion was not a major part of Barbara's life. She attended Sunday School in the LDS Church for a while, but for most of her life she was not attracted to formal religion.

A High Fever—Out-of-Body

Barbara began to tell her story. "When I was fifteen years old and a sophomore in high school, I had difficulty with tonsillitis. My father was the type of person who rarely took any of the family to the doctor or to the dentist. We normally toughed-out our illnesses.

"The tonsillitis bothered me off and on, and it got bad enough, with high fevers, that I missed about a month of school. At one point, my mother later told me, my fever was so bad that I didn't wake up for two days. She decided she was going to force the issue with my father and get me to a doctor.

"During the period that I was asleep, or unconscious, I suddenly found myself floating above my body. My body was just lying beneath me in the bed, and I was floating up near the ceiling.

"Looking around the room, I wondered about the strangeness of the scene. It was early afternoon, and my room was full of sunshine or some other brightness. Then I saw another man standing in the room—he was my grandfather on my mother's side. He had died several years before, when I was about eight years old, and I was very close to him.

"Grandfather was dressed all in white. His clothes were tailored like the farm-bib coveralls that I was familiar with when he was alive, but they were very white.

"Sitting on the edge of the bed, he raised his arm, took my hand and pulled me down to sit with him. We both sat at the foot of the bed, he being closest to my physical body. Then he started talking to me and explaining why I could not go with him. The overwhelming feeling that I had at the time was to go with Grandfather, wherever he was going. I really loved him.

"Talking to me for some time, he continued to explain why I couldn't come. My mother and father would be badly hurt if I left, he told me, and besides, it wasn't my time. He said I was young and still had things I had to do—and he would see me again when it was my time.

"He finally convinced me that I should return. That was the last I remember until I woke in my bed. My mother then got me in to see the doctor, and they took out my tonsils."

Questions Concerning Barbara's Experience

Barbara agreed that I could ask her some questions. "When you first came out, you said that you could see your body below you?"

"Yes. It was as if I were floating in the room, and there was a movement-oriented feeling. After floating about for a bit, I got stuck up near the ceiling. Looking down, I saw my body and realized it was I."

"How did your body look?"

"As though it were asleep."

"How did you feel about being up near the ceiling?"

"It wasn't really scary. I was kind of amazed, and curious, and that's when my grandfather appeared."

"How did you feel when you were out of your body?"

"Good. There was no pain, and I wasn't afraid."

"Did you say anything to your grandfather?"

"Yes. Throwing my arms around him, I told him how glad I was to see him. Then he spoke to me. Repeating what he used to call me, he said: 'Nuisance, I still love you.' Then I asked if I could go with him. I also asked him where he had been. Never answering my question, he told me why I should return. He seemed to be avoiding questions about himself."

"What did he look like?"

"Exactly as I remembered him, only younger somehow. There was a glow about him, though, and he was dressed in pure white with pure white hair."

"When you communicated, how did you do it?"

"I don't remember talking with our lips. We seemed to be reading each other's mind."

"Did you hear his voice?"

"Yes. I could swear I heard his voice—in my mind."

"Did your grandfather tell you what it was you had to do?"

"Not that I remember."

"Why didn't you want to come back?"

"Grandfather was fun, and I wanted to be with him. At the time I was a typical rebellious teenager, and I wanted to stay with him. I was an unhappy and frustrated teen, and he made me happy."

"When you came back, did you still hurt?"

"Most certainly. My throat was really infected, and my fever was still high."

"Did your experience seem like a dream or a hallucination?"

"No. It was real. It wasn't anything like a dream."

"Are there any messages you would like to leave others?"

"I don't think people should be afraid of dying. I've lost all fear of death since my experience."

"What about getting through death, though, aren't you fearful of the pain of dying?"

"Well, you see, I am HIV positive; I have the AIDS virus. I understand that there can be a lot of pain and misery on this earth. But I really feel that the afterlife will be a reward—free from all pain and emotional hurt."

Patricia

She was waiting in her lovely apartment, decorated with several paintings that she had created, when Carol and I visited her in the spring of 1993. Her even features, blonde hair and cultured manner bespoke a previous career in modeling.

Patricia made us comfortable and began to tell us of her background. She was born in Brigham, Utah, in 1956, and she was raised with her brother and sister in the Salt Lake City region. Attending Weber State College after graduating from high school, she studied elementary education and art. At the time of our interview, Patricia had two teenage children, and she was unmarried.

During her youth Patricia was exposed to several religions. Her mother was an active member of the Jehovah's Witnesses faith, her grandparents were members of The Church of Jesus Christ of Latter-day

Saints, and her father was an inactive member of the same church. Because of the divorce of her parents, she was partially raised by her grandparents.

Having worked in New York, Arizona, and Houston, and having traveled as an adult, Patricia had exposure to various cultures. She said that she had no strong commitment to any particular faith or religious belief.

A Dangerous Experiment—A Strange Outcome

Patricia began to tell her story. "When I was thirteen years old and attending Davis High School, a speaker came to our school to tell us about drug abuse. He told us that students in our school had experimented with drugs. Some students had sniffed glue, others had sniffed gasoline, and he explained some of the ill effects that could result from sniffing these materials.

"A group of popular girls that usually did not get in trouble—two of them were cheerleaders—decided to try sniffing drugs. Our curiosity, after we heard the lecture on drugs, about what happened when you sniffed them got the better of us. So, a group of us siphoned some gasoline out of a lawn-mower.

"Not being quite sure how to sniff gasoline, we put the gasoline in a plastic milk container. Taking the container with about an inch of gasoline in it, I shook it up to get a good mixture of gasoline vapor in the carton. Then I exhaled all the air from my lungs, put my mouth over the carton opening, and squeezed on the carton as I inhaled.

"Instantly, my lungs burned fiercely, my head ached enormously, and I couldn't catch my breath; unconsciousness followed. My girlfriends tried to hold me up on the picnic table where I was sitting when I went unconscious.

"Watching my girlfriends struggle to hold me on the table, from an elevated position, I became aware that I was out of my body. They failed to keep me on the table, and I saw my body tumble to the ground. As my body fell, it tipped over a jug of gasoline that was sitting on the lawn. Trying to warn the girls to be careful, I told them to pick up the jug and put it on the table. I was frustrated because they didn't listen to me. My concern was that we would get in trouble from a gasoline spot on the lawn.

"The girls started giving me mouth-to-mouth resuscitation, and I could tell that I didn't look good. My body had turned a bluish color.

"Floating around above the girls, and watching them, I felt really good. There was no pain, but it didn't make sense to me. For a moment or two I went fairly high above them. Then, for no apparent reason, I snapped back into my body.

"It was as if I slammed back inside my body. As I did, I took a large gasp of air. My lungs were burning, my head hurt, and my ears were ringing. It felt awful. We never sniffed gasoline after that."

"When you were out of your body, Patricia, did you see what your spirit-body looked like?" I asked.

"There was form to it. It was a whole body, and I had hands, for example."

"What did your spirit hands look like?"

"They were not like the hands on my physical body. They were more . . . they had shape, but it was like they were luminescent, not flesh and bones. It's hard to explain, but they seemed sort of lit up."

"Are you sure it wasn't a drug-induced type of hallucination that you had?"

"Everything was clear and real. The lawn and my girlfriends were clearly visible, and I could tell what the girls were doing. It was not a hallucination; it was real."

A Strange Force

"Up until I had that out-of-body experience, I didn't really believe there was a life after death. Even after my initial experience I didn't believe in concepts such as evil or good. My idea of a spiritual world was poorly formed, and I tended to accept only what I could see and feel in the physical world. Then I had another experience which, together with the first one, convinced me that there were spiritual forces.

"When I was twenty-five years old, I was going through a divorce. Depression was really bothering me; my husband had left me for a young model, and I had two children. My thoughts were almost suicidal.

"One night, as I sat in bed reading, a strange feeling came over me. It was as if someone, or something, had come into my room. And whatever it was felt evil.

"In my bed, while I was wide-awake, I was suddenly pinned down—I couldn't move. It felt as though some evil presence was trying to get into my mind. There was pressure so that I couldn't breathe, and my hands were immobile. I wanted to reach for the phone and call for help, but I couldn't.

"Something seemed determined to get into my mind or body. I was terrified. It felt like a see-through dark cloud that was overwhelming me. The only means I had of fighting the force was by thinking. My grandmother had earlier tried to teach me that if an evil presence ever came around I should command it to depart in the name of Jesus Christ.

"As I thought of my grandmother's words, the force pulled off of me. Released from the force, I sat up, and I cursed with relief. My uncle was a religious man, and I called him. He came over, and he suggested a blessing on the house, but I wanted to leave—and I did. The incident, whatever it was, fortunately never repeated."

Chapter 14

LEARNING EXPERIENCES

Elizabeth Marie

She was waiting in the beautiful old home of her mother when Carol and I visited her in the spring of 1993. Elizabeth was a shy young blonde lady who agreed to be interviewed after we met her at a local meeting of the International Association for Near Death Studies (IANDS). Her mother joined us after we exchanged greetings, and she seemed quite interested in listening to her daughter's interview.

Elizabeth was born in December 1964 in American Fork, Utah. Her upbringing was in Pleasant Grove, Utah, and she had two brothers and four sisters. She graduated from high school in Pleasant Grove. On a rock-climbing activity with some friends, she met her future husband. At the time of our visit, she and her husband had four children. As a child she was raised in the LDS faith, and she was still active in that faith, with her husband and family, at the time of our visit.

A Youthful Mistake

Elizabeth began to tell her story: "When I was fourteen years old, I got involved with drugs. On one particular day I was smoking marijuana with a boy I knew, and I accidently took a drug overdose. Without my knowledge the marijuana had been dosed with opium. The boy and I were having a contest to see who could smoke the greater amount. He passed out, and when he did I went in the house and managed to get back to my room.

170

"Upon reaching my room I lay down on my bed—I was stoned. After a time I noticed that I was looking down on myself on the bed. My immediate thought was: *I'm in trouble!*"

An Astonishing Experience—Indescribable Love

"There was no sensation of still being under the influence of the drug; my mind was clear. I knew exactly what had happened. The perspective I had was that of a fourteen-year-old, knowing I was in trouble, and I was very upset. My next thought was: *How will I ever explain this one to my parents? Mom will really be upset.*

"While in this disturbed state I found myself drawn into a tunnel and through it at a rapid rate of speed. Upon reaching the end of the tunnel I entered a room with many people in it—people sitting on chairs, and laughing at me. They were laughing because I was trying to hide. The embarrassment I felt as a fourteen-year-old—for having done what I did—was severe. Since there was no place to hide I was doing the best I could by crouching down and putting my head on my knees.

"Someone called my name, and I looked to see who it was. Everyone that had been in the room was gone, and I could see a light in the distance coming toward me. It was a very bright light. When the light got close to me He put His arms around me. And He . . . " Elizabeth was unable to continue for a moment while her mother got some Kleenex. When she regained her composure, I asked: "He? . . ."

"Yes. He put his arms around me and asked me if I had known that what I did was wrong. I told Him that yes, I had known it was wrong.

"The amount of remorse I had, I'd never felt before. It was remorse over what I had done. I felt so sorry; there was a deep disappointment over my previous activities. The feelings of remorse and disappointment were pure feelings that permeated my body.

"I was asked if I had known what was right and wrong—and I had. My knowledge, in the presence of Him, was that I couldn't progress from the place I had positioned myself. Knowing that I was stopped in my progression, and feeling great remorse, I asked if I could return and help others to come back to Him. There was an intense desire within me to amend for the pain and suffering that I had caused others.

"The love I felt from Him during this period was extremely intense. Love traveled from my toes to my head, filling my entire body. There are no words that can adequately describe that love. It was a fatherly type of love, and I knew that He was pleased when I acknowledged my sins and asked if I could amend for them.

"He held me in His arms the whole time, and . . . and the feelings were so intense. The love I felt was beyond belief. And while I was embraced by Him and felt of His great love, He asked me if I would help others to come back to Him. I said I would.

"Since my experience, though, I haven't known who it was that I was supposed to help. I've wondered if it was one person, or many persons. I understood that it was to help someone, or several people, who had lost their way, to return to His presence, but I still don't know who they are.

"We had hugged each other for a while, when I knew that I was to return—I was put back in my body, although I don't remember that event. That was the end of the experience."

Questions of Elizabeth Marie

Elizabeth agreed that I could ask questions of her experience. I began: "When you first found yourself out of your body, how did you feel?"

"I felt okay, but I was concerned because of what I had done."

"Did it feel like a dream, a hallucination, or a drug-induced experience?"

"Heavens, no. It was a real experience, not like the stupor I had previously been in from the drugs. The drugs depressed my system and caused me to die. My senses during the out-of-body experience were alert and awake."

"And you could see your physical body lying there?"

"Yes. The picture of my body lying there, and the position it was in, is still vivid in my mind."

"Why did you call the next part of your experience a tunnel?"

"It was round, and I was moved through it very rapidly. There was a sound . . . like wind rushing by me."

"Did you feel alone in the tunnel?"

"There was no fear, and there was a light at the end of the tunnel. The sides of the tunnel, though, had some light. I could see the walls. It was big enough that if I had put my arms out they wouldn't have touched the walls."

"Did you have arms?"

"Yes."

"Did you see them?"

"Yes. My feet and my hands were visible to me."

"What did your hands look like?"

"Just like my hands do now. There was a white robe that covered my arms down to my wrists. The robe started at my neck and went to my ankles—it was a pure white. There are no words to describe that kind of white."

"When you came out of the tunnel and entered the room, did you know the people that were there?"

"I'm not sure. I didn't really want to know them because of my feelings of embarrassment. They seemed to think it was funny that I was trying to hide."

"Why were you so embarrassed?"

"It was because of what I had done—and because of the marks on my robe."

"What marks?"

"The robe I was wearing was white, a pure white, but it had black spots on it."

"Where were the spots, and why did they bother you?"

"There were several of them on my left side, down to my ankle. They bothered me because I knew that they represented some of the things I had done wrong. When I bent down I was trying to hide them, and that's what the people were laughing about. There was no way I could hide them."

"How were the people dressed?"

"They were also in white."

"Could you see the people very well?"

"Yes. There was this one person in particular that I remember."

"Describe that person, if you can."

"It was a male, with dark hair, and he had pointed at me."

"How old were the people?"

"They all seemed to be . . . gosh, about . . . there didn't seem to be any age to them, except the people seemed young."

"Describe the light in the room."

"It was light like in the tunnel. It was bright, but not nearly as bright as the light that came after He called my name."

"Where did the bright light come from?"

"It was high up and distant when I first saw it. The room boundaries seemed to disappear."

"What did the light look like?"

"When it got close to me, it was brighter than the sun. The sun is yellow, but the light was white. Yet I could look at it with my eyes."

"What happened to the light?"

"It came down and stood a few inches in front of me. It was a man."

"There was a man in the light, then?"

"I didn't see a man, but I knew He was there."

"Who was He?"

"It was Jesus."

"How did you know it was Jesus?"

"I just did." Elizabeth paused for a period to control her emotions. She continued: "I don't have words for it, but I knew it was He."

"You felt Him embrace you?"

"Yes. He put His arms around me and hugged me, just as my father would. The feelings I had at that point were extremely intense. My children and my parents, for example, I love with all my heart. Yet in this life I couldn't produce a small portion of what I felt in His presence. The love was a mutual feeling between us, and it went through my whole body."

"Did you have a life's review?"

"When He asked me if I knew the things I did wrong, they were brought back to my memory with full emotion. There was a clear understanding of each wrong event, and I felt remorse. The memories were very painful."

"What was His reaction when you remembered each event?"

"There was just love coming from Him. The sorrowful feelings were coming from me."

"In a sense, then, you were your own worst judge?"

"That's true, and it was extremely painful. It was clear to me what I had done wrong, and I suffered emotional pain as the memories came to me."

"Did you ask to come back, or were you told to come back?"

"I knew that He wanted me to, and I asked if I could. It was my choice, though; I could have opted to stay."

"How did you know he wanted you to return to this life?"

"By the feeling I had."

"How did He and you communicate?"

"Through my mind. I didn't speak, and I know that He didn't speak with His mouth. It was completely through thought."

"Was it as clear as you and me talking?"

"It was clearer. There was no mistaking what either of us was saying—there was no possibility of misunderstanding."

"That was the end of your experience, then?"

"There was one other thing that happened, but I don't remember everything from it."

"Tell me what you remember."

"There was a tall window. It was made of a purple stone with marble marks in it. It was crystalline-clear, and it was beautiful. Light shone through it, but I couldn't see through it. While I was in this room with the window there was someone that I talked to."

"Do you remember what you talked about?"

"Part of what happened was taken from my memory. I remember that we were making hard, important decisions about my future life, but I can't remember what they were. I've tried, but it's as if I'm not supposed to remember everything."

"When you returned to your body, what was the next thing that you remember?"

"It was morning, and I was on my bed."

"How long do you think your experience took?"

"I don't know. I didn't really have a sense of time."

"How did you feel when you woke up?"

"I was fine, but the experience changed my life completely."

"How did it change your life?"

"My decision, at that point, was that I would not do the bad things I had previously done. There would be no drugs or other bad things. And I changed. Someone told me that I couldn't change overnight, but I did. Even my friends were from a different group."

"Did you tell anyone about the experience?"

"I tried telling one of the counselors in the bishopric, at the time, but he said it was a dream. I knew that wasn't true."

"Did you tell anyone else?"

"Not for a long time. The fear of ridicule prevented me from saying anything. Much later, I told my mom. About six years ago I told my husband."

"Did they believe you?"

Elizabeth looked at her mom and asked: "Did you believe me?" Her mother smiled and shook her head yes.

"Had you read anything about out-of-body experiences when you had your experience?"

"Not at that point. Not for several years. Even when I did hear about others having such experience, I was excited, but I didn't dare tell about my own experience."

"Why did you approach me for this interview?"

"I don't know. I just felt prompted to talk to you. It was difficult, though, because I remember the problems I had after my experience, and I didn't want to relive those feelings. Initially, for example, there was a period of depression—because I felt unloved. The love with Him was so great that every other form of love seemed weak in comparison. Nobody could come close to what He gave me. It took me a long time to overcome the longing for that type of love."

"Are there any other experiences of a similar nature that you have had?"

"I have had other out-of-body and spiritual experiences, but they were for different reasons."

"Tell me about them."

Other Spiritual and Out-of-body Experiences

"For the last ten years I have had a serious heart problem. My problem is the result of blood vessels that are too small to deliver the blood my heart needs. The doctors call it Syndrome-X, and there isn't much they can do for it except to treat me with pain killers. They put a pacemaker in me sometime ago to help my heart keep a normal rhythm.

"Whenever I exercise, or put my heart under any kind of stress, I feel pain. The pain is similar to what happens in a heart attack. In late 1991 and 1992 I was pregnant with my last child, and the pain with my heart became severe.

"One night, during my pregnancy, I became ill and the pain was really bad. Medication had been given to me by the doctor to ease the pain, but nothing seemed to help. At one point I despaired, not knowing what to do, and I prayed to our Heavenly Father for help. As I did, I looked up and there were three men in my room.

"The men stood there looking at me, and I had a feeling of peace. One of them whispered something in my ear and kissed me. It was a most comforting feeling, and my pain was gone. Then the men disappeared."

"Did you know who they were, Elizabeth?" I asked.

"I didn't know their names, but they seemed familiar to me."

"Do you know what the man whispered to you?"

"I don't remember, except that it made me feel good."

"Tell me about your other experiences."

"My baby was born in July 1992. The birth was difficult and I hemorrhaged badly—I lost about half of my blood. There were severe chest pains from my heart, and the doctors couldn't do much for me. Pain killers didn't work. It reached a point where I couldn't stand the pain.

"Suddenly a strange feeling came over me—and I knew what was going to happen. There was a floating feeling as I left my body and floated above it. All pain left me, and I had a wonderful, restful feeling of peace. It gave me sufficient respite that, when I returned to my body, I was able to cope. The experience lasted just a few moments, but the relief was marvelous."

"What were your other experiences?"

"There were a couple of times when I had brief out-of-body experiences—all related to my heart problem. On one occasion after I had my baby, when I was in severe pain, I felt myself leaving my body again. It kind of scared me, and I said to myself: *No!* That stopped it, and I haven't had any repeat experiences since then."

A Message for Others

"The initial experience I had was profound, and it changed my life forever. The love I felt there was beyond expression, and that love, or a portion of it, came back with me. Permeating every cell of my body was a feeling of love, a feeling of peace, and a relief from pain. Heavenly Father loved me with infinite love, despite the wrong things that I had done.

"An important message, therefore, is that we should be kind and help others. Since my experience I have found that it is easier for me to accept people for what they are. Even people whom others shun; to me, they are okay people. We can't know the circumstances that cause people to behave as they do, so we should accept and love them for the fact that all of them are children of God.

"And we should love Heavenly Father and keep His commandments. To the extent that we disobey Him we will feel intense emotional pain—as I did. It is okay to make mistakes, though, if we learn from those mistakes and stop repeating them. He is a loving God, and He is willing to accept and forgive us if we reach out to Him."

Lori

It was a spring day in 1993 when Lori came to our home. She was a slight, dark-haired young lady with penetrating green eyes, and she had an intense manner of speaking. Her birthplace, in 1964, was Burley, Idaho, a small town in south-central Idaho. With two older sisters and a younger brother, Lori had a happy childhood with her family and with the horses that they kept.

Graduating from high school in 1983, Lori went two years to the College of Southern Idaho, in Twin Falls, where she took accounting. When she was young, she went to the Lutheran Church; in the sixth grade she converted to the Catholic Church, due to the influence of a friend. Lori had been married and had two boys, twelve and six years of age, at the time of our visit. She came to Salt Lake City in 1991 and was employed in the accounting department of a Salt Lake-based airline.

A Serious Illness

Lori began to tell her story: "At sixteen years of age, I had a child that was born with a partially cleft palate. Depression bothered me from the many pressures; school, work, and my child. Fortunately, I had a supportive family.

"Waking one morning I felt worse than usual, and I thought I had the flu. My back hurt badly, so I called in sick at work. Not wanting another doctor's bill, I didn't go to the doctor. By evening, when I went to the bathroom, I fell to the floor and couldn't get up.

"Someone, my mother or my girlfriend, found me and took me to the doctor. After a brief examination, he put me in the Cassia Memorial Hospital in Burley.

"During the period that I was in the hospital, I kept going in and out of consciousness. On several occasions I woke to find myself above my body, in the corner of the room, looking down on myself. There was a feeling of floating as I viewed myself. While I was in this elevated position I remember thinking: *Why am I up in this corner?* Often, when I was up there, I saw a tall, handsome man sitting in a chair next to my bed, and I wondered who he was. Later I found that he was my sister's boyfriend.

"At times I would want to stay in my body, and I would feel vibrations. The entire bed seemed to move with me at one point. There was a part of me that wanted to stay, and there was another part that wanted to leave my body. I was kind of in and out. After the first time that I left my body, the intense pain I had felt in my back left me. There was no pain after that.

"One of the times when I was out of my body, I became conscious of another man in the room, not my sister's boyfriend, but another spirit-person. He had form, and I could feel his presence, but I couldn't recognize specific features. It was as if the being were in silhouette form; there was a feeling of peace associated with him.

"This spiritual being placed his hands on my chest—I could feel them—and there was a feeling of warmth. The emotional feeling associated with his presence was overwhelming. Every emotion I had was involved; every fear was released, every anger was removed, and every joy was magnified. There was an intense sense of peace. Then I felt my spirit returning to my body. The spirit-man seemed to be there for that purpose, and to give me a feeling of security and peace."

"Did you know who this spirit being was?" I asked Lori.

"At one point, I remember asking who he was, and he said that he was a spirit guide."

"Was that the main extent of your experience?"

"Yes."

"Did you feel yourself reentering your body?"

"There was this gigantic feeling of peace, and I felt myself going back. As I was returning, I had the exploding-emotion feeling that I told you about."

"Were you out of your body for a long time?"

"A single event may not have been long, but I was in and out of my body over a period of days. Frequently, I found myself up near the corner of the room, looking down on me. This caused me to wonder what I was doing up there. And I wanted to come back."

"Did you have form and shape when you were out of your body?"

"Yes. That's the strange thing, I could see my body lying below, yet I could also see my hands and feet on my other body from my elevated position in the room."

"What did your spirit hands and feet look like?"

"Just like they do now. There was a bright beam of light around my spirit body. My spirit body was surrounded by . . . colors."

"What happened when you returned to your physical body?"

"After I returned, and after the emotional feeling, I remember waking up and feeling hungry."

"How long were you in the hospital?"

"Fourteen days."

"Did they tell you what your illness was?"

"There was a kidney infection, brought on by the flu, and I became dehydrated as I didn't replenish fluids. I got too sick to drink, and my kidneys failed to function properly."

"Were you okay when you left the hospital?"

"It took a couple of months to recover my strength—I had lost a lot of weight. Sleep helped me to recover during that period."

"Have you had other experiences of this nature?"

"During the two months that I was recovering my strength I had vivid dreams. One recurring dream was of a wise Indian man who came to help me.

"Several times during the recuperation time, it seemed that I started to leave my body again. There was vibration, and I could feel myself leaving. It was a frightening sensation—I consciously resisted it and pulled myself back into my body. For a time, even the coming of night frightened me.

"One series of out-of-body events was somewhat amusing. After my illness I stayed at my mother's house. Still recovering from my illness, I slept on the couch frequently. Almost every morning I would leave my body and go into the kitchen to see what time it was. Then, when I awoke I would say things such as: 'Mom, why did you let me sleep so late? It's eight o'clock already.'

"My mother, at first, insisted that I couldn't know the time. The clock was in a location in the kitchen where I couldn't possibly see it from my position on the couch. Later, my mother and sister would tease me if we were driving somewhere. They would ask me to send my eyes up the road and tell them how much farther we had to go. I couldn't, of course, do what they asked since these particular out-of-body events seemed to happen spontaneously while I was sleeping."

Other Out-of-Body Experiences

When we finished discussing Lori's near-death experience, I asked her if there were other occasions when she left her body. She said there were, and she began to explain what happened: "Sometime ago I was dating a young man, and I felt he was not being honest with me. When I went to sleep, one night, I was disturbed because I believed he had lied to me about where he was going.

"In the middle of the night I became aware that I was no longer in bed. To my surprise I found myself at a strange house. I could see the street signs, the address of the house, and the lights—and I saw my boyfriend in the house with another girl."

"Had you ever been to that address before?" I asked.

"Never."

"Did you accuse your boyfriend of being with the other girl?"

"The next day I confronted him with what I knew. I asked him who lived at that particular address."

"How did you explain your knowledge?"

"By a dream—I said it was a detailed dream."

"Was it a dream?"

"No."

"What was the reaction of your boyfriend?"

"He was very quiet, and he went white."

"Are there other similar experiences?"

"Yes. My mother and I have always been close, and after I moved here from Burley I was concerned about her. This one night I found myself by her bed, and she was crying. When I called her the next morning and asked her if she were all right, she said that she had cried all night. She said that she was sad because she missed me."

"Are there other experiences?"

"There were several smaller instances, and one that was about like these two, except that it was in a beautiful setting."

"Tell me about it."

"About six months ago, I had been angry and hateful toward a particular person. Knowing this was wrong, and that it was consuming me with hateful thoughts, I decided to get rid of the anger and hate and replace it with love. So I called the person and apologized.

"After I apologized, I felt much better. On a particular evening after going to sleep, a sense of peace filled me, and I felt myself leave my body. Awakening, I found myself soaring over a beautiful valley. It extended for miles, and it had long grass in it and extremely colorful flowers. The flowers were vivid reds, yellows, and golds."

"Was it daylight where you saw the field and the flowers?"

"Yes it was."

"Do you remember going back into your body?"

"Yes. When I returned to my room, the light was dim. It was just turning daylight. The thought that crossed my mind when I returned was that it would have been nice to stay in that beautiful place a little longer. Then, instantly, I was back in my body."

"Do you know where you were?"

"I have no idea, but it was gorgeous. The grass was longer than I had ever seen before."

"Were all of these out-of-body experiences after you had your near-death experience?"

"I think so. I'm not sure, but I believe they were after my experience. The more extensive ones certainly were."

"Have all of these out-of-body events been pleasant?"

"No. The one where I found my boyfriend with another girl wasn't pleasant. Also, when I was under stress, sometimes, I felt an evil presence. Pressure on my chest accompanied this evil feeling, and it was as if someone or something were trying to get me out of my body. These events were very frightening. During one of these episodes I remember that my mother couldn't wake me for a long time. On another one I heard a terrible growling noise."

"How did you combat these negative events?"

"By prayer. Prayer and peaceful, pleasant thoughts keep them from happening."

"Have all of these events had an impact on your life?"

"Yes they have."

"In what way?"

"I am very non-judgmental of others. Most important, though, I have a strong belief in the Lord Jesus Christ."

"Are there any messages you would like to leave for others?"

"Nothing is impossible."

Chapter 15

THREE WHO FELT THE LOVE

Mary

Mary was waiting as Carol and I drove up to her home in the Salt Lake City area, on a spring day in 1993. Her two dogs greeted us, and while she seated us, she began to tell us of her background.

She was born in Utah in 1934, in the Salt Lake City region. Her family moved around somewhat as she was growing up so that her stepfather could pursue his occupation as a miner. By the time she reached the sixth grade she had gone to fifteen different schools. When she was in the eleventh grade she quit school and went to work. She had eight brothers and sisters.

Mary and her husband have two daughters, and two grandchildren, all of whom lived in the Salt Lake City area. Mary's husband, John, is a construction foreman, and he also has an interest in rodeos. Mary showed Carol and me many mementos and pictures from the rodeos they attended.

During her youth Mary was exposed briefly to the LDS, Assembly of God and Baptist religions. As an adult she has a very strong Christian belief in Jesus Christ as our Lord and Savior.

A Hunger for Love

Mary began to tell her story: "In 1968 I was very depressed. My life seemed to have no meaning, and I hungered for love, but I didn't seem to know how to get it. Worldly events and material things were all that mattered to me, and there was no spiritual satisfaction in anything that I did.

"On one particular day I decided that I had had enough of this life; I wanted out. So I wrote a note asking the Lord to forgive me, and I left the note for my husband to find. Then I took every pill I could find in the house, and I lost consciousness.

"When my husband came into the house, he found me and rushed me to the Cottonwood Hospital in Salt Lake City. The doctors told him they didn't give me much hope. It was especially bleak because there was no fight in me—I didn't want to live."

A Tunnel, and a Rainbow-colored Room

"My first memory after losing consciousness was to awaken and realize that I was speeding down a dark tunnel. There was a light at the end of the tunnel, and I was moving toward it. Suddenly I came to the end of the tunnel. Entering a beautiful room that was filled with a rainbow color, I stood in awe and wonder at the beauty of it all. Then a bright light came down upon me, and I knew it was something special.

"The peace I felt was wonderful, a perfect tranquility and warmth, for I was surrounded by an unconditional love. The love was everything that I had hungered for but seemed unable to find in life. All the anger, hate, pain, and fear that I had previously felt were removed. Pure love and peace were all around me.

"Wanting to stay in the presence of that love forever, I continued to stand in the light. Suddenly, though, I knew I couldn't stay—and I was sent reeling back through the tunnel of darkness. It was not a pleasant feeling coming back. Opening my eyes, I discovered that I was again in the hospital. Leaving that beautiful place of peace left me furious. Instead of a place of peace and love, I was greeted by a nurse who gave me a painful shot. And I was cussing mad.

"When I came home from the hospital, I still had the memory of the wonderful love and peace that I felt in the rainbow-room. Only my husband was aware of what had happened to me. In those days it was not acceptable to talk about what I had experienced or witnessed. People seemed to be afraid to hear me talk about it. So it became my private knowledge."

A Second Experience

"In January 1986 I entered the hospital with pneumonia. It was particularly dangerous for me because I was a heavy smoker, and I had not stopped—despite having been told that I should stop. After being treated for pneumonia and related respiratory illnesses for a week, they talked of releasing me. Things weren't quite right, though, so they kept me somewhat longer.

Finding myself in darkness on one occasion, but conscious, I tried to figure out where I was. Looking down from an elevated position, I saw a lady, in bed, dressed in blue. Medical people were clustered around this poor lady in blue, and they were attempting to put a ventilator on her.

"At first I couldn't imagine who the lady in blue was. The view I was seeing was from the upper corner of a hospital room. I continued to watch the scene, feeling empathy for the patient, when things went dark again. Much later I figured out that the poor lady was I.

"My next conscious memory was to awake in bed, and to see my sister, who had died in 1980 in a car wreck, standing at the foot of my bed. Her hands were folded and she was smiling at me.

"It seemed strange to see my sister, and I wondered what she was doing there. Then I felt the presence of someone else on my right side. Looking in that direction, I saw my Savior, Jesus Christ." Mary paused in her discussion as she attempted to control her emotions.

"Jesus was looking down at me, and I knew that He wasn't too happy with me because I hadn't quit smoking. He was so full of love, though, and He turned to my sister and smiled.

"The moment Jesus smiled at my sister, I knew that I wasn't going to die. He turned back to me, and. . . . Now He didn't talk to me like you and I talk. The message He sent to me, it was. . . . I heard Him in my head.

"As He turned to me, there continued to be this unconditional love, and He said: 'Tell your family about Jesus Christ.' That was the only message. Then He smiled at me and left.

"My sister continued to stand there for a time. She was dressed in a brown dress with a white collar. Her dress, in that environment, seemed to symbolize scholarship.

"After a short period my sister left; and I was back with the nurses, the ventilator, and all the medical equipment. They had me tied to the bed—the ties were to keep me from removing the tubes that they had me plugged into.

Recovery

"My recovery was very fast. My brother, whom I had not seen for some time, came to see me during my recovery period. Because of my experience I felt a necessity to tell my family of Jesus. Also, I wanted my brother to read from the 23rd Psalm. We joined hands as he read it; then we said the Lord's Prayer together.

"The hospital kept me for one week after that. Returning home, I continued to feel the love of my Savior, and I knew that my immediate medical emergency was over. My overall health, though, still suffered from the years of smoking that I had done. Chronic Obstructive Pulmonary Disease (COPD) was a continuing problem. At night, even now, I have to use oxygen because of the limited capacity of my lungs."

Questions About Mary's Experiences

Mary agreed to being questioned about her experiences. I began: "In your first experience, when you went through the tunnel and came out in the room, can you describe the room?"

"It was just like a rainbow. I think the colors were representative of God's promises to us."

"Was there any furniture in the room, or were there other distinguishing features?"

"Nothing. Just the rainbow-colored light. There were pastel colors, and it wasn't exactly like our rainbow, it was just . . . We don't have the kind of beauty that I saw."

"Did you hear anything?"

"No."

"In your second experience, when you were up near the corner of the room, how did you feel?"

"It didn't seem strange to be up there—I didn't even question it. There was no pain, and I felt great."

"When you saw Jesus, what were the circumstances?"

"It was a different place than the hospital. I was in bed, and my sister was there, but I didn't have the ventilator or other equipment on me from the hospital. It was a different dimension, or something. Jesus was standing on the right of the bed."

"How do you know it was Jesus?"

"I just knew. I know Jesus."

"What did He look like?"

"He looked just like Jesus. His robe was in the style of the biblical times, and it seemed to be made of homespun material. There was no question about His identity. When I later tried to tell someone about it, I just broke down and sobbed—from the feeling I got remembering Jesus."

"Did you say anything to Jesus?"

"No. I didn't talk. He just asked me to tell my family about Jesus Christ. That was all, and then I was back."

"Were you angry, this time, when you came back?"

"No, because this time I had something to do. There was an important reason for my being here. And I am telling my family and others about Jesus Christ."

A Serious Illness and a Healing

As Mary finished telling of her second out-of-body experience I asked her if there were any other similar events in her life. She said there were not any others where she left her body, but she did have an unusual experience related to her health. I asked her to tell me about it.

"In 1978 and 1979 I had lots of problems with tumors. The doctor had been trying to get me to stop smoking, but I also had these tumors that kept growing in my breast. He had removed several of them, but they kept coming back. It reached the point where I was completely frustrated.

"One of my friends knew how I was suffering, and she belonged to the LDS Church. Her son had returned from a mission, and she talked to me about having him give me a blessing. At first I told her no, but she persuaded me that I should do it.

"Her son came and gave me a wonderful blessing. At one part of the blessing, I still remember, he said to keep my faith. Following the blessing I felt an inner warmth.

"The doctor had me scheduled to come in and have a tumor, about the size of a quarter, removed. The operation was scheduled for the following day. When I awoke on the day of the operation, the tumor was gone. I didn't have to go through the operation. The doctor said that I was living proof of a miracle. There was no other explanation."

"Later, the doctor still had me scheduled for a bilateral mastectomy, but I said no. Seeking other medical advice, I finally found an oncology expert who told me that I could avoid a mastectomy and just treat the tumors if and when they appeared. So, after praying about what to do, that is what I did—there was no mastectomy."

Final Thoughts from Mary

"Did you ever quit smoking, Mary?"

"Yes. In 1988 I got to the last cigarette, and I prayed to the Lord to help me. After that I never had the desire to smoke again. Unfortunately, the damage had been done and I got COPD. It's a combination of emphysema, bronchitis and asthma. So I now have to take lots of medicines for it."

"Are there any messages you would like to leave for others?"

"Yes. Life is a beautiful gift from God. Suicide is never the answer to our problems. We should trust in God, and love the Lord with all our heart. We should also love our neighbors. Once I had a question: 'How big is my family?' The answer just came to me: 'My family consists of all the people that Jesus Christ leads into my life.' And we should understand the message given in John 3:16."

Maria

Maria was a friend of Mary's, and Carol and I visited with her at Mary's home. Mary arranged for our meeting after informing us that Maria had also had a near-death experience.

We visited for a while, and then Maria began to tell us about herself. Having been born in 1915 in Salt Lake City, Utah, she and her two brothers were raised in the Salt Lake region. She went to school at the Hawthorne School. Her marriage was in 1936 and she had six children, twenty-seven grandchildren, and six great-grandchildren.

At the time of our visit, Maria and her husband were raising three of her grandchildren. One of her daughters became ill, so Maria and her husband volunteered to raise the grandchildren.

Maria was raised as an active member of The Church of Jesus Christ of Latter-day Saints, and she and her husband remained active throughout their lives—they were active LDS temple workers.

A Ruptured Appendix

Maria began to tell her story: "In 1956, when my oldest boy Jim was on his mission, I became ill. One day I got this horrible pain in my left side. It got bad enough that I went to the doctor.

"The doctor thought something could be wrong with my colon, and they said they might have to operate. They sent me home for a period, and when I was walking up some stairs I felt something break. I became very ill and had to go to the hospital.

"My husband took me to the hospital. When the doctors operated on me, they thought it was for a ruptured colon, or something else. In actuality they found that my appendix was on the wrong side, and it had ruptured.

"It was the LDS Hospital, and I was so sick I hardly knew what was going on for a while. The doctors were very concerned about me, and one night I felt so bad I didn't think I would make it."

A Beautiful Experience

"Suddenly I heard the most beautiful music imaginable, and I felt somebody holding me in their arms. There was so much peace and love. It was a tremendously comforting feeling. The pain left, and I felt wonderful.

"I had the sensation of being carried up someplace, until we got to a location that had a veil (like a curtain). A voice said: 'Do you want to go in?' and I asked: 'Is there more for me to do?' The voice then answered: 'Yes.' Immediately afterward I awakened in my bed. That was the end of my experience.

"My recovery, due to peritonitis, phlebitis, and other complications was extended. I was in the hospital for sixteen days."

"May I ask you a few questions about your experience, Maria?" I asked.

"Yes."

"When you were first ill, was it very painful?"

"My, yes. It hurt so much I told my husband to take me out and shoot me. My little girl cried when I did that. She told her daddy not to shoot me." Maria laughed as she thought back on the incident.

"When you went to the hospital, did it still hurt?"

"By that time I was weak, and I felt sick to my stomach."

"Then when you had your experience, how did you feel?"

"There was no illness or pain, and I felt as though someone were holding me. The music was the most marvelous sound I had ever heard."

"What did it sound like?"

"It sounded like a choir singing wonderful church music, and it surrounded me."

"Was it like cowboy or rock music?"

"Heavens, no. If you listen to the Mormon Tabernacle Choir, it sounded like they do. There was a feeling of peace that went with it."

"Then you were carried somewhere?"

"I was carried to a veil."

"What did the veil look like?"

"It resembled a white curtain, or a drape. Then they asked me if I wanted to go through."

"When you say *they*, what do you mean?"

"I was carried by someone, and a man was standing by the veil. He asked me if I wanted to go through."

"What did the man look like?"

"Like they do in the temple—he was dressed in white."

"How did you feel when he asked you that?"

"My thoughts went to my children, and I asked: 'Isn't there more that I should do?' At that time, my oldest boy was on a mission; the second boy, Steve, was six years younger; and then there were George, Judy, Nola and Charlotte. They needed me, and I knew it. I had to come back."

"When you came back, did you hurt again?"

"Yes. It hurt all over my body."

"Are there any messages you would like to leave for others?"

"I've heard all my life that Jesus will win. There is so much sin in the world, today, that I worry the devil will win. I want everyone to get on the Lord's side."

Debbie

She was a tall, young blonde woman with a delightful southern accent. She greeted Carol and me graciously when she came to our home in May 1993.

Debbie was born in Chicago, Illinois, in June 1961; she was the oldest of five children. The family moved from Illinois to Ohio, and then back to Alabama, their previous home, where Debbie was raised.

Most of her youth was spent in a backwoods region of Alabama. Despite no tradition of formal education in her family, Debbie graduated from high school. In 1979, before graduation from high school, she enlisted in the Air Force, and she became an active member immediately after graduation. As an adult, at the time of our interview, she was attending college and taking pre-med courses.

Debbie's youth was not entirely happy, since she had an abusive father. Her mother, however, was a spiritual woman, and she took the children to church whenever she could. They attended a fundamental Baptist Church.

After entering the Air Force, and completing basic training in Texas, Debbie was assigned to Hill Air Force Base in Utah. She met her future husband there. When she became pregnant, she obtained a discharge from the Air Force. At the time of our visit, Debbie had two children, and she was divorced.

As Debbie visited with Carol and me, she exhibited some nervousness, typical of many who tell their experience for the first or second time. She informed us that she had not often told her story. She seemed to be under considerable emotional pain.

A Difficult Operation

Debbie began to tell her story. "Before I joined the Air Force, I had braces on my teeth. In order to be allowed in boot-camp I had to remove the braces. The recruiting officer signed a statement, however, that after basic training the Air Force would continue my treatment.

"At my first duty station I visited the military dentist on the base, and he examined me. After the examination he scheduled me for cosmetic surgery, known as malocclusion surgery, to correct a severe overbite problem.

"They flew me to Texas, where the surgery was to take place, on Christmas eve, 1980. My surgery was scheduled for January 3; the delay was so that dentists and doctors could be flown in from other Air Force installations. This was to be a major operation, and it would be filmed for later training purposes.

"The doctors were nice to me, and they gave me a complete physical before the operation, which they said would take six hours. Joking with them to relieve my nervousness, I told them to be sure and wash their hands before they worked on me.

"A number of complications arose during the surgery. They put a tube down me, and that apparently caused severe bleeding of an ulcer in my esophagus. The worst problem, though, was from the anesthetic. It turned out that I was allergic to it, and I went into cardiac arrest during the operation. They were able to restart my heart using resuscitation techniques, but in the process they ruptured my diaphragm."

Cradled by Christ

"While the doctors were having these problems I suddenly felt warmth all around me, and I knew that somebody was holding me. The area I was in was surrounded by light.

"It felt as though I were being cradled by someone, and when I saw all this light, I looked around to see what was happening. As I lifted my head I found myself looking into the eyes of Christ. He was carrying me, as a child would be carried, in a cradling fashion.

"There were no fear and no pain, just a feeling of lightness and security—and I kept staring at Him. He was walking with me; then, strangely, He carried me through a wall, or something, and we went from the light into darkness.

"Christ's lips never moved, but He communicated with me, and He asked: 'Do you know where you are? Look around the room.'

"Looking around, as He directed, I saw that we were in the hospital room and He was carrying me toward my body. The darkness frightened me, and I looked back at Christ's face where there was light. Looking at Him calmed me, and then I noticed that we were again moving toward my body.

"Having a sense that I would have to return to my body, I asked Him repeatedly, 'Why? Why?'

"In a soothing way He told me that it was not my time yet. While He stood there holding me, I could see my body plainly. But at the same time, I knew I had a semblance of a body, or a spirit body, that Christ was holding. And I could feel His strength while He held me.

"When He went to lay me down into my body, I tried to resist by grabbing at Him. Crying desperately, I kept repeating: 'Please don't. I don't want to go back.'

"Struggling with my emotions, and crying continuously, I asked Him what I must do. He smiled at me and responded: 'Shhh, everything will be all right.' My gaze was riveted on Him, and He began backing away.

"Christ was moving slowly in a gentle manner, but, as I cried, I wanted Him to stay and talk to me. He addressed me again, saying: 'Keep focused—stay focused!'

"Then the light sort of followed Him out of my room. He was gone.

"Continuing to look for Christ, I saw a light a short distance away, but it was only the light from the area where the nurses were. One of the nurses saw me look, and she announced to the others that I was conscious."

Questions About Debbie's Experience

Debbie agreed that I could ask her some questions. "Can you describe what Christ looked like?" I asked.

"His hair was long and sandy-blonde, with a nice wave in it. He was bearded with a smooth face, and His eyes . . . His eyes were the bluest blue I had ever seen; they were a clear see-through blue. There was warmth, there was love, there was compassion in his eyes. I couldn't look away from Him—He was the one that told me to look around."

"So you did, then, look around?"

"Yes, and when I did I felt fearful."

"How was Christ dressed?"

"He was wearing a white gown."

"Was there light associated with Him?"

"Oh, yes. There was light all around Him; it actually stood off of Him. It was an energy."

"What color was the light?"

"It was white, with a blue tint."

"When you were carried through the wall, where did you wind up?"

"I don't know; I wanted to ask Him how He walked through the wall." Debbie laughed as she thought back on the event. "I don't know where we were because, at that time, I didn't look around. Gazing into the eyes of Christ, as much as I could, there was just light around us. It was a brilliance that filled everyplace."

"How did you know it was Christ?"

Debbie sighed as she gathered her thoughts. "Knowing that my heart was at that much peace, and that I felt so drawn to Him, it had to be Christ. If it wasn't Christ, I guess I could say, that's where I want to go. He understood me, and He loved me—it was a love that I had not felt previously nor since, anyplace on earth."

"Why did you use the word: *peace*?"

"Perhaps it was because I've had such a lack of it in my life. There's always been turmoil and difficulty. With Christ, I finally found peace."

"You mentioned that when you saw your body, you existed in another body. What was your other body like?"

"That's hard to explain, because I was in full body. There were limbs, and I knew Christ was carrying me. But it was without the bulk I normally felt in my earthly body. I felt light, and I also felt as though I had light around me. When He placed me back in my body, it was as if this light, transparent something was entering a bulky body."

"When you saw your body, did you have any feelings toward it?"

"Yes. I didn't want it."

"Why didn't you want it?"

"I didn't want to leave, and when He put me back into my body, I felt as if I couldn't move in that bulky thing. Trying to grab for Him, I reached out, but I couldn't touch Him anymore. There was no way I could get back in His arms."

"You didn't feel pain when you were out of your body?"

"No. Trying to find words in the English language that express the feeling is impossible—I've tried. All the positive thoughts you've ever had will not explain the feeling that I had. The word that most expresses it is: *peace*. I was deliriously happy while I was there. I never wanted to return here. Later, when I was back, I was ashamed at the way I clung to Christ and cried while He brought me to my body. It must have been hard on Him to have to return me under those circumstances.

"My feelings haven't changed much about this life, since my experience." Debbie began to cry as she attempted to explain her feelings.

"In that environment of love, and in my innocence at the time, I was fed up with the world and its mixture of hypocrisy, hate, envy and pain. I still feel that way. My anger at returning to this cruel world spills over at times, and the only relief I get is from prayer. Praying long and hard is my solution."

Debbie's Recovery, and Her Final Thoughts

"The film of my operation was a documentary of medical history. They had to cut my jaw in two places, and my jaw was wired shut after the operation. The wires weren't supposed to come off for at least four to six weeks. They un-wired me in two-and-a-half weeks, and my jaw was healed. During the healing process, I didn't feel pain with my mouth—Christ healed me.

"My jaw healed well, but I did have a relapse. Since my jaw was wired shut, they could only feed me through straws, and they gave me this terrible protein stuff. I hated it, so when they gave it to me I hid it in the closet; I wouldn't drink it. After a few days I passed out, and they found out what I was doing. They put tubes back down me and fed me that way until I recovered."

"How long were you in the hospital?"

"It was the Wilford Hall Medical Center in San Antonio, Texas, and I was there for two months."

"Did you tell others about your experience when you regained consciousness?"

"My mouth was wired shut, so I had to write messages to talk. I wanted to tell my doctor, but he wouldn't let me. He just said: 'Honey, I know you are blessed,' and he kissed me on the lips. After that, I sort of shut the experience inside of me."

"Do you think your experience could have been a dream or a hallucination?"

"No. It was too real—as real as my sitting here next to you."

"Are there any messages you would like to leave for others?"

"Yes. The Bible says not to judge others, and that is the primary message I would like others to have. We can't know the circumstances of others, so we shouldn't judge them."

Chapter 16

A PROFOUND EXPERIENCE

David Chevalier

It was his hair and beard, both a carrot red, that distinguished him when I visited him at his home in the spring of 1993. He smiled and explained that he had been taking a short nap to recover from an early session preparing for and teaching an English class. The morning had started for him at 4:30 a.m.

After exchanging greetings, David told me of his early life. He was born in Council Bluffs, Iowa, in 1953. His father was a railroader, and they lived on a small farm just outside the city limits. When David was two years old his father and mother were divorced, and David lived with his grandmother for three years. David's father remarried, and the Chevalier family ultimately consisted of the father and step-mother, one full-blooded sister of David, and twelve half and step-brothers and sisters. When David was fifteen years old, the family moved to Southern California where his father's job on the railroad took them.

Graduating from high school in Rialto, California, in 1971, David also attended junior college part time. His schooling was interrupted by three years in the army, until 1975, when he returned to junior college. He met his wife, Christine, in San Bernardino while they were working and attending junior college. They married and moved back to Iowa where David went to work for the Chicago and North Western Railroad until 1981. He completed his college education with a B.A. in business in 1985, and later, an M.A. from Northern Arizona University.

They lived in Flagstaff, Arizona, near Chris's parents, until 1991 when Chris's father had a heart attack and had to move from Flagstaff because of the altitude. Chris's sister had a house in Utah, and David and Chris liked the area, so they moved Chris's parents and themselves to Utah. David obtained a job teaching English at a local college, and Chris found employment as a conductor for AMTRAK.

During his youth, David was encouraged to decide for himself what kind of religious experience he wanted. As a consequence he attended the Lutheran, the Presbyterian, and the Baptist churches. At the time of our visit David and Chris had one small girl and two older boys.

A Terrible Wound

David began to tell of his experience: "It was Friday, November 13, 1981, and we were living in Iowa where I was working for the railroad. On that morning I had driven Christine to work, and I was dressed up to attend the funeral of a friend from work who had been killed in an auto accident. For some reason I felt it was necessary for me to attend the funeral, even though I normally didn't go to funerals.

"After taking Chris to work, I stopped by my grandmother's house in Council Bluffs to say hello. Offering me breakfast, she proceeded to cook it while I sat at her kitchen table. My uncle (on my father's side), who was living with my grandmother, came into the kitchen. He had a serious life-long drinking problem and apparently was in an alcoholic haze when he got up, because he immediately began to argue with me.

"Not wanting to get into a family argument with my uncle, I told him to leave me alone. Storming from the room, he left, returning shortly with a center-break single-shot twelve-gauge shotgun. Carrying the gun in his hands near his hip, haplessly, he pointed it at me and pulled the trigger as I sat at the table.

"The shotgun blast hit me in the lower right abdomen and blew me backward into the back door. Finding myself on my back looking out across the table at my angry uncle, I realized I had been shot. To my horror I saw him break open the shotgun and load it with another shell. My grandmother, who had just witnessed her son shoot her grandson, was in shock and unable to do anything.

"While lying on my back, I grabbed the nearest kitchen chair and used it as a device to fend off the shotgun—in much the same manner that a lion tamer would fend off a lion. With the end of the barrel caught in the rungs of the chair I was able, for a period, to keep the gun from pointing directly at me. Struggling to my feet, I managed to grasp the barrel with my free hand.

"Pleading with my uncle to stop what he was doing, I continued to wrestle with him over the gun for some moments. He finally seemed to understand what he had done, and he stopped fighting. Breaking open the gun and ejecting the shell, he convinced me that I could let go. The tone of his voice showed that he was again rational, so I released my hold on the gun. After dropping the shotgun, my uncle ran from the house.

"Having been in the military, my excellent training concerning the treatment of wounds was instantly called to mind—not looking at the wound; treating myself for shock; and making sure that I wasn't bleeding to death. These were all issues I was concerned with. Putting my hand on the wound, I withdrew it and saw that there wasn't much blood—just a circle, an outline, of blood where the shot had entered my abdomen. Because of the lack of surface blood I knew that I was bleeding internally.

"As the enormity of my situation became clear I fell on my knees, crying, and I began praying. I prayed for repentance of my sins. Upon completing a quick prayer, I recovered sufficiently to dial 911. Shortly thereafter the operator let me know that help was on its way.

"Knowing that help was coming, I lay on the couch in the front room, propped my feet up to treat myself for shock, loosened my tie and my shirt, and continued with my prayer. I'm not sure how long it was, but I next remember a detective from Council Bluffs coming through the door in a crouched position with a drawn .357 Magnum. When he saw me, he asked: 'Where is he?', and I pointed out the back door. He rushed out the door with his gun drawn.

"Following the detective were two paramedics. They treated me at the scene, putting balloon pants on me and inflating the pants to keep the blood in my upper body. When they got me into the ambulance and started the siren, I heard them radio to their dispatch and say that they were heading for Jennie Edmonson Hospital. There are two hospitals in Council Bluffs. I was born at Mercy Hospital, and I figured if I were going to die that's where I should be, so I redirected them to Mercy Hospital.

"At the emergency room of Mercy Hospital, I remember the nurses asking my name and other vital information. My thoughts were: *Here I've had the worst wound of my life, I may not live, and the nurses must still fill out the forms*. I carefully spelled my last name for them, because I wanted to make sure it was not misspelled if I didn't live. Upon getting all the information they needed, the nurses released the air in the pants—and I lost consciousness."

Medical Treatment, and Strange Happenings

"My next memory was of hearing a nurse read my blood pressure. Hearing her read it, I could see two nurses on the left-hand side of my bed, and the doctor on the right side. This view of the nurses and doctor working on me was despite the fact that I wasn't conscious. I was seeing this scene as if I were somewhat above a prone position in my bed. It was almost as if my ethereal body were holding and consoling my physical body's head in its lap.

"The nurse said that my blood pressure was sixty over zero; then she said it was fifty over zero. The doctor told them to alert the family and the clergy.

"As the doctor made his comment about the clergy, I heard another voice, my voice, but coming from outside me, saying: 'No. I'm not ready yet.' Instantly upon hearing that voice a feeling came over me that I could make it. It was a similar feeling as that obtained on getting a second wind when running a long race. I knew I could survive—and then I was in blackness again.

"During this unconscious period they operated on me. They told me later that I was initially in surgery for eight-and-one-half hours. There were two gurneys, one with me on it, and another at right angles. To repair my intestines the doctor removed and spread my entrails and laid them out upon the other gurney. In that manner they searched, cleaned and sealed those penetrations of my intestines by bird-shot that they could. Other portions of the intestines that they couldn't repair, they removed. They learned, during this process, that the shotgun pellets were size number 8 bird-shot. Some of that bird-shot is still in my body—even in my heart.

"Upon waking, later, I heard someone ask me if I wanted a respirator. Breathing was a problem for me, and I nodded, yes, I wanted one. It felt so good when they put the respirator on, and I drifted back into unconsciousness again.

"The next memory was of waking in Intensive Care with my father and my wife close by, and several nurses attending me. Seeing my father gave me a sense of relief. He had been in Arizona, and in order for him to be in Iowa it was clear that substantial time had passed—and I was still alive.

"Wanting to communicate, I motioned for something to write on. Because of the many tubes going down my nose and throat, and the respirator, I couldn't talk. When they gave me a clipboard with paper and a pen, I wrote in capital letters: *WHY?* My mind was obsessed with the thoughts: *Why did this happen to me? What did I do to cause this to happen?* After thinking those thoughts I became unconscious again.

"When I lost consciousness this time, the doctors discovered that there were still bleeders in me, so I was again returned to surgery. While I was in this second surgery my heart flat-lined, and they had to use the resuscitation paddles to restart it. This whole period, the second surgery, and recovery in Intensive Care were just a fog to me. I was unaware of what was happening.

"Five days after I entered the hospital, at night when the lights were low, I awakened in the Intensive Care unit. The respirator had been removed, and I only had one tube going up my nose and down my throat. My mouth felt as if an army had marched through it with muddy boots. Looking around the room I spotted a bottle of sterile water nearby. I grabbed it and took some long delicious swallows of water. The nurse happened to come into the room as I was drinking the water, and she was horrified.

"Apparently when you have a stomach wound you are not supposed to have water. In my case the water started massive internal bleeding, and I slipped into unconsciousness."

The Savior—An Amazing Valley

"One night, about a week after entering the hospital, while in Intensive Care, I slipped away and they again had to resuscitate me with the paddles. During that night, with my room darkened, I became fully aware of what was going on in my room. Looking around the room I could see everything—and standing by one side of my bed was my Savior. He was as plain to me then as you are now.

"Reaching over to me, He ran His hands up and down my body, and all the tubes, all the staples and other attachments to my body were gone.

His right hand reached out, as if to beckon me; I reached back to touch His hand.

"As my hand touched His, instantaneously we were on the rim of an incredible valley. It was a huge valley, on the order of Yosemite or Zion National Park in size, and it was verdantly green. There was water; there were rivers, there were lakes—and the valley was filled, almost shoulder-to-shoulder, with people.

"Gazing on this astonishing scene, I had the feeling of eager anticipation emanating from the multitude below me. The mood of this enormous crowd, the feeling that I could also feel, was as if in expectation of some marvelous event that would soon happen.

"The breadth of the scene was breathtaking, and I stood there trying to absorb what I was viewing. People were milling about, some of them speaking in soft tones, and there was a calmness about them despite the feeling of anticipation.

"Turning to my Savior, I asked: 'What are we waiting for?' He said something that I've later had to reconstruct, because the moment that He spoke I found myself back in Intensive Care with all the tubes and staples attached to me. My sense, upon returning, was that I would not only survive my physical ordeal but I would be better for it. I was overwhelmed by a glow within me, almost a fire, and a complete feeling of well-being.

"Thinking about the Savior's reply to my question, I had difficulty translating what He said into English. He communicated, and I had a sense of what it meant, but it was a form of communication that English doesn't cover. When He spoke, a number of thoughts were conveyed simultaneously. One thought was that we were waiting for the second coming; another thought was that we were waiting for the resurrection; a third thought was that we were waiting for redemption. And all of those thoughts entered my mind instantaneously."

Recovery

"When I found myself back in Intensive Care, I could hardly wait to tell others what I had seen. Seeing Chris and my father the next day, I wanted to tell them everything—and they believed me when I told them. Some of the people I told, though, thought I was affected by the morphine and demerol that I had been taking. I knew better. It was too real.

"Father Burns, the Catholic Priest who was the chaplain for the hospital, came to see me, and I told him about my experience. His response was that my experience was very special, and it had a reason. He told me that I should take it for what it was, and he said it was not the first time he had heard such a story.

"It took another month-and-a-half in Intensive Care before they moved me to another wing. Then there were another three weeks in a regular care unit before they let me go home. My recovery was truly a miracle, I wasn't supposed to live; or at least that's what the doctors said. One of the doctors told my wife that I only had a one-percent chance to live."

Questions about David's Experience

Dave agreed to some questions, so I began: "On the first incident, when you heard the voice, it was your voice yet it seemed to come from elsewhere—was that it?"

"Yes. There were obviously no vocal cords involved, but I could hear myself say that I wasn't ready yet. It was a real voice coming from outside myself, but it sounded like me."

"On this first event, could you see your body?"

"I could see my body, I could see the bed, I could see the sheet, but I couldn't see my face. The nurses were all clearly apparent and recognizable. Later, I told one of the nurses, for example, that she was reading my blood pressure when the doctor told them to get the clergy. She agreed that my memory of what happened was exactly right, and she wasn't surprised at what I told her. She had apparently been through such incidents previously."

"In the next event, Dave, you said that your Savior was standing near the bed?"

"Yes, He was on my left as I was lying in bed."

"What was He wearing?"

"Exactly as I imagined my Savior would look, with a white robe, and a sash tied in the center of the robe. He had a beard and long hair."

"Was He, or was the room, bathed in light?"

"Not that I noticed—except when He put his hands on me. The sheets seemed to get brighter during that instant."

"What were your feelings when He put his hands on you?"

"It was comforting. There were no feelings of fear or pain."

"How did you know it was your Savior?"

"I know Jesus Christ when I see Him."

"How did you know?"

David chuckled as he thought. Then he said: "Probably it was the sense of goodwill and the sense of comfort that I felt—together with the other events that I witnessed. The fact is, I just knew. I knew!"

"When you found yourself at the rim of the giant valley, and saw the people, how were they dressed?"

"In white."

"Were there any sounds associated with the valley?"

"Only the sounds of nature, and the gentle speaking of some of the people."

"What were the colors like?"

"Vivid blue and green. It was the greenest forest and grass that I had ever seen. The sky was the deepest blue I had seen, and the water was crystal clear. Perhaps the most remarkable thing about the scene was its intense clarity. It was as if someone had cranked the focus up on a remarkable camera or TV screen."

"Did you have any special feelings during this event?"

"Just the overwhelming sense of anticipation; and I was getting that sense from all the people who were present."

"And He communicated with you about that anticipation?"

"Yes, in response to my question: 'What are we waiting for?' Then I was back in my room."

"How did you communicate?"

"I spoke just as I do now, by voice. But His communication was different—it was not English—it was communication of thought. When He spoke, words were used, but I can't tell you what they were. It was more a conveyance of knowledge. Later, I was able to recollect the ideas of the second coming, the resurrection, and the redemption."

"Has this experience affected you?"

"Very much so. People who knew me previously, and who know me now, say that I am two different people. My life changed completely after the event. Prior to the event I was a typical hot-tempered, redheaded Irishman. Since the event I have obtained a new appreciation for people, for my family, and for my associations with people. If you had said before the incident, for example, that I would be teaching college classes, I would have responded that you were out of your mind. Now, I love the interaction I get with the students."

"Has life been easier or harder since your experience?"

"With Post Traumatic Stress Disorder (PTSD) induced by this event, I have been faced with a great number of difficulties since the experience in 1981. Schooling had to be completed while supporting a wife whose health was fragile. There was pressure to support kids and family, and lack of success in finding full-time employment, but despite those and other difficulties, life has been rewarding."

"How has your health been?"

"My current doctor in Utah was completely surprised when he examined me after I told him about the gunshot wound. Since 1981 when I was finally released from the hospital, I've had two instances when I've had to go back in the hospital. The doctors tell me, though, that based on the extent of my injuries I should have had to return to the hospital at least annually. They tell me that scar-tissue, alone, should keep me in a constant state of distress. That hasn't been true; I don't have recurring complications.

"My doctor, the one who operated in Iowa, talks about me as his proudest achievement. Originally, after the operation, he told Christine that I only had a 1 percent chance of living. He said I beat all the odds, and he later wrote a paper on me."

As David told me of his injury and recovery, he opened his shirt and lowered his trousers so that I could see the scar. There was a one- or two-inch-diameter semi-circle of scar-tissue on the lower right abdomen, peppered by surrounding dots of scar-tissue. There was also a scar from the operation, starting at the solar-plexus, running down Dave's center-stomach, skirting around his navel, and ending two inches below his belt-line. The evidences of a massive wound were obvious.

Thoughts on the Meaning of the Experience

"Have you any sense of why you were allowed to come back?"

"That question has plagued me since I was shot. Initially I thought it might be to help my wife and my two sons. Then, after I completed my education and started teaching, I thought it might be because I am able to express myself and to teach others well. Recently, when my daughter was born, I suspected it might be to help nurture and raise her. Maybe it's all of those things."

"Has your religious perspective changed?"

"Very much so. During the '50s and '60s, my generation was filled with doubters. Even though I went to different churches, I still had a skeptical, show-me attitude about religion. About one year prior to my getting shot, Christine and I took the boys and attended The First Christian Church. At that time I was baptized and surrendered myself to Christ.

"When I was shot, therefore, my first thought was for my spiritual well being rather than my physical survival. My prayer was for repentance, not survival. The appearance of my Savior, I think, was in part due to my prayer for repentance.

"When we moved to Utah in 1991, the LDS missionaries called on us. Back in Arizona, our oldest boy, Leon, was the first of our family to be baptized into The Church of Jesus Christ of Latter-day Saints. Christine, our youngest son, and I followed in June of 1992. Since joining the LDS Church I've had the opportunity of telling my story to several groups, and it has been a refreshing change to speak to those who believe. When I first had the experience, and was exposed to all the doubters, I became very private about what had happened.

"Had you read much about near-death experiences when you had yours?"

"Nothing prior to the experience. After it happened I became very curious and searched for material. About two years later I read Raymond Moody's *Life After Life*, and it helped me. Just this year I read *Return from Tomorrow* by George Ritchie."

"Could your experience have been a dream or hallucination?"

"No. It was the most real thing that ever happened to me—more real than being here now in my conscious state."

"Are there any messages you would like to leave for others?"

"My message involves faith. People are often told to have faith; to have faith that there is life after death, to have faith that Jesus Christ is real and is our Savior, and to have faith in a living God. I would like to offer myself, to those who struggle with their faith, as a living testimony that He does exist. I have seen Him, and I know that He is there. If people can't believe based on their own faith, then believe because of my witnessing—it is the truth. Please listen to me as someone who is a first-hand witness that Jesus Christ lives and is our Savior."

Chapter 17

A GENEALOGY EXPERIENCE

Renee Zamora

She visited our home in the spring of 1993. Renee seemed especially anxious to talk to us about her experience; she appeared to have a number of questions concerning what had happened to her. Carol and I promised to answer questions, to the best of our ability, after we completed the interview.

Her birthplace was Glens Falls, New York, in 1961, and she had three brothers and one sister. When Renee was four years old, her parents joined The Church of Jesus Christ of Latter-day Saints; later her father served as Branch President, then Bishop, of the local church unit.

Being raised in New York, Renee attended schools in that state, and she met her husband in a young-adult camp-out for members of her church. They were married in the Washington, D.C. Temple in 1982, and at the time of our interview they had two boys and a girl. Living in Massachusetts, where his work was, they had problems during the recession, so they moved to Utah in 1989.

A Precursor Experience

Renee started to tell her story: "When we moved to Utah, my husband was having trouble finding work, and he was depressed. The landlord, where we were living, kept some money from us that he was supposed to return, but didn't. The combination of no work and no money was more than I could handle.

"Lying on my bed one afternoon, crying, I remember thinking: *Life is too difficult—I can't handle it anymore. How could I kill myself without causing pain to others or without hurting myself?* Obviously, it was impossible to do what I asked myself, but the point is that I was seriously thinking of suicide.

"My grandmother, who had died some months earlier, suddenly was present in my room; I could feel her. She spoke to me, saying: 'It's only money!' As soon as I heard those words, I thought: *Of course. It's not worth it.* After that my suicidal feelings left me."

An Improperly Diagnosed Illness

"In 1991, here in Utah, my husband was working two jobs trying to make ends meet, and I was home with the children. Because of our lack of resources we did not have medical insurance.

"For some reason I got a really bad headache that wouldn't go away. Thinking it was just the onset of the flu, I had people give me blessings, and I tried to cope with how badly I felt. Finally, when I didn't get better, I went to see the doctor; the practitioner nurse who was there told me they would have to do tests.

"Without medical insurance we couldn't afford the tests, so the nurse gave me some antibiotics to take in the event it was some type of bacterial infection. The antibiotics seemed to affect me adversely, with an extensive rash, and I got worse.

"My illness progressively got worse, with high fevers, rashes, headaches, and exhaustion, so the doctor began to perform tests. After about two weeks they put me in the Utah Valley Regional Medical Center in Provo. A specialist was called in, and his initial diagnosis was viral-encephalitis.

"Things didn't get any better, and when my temperature rose to 106 degrees they packed me in ice. Due to the headache I had, and the way light hurt my eyes, they kept a cold, damp cloth over my eyes.

"Testing of my various functions continued; they performed an MRI, a CAT scan, a spinal, and many other tests. My headache continued to get worse, and I felt a growing numbness throughout my body. It seemed an effort just to remember to breathe.

"After two days of this in the hospital, they hooked a strong antibiotic to my I.V. apparatus; it caused another reaction in my body. My illness got worse, with vomiting and diarrhea. They kept me on the antibiotic treatment for three more days, until I got so bad that they stopped using it. During this period I had my experience."

Strange Visitors

"While I was feeling so bad, the nurses had to keep taking blood samples. It disturbed me, and I didn't like it, but I kept the cloth over my eyes because of how the light hurt them. Strangely, after a time, I was able to see the nurses coming and going, even though the cloth was still over my eyes. Wondering about it, I decided it must be the illness that was affecting me.

"Feeling so bad, I asked that no visitors be allowed—I just wanted to be left alone. My mind pondered the thought: *Am I so sick that I am going to die? What about my children?* I decided that if I were going to die my grandmother would come for me.

"While struggling to survive, and pondering these questions, something really peculiar happened. Passing through the door, and into my room, was a family. Their clothing was in the style of the late 1800s or early 1900s (I later looked it up). Walking past the foot of my bed, they stopped near my side. For some reason I understood the relationship that each person had to the other.

"As I watched, amazed, the father and one of his sons began playing checkers. The whole scene irritated me terribly. My thoughts were: *Here I am, so sick that I've asked for no visitors, and these rude people come into my room and play checkers.* What made matters worse was that they were talking to each other and ignoring me.

"Because I was so disturbed by the people, I decided that I would pay no attention to them. They must be figments of my imagination, I thought. Despite my trying to ignore them, they continued to stay in the room and annoy me—until the nurse came in. Whenever the nurse would enter, they would disappear.

"Unfortunately, when the nurse would depart, they would reappear. Another strange phenomenon occurred. I became aware that I knew the names of all of the individuals that were there, and I understood their specific relationships to each other. They seemed completely oblivious to my presence, continuing with their family small talk, and continuing to ignore me. It was interesting that they chattered away happily, but they did not move their mouths when they talked.   Their laughs and their smiles—the expressions on their faces—denoted their states of mind, as well as their conversations.

"About the second or third time I saw them, other family members joined them. Again, I understood the relationships, and this time it was the father's father, his spouse, and other relatives. The age appearances of the family members were as if they were all in their early 20s. The father might be a few years older than a child, and his father might appear a few years older than him, but they all looked to be young adults. Yet I knew instantly who was related to whom. Other knowledge about them came to me. One person, for example, had died as a child, and I knew it.

"This knowledge came to me despite my annoyance with the whole scene. My head continued to hurt desperately throughout the experience, and I wanted the people to leave. They were not dressed in white, and this bothered me. I was not interested in learning more about them.

"This process repeated itself for perhaps twenty times over the next two or three days. Gradually, the original family was joined by so many people, always their relatives through birth or marriage, that no more people could fit in the room. When this occurred, I watched, astonished, as the wall to the room vanished—except for the main beams in the walls."

Trip to an Unusual Place

"As the wall disappeared, the people in the room walked through it. They didn't even see the wall; they just walked off in the distance. I didn't want to go with them, but I had no choice. It seemed that I just floated off my bed, still in the horizontal position, and traveled with the people.

"Floating through the wall, I entered another of the hospital rooms. Looking down into this room as I floated through, I saw a frail old man in his bed. There was an oxygen tube in his nose, and his eyes were alternately open and closed.

"The people continued their journey through the hospital walls with me alongside them. When we reached the boundary of the hospital we sailed through, and suddenly it was as though we had gone to a park. I remember wondering: *What happened to the city of Provo?* As the thought entered my mind, I seemed to understand that the park was somehow overlaid upon the city, but slightly above it.

"It was a pretty park, with green grassy areas, and trees. My head kept aching, though, and I continued to resent having to go with the people. None of them recognized that I even existed—not that I wanted to be recognized by them. If I had been recognized, my fear was that I would have had to admit that I was dead. Moreover, I still had not seen my grandmother, the only one I would have been glad to see.

"When we traveled into the park area, I noticed people in the distance playing croquet. My thought was: *Why are people playing croquet?* It didn't make sense. None of it met my expectations of what I thought might happen on the other side. People were dressed in period clothes, not in white, and my grandmother was not among them. Even more peculiarly, they were engaged in activities, checkers and croquet, which to me seemed to be trivial.

"New groupings of people came to my attention, and I instantly knew their relationships to the others. Looking at one young woman, I understood that she was the sister-in-law's child from another group. And I knew their names. The people I identified often had an obscure and remote relationship to someone else—not a direct relationship.

"Beyond the area where the people were playing croquet was a sloping hill and a large tree. Several people were gathered near the tree, and they were having a picnic. A strange thing happened as I got near the people having the picnic; my headache left me. Again, I understood everyone's relationship, except one man who stood directly under the tree. For some reason I was not given his relationship.

"The headache pain had been so terrible that when it stopped I became very conscious of its departure. The moment that my consciousness acknowledged the departure of my headache, I was instantly back in the hospital with a splitting headache.

"This particular experience was repeated about three times before it dawned on me that if I wanted relief from my headache, I would have to stop thinking about it. I didn't particularly want to repeat the voyage to the park area, but since it was the only relief I got from my headache, I figured, okay, that's where I'll go. It also became clear that, whether I wanted to or not, I would have to focus on the relationships of the people in the park—otherwise I would bounce back into the hospital and my head would ache again. In effect, the headache was forcing me to make trips to the park and to concentrate on the different relationships."

A Frightening Man

"During each of these trips to the park and to the picnic area near the tree, I was still exasperated by the fact that no one could see me. Finally, on one trip to that area, I looked at the man whose relationship I didn't know. He looked back at me—he could see me—and I felt an impact in my heart that was indescribable. It was as if some physical object violently hit me.

"Instantly, upon receiving this jolt, I wanted to remove myself from the proximity of the man who could see me. I wondered who he was, but I knew that I wanted to be as far away from him as possible. The thought came into my mind: *He knows me.* And I didn't want him to know me.

"Repelled by the man who knew me, I looked at the people around him. They seemed to be oblivious to what was going on. The unpleasant man was able to see me, and my side of existence, but the others could not. They could only see themselves and the park area.

"Leaving the picnic area to distance myself from the man who knew me, I went down a hill and saw a wooded area in the distance. People wandered from the wooded area in groups, enjoying each other, and I immediately knew their relationships and their names. Despite knowing all the relationships they had to each other, I never was told whether or not they were related to me.

"Below me, in a distant part of the field, there was a depressed area with a stream of running water. The sound from the water reached me, and it was magnificent. The noise from the water soothed and helped me. In a way I wanted to proceed further, toward the water, yet I hadn't seen my grandmother, so I wouldn't go beyond where I was.

"There were many trips that I made between my hospital room and the park area. Whenever a nurse came into my room, I came back. It occurred over a period of three days, yet a puzzling aspect of the experience was the fact that time didn't seem to pass as fast for the people in the park area as it did for me. My three days were like five minutes to them, and I wondered how that could be."

The End of Renee's Experience

"All of the men in my ward bishopric were aware that I wanted the group of them to come and give me a blessing. On one Sunday afternoon they came, and after their blessing, I never saw the people again.

"The day after the bishopric gave me a blessing, the doctors told me that I had Epstein-Barr virus, and I could go home. After my release, it took me more than a month before my strength began to come back. According to some information I received, later, antibiotics should not be taken with Epstein-Barr virus, and this may have explained my serious illness.

"While I was in the hospital, and for some time afterward, I never told anyone about my experience. I was afraid they would think I was crazy. There was another problem—it was the fact that I didn't see my grandmother, and none of the people I saw were dressed in white. There was no way I wanted to be with them, and I didn't want to talk about it."

Thoughts on the Experience by Renee

"For a long time I wondered about this experience, and why it happened to me. It seemed real, yet I couldn't explain it. During my release from the hospital, though, something happened to convince me that it was real.

"They put me in a wheelchair to take me to the hospital entrance. At one point, while they went to get something, they parked me in the wheelchair at the doorway next to my room. Knowing I was just outside the room where I saw the frail old man in bed with the oxygen tube in his nose, I leaned around the corner and looked in. It was the same man—I saw and recognized him. From where I was lying in my room it would have been impossible for me to have seen him.

"The man whom I had seen under the tree, and who knew me, bothered me immensely. His image stayed with me, and I disliked the thought of it. For months afterward, I wondered who he was and why I wanted to run away from him. Yet I was fascinated by the thought of him. He was a good-looking man.

"One of my friends, Tami, was an artist, and I once explained my experience to her. We discussed the man who knew me, and I tried to describe him in sufficient detail that she could paint a picture of him. As our conversation evolved, she finally said: 'Renee, you don't want a picture of him. You know who he was, don't you?' At that moment, I did, and I said: 'Yes. It was Satan.'

"Not only did I know who the man was, but I understood that I should read the 138th Section of the Doctrine and Covenants in order to understand my experience. Also, I knew that I would find further answers by attending the temple.

"Many of the answers came in the temple, and some of them are too sacred to discuss here. It became clear to me, though, that the people I had seen were those who had passed on, but were confined to this earth, and who needed further work done for them in order to progress beyond where they were. I also understood why Satan was there, why he knew me, and how privileged I was to see what I did. Much of what I saw had symbolic meaning beyond the outward appearances of the events themselves.

"Since that experience, I have become a fanatic concerning genealogy and temple work. The patience of my husband is sometimes tried as I work on genealogy.

As a final thought, Renee said: "The genealogical and temple work that we do is enormously important. We should work diligently to find those people who are not necessarily on our direct genealogical line, and we should perform the work so that their temple ordinances can be done. Since my experience I have been driven to locate all the people I saw that needed their temple work done. Each person is important in the sight of the Lord."

Chapter 18

A LIFE'S REVIEW IN THE LIGHT

Roger Smith

Carol and I first met Roger at a meeting of the local International Association for Near Death Studies (IANDS). He agreed to be interviewed for this book, and he came to our house in the spring of 1993. I was indisposed with the twenty-four-hour flu, so Carol proceeded to interview Roger.

He was born in North Carolina on January 6, 1944. Most of his early life was spent in West Virginia until age sixteen, when the family moved to New Mexico. Serving in the military for a time, Roger moved to Utah after his release from the military in 1965.

Attending a number of Protestant churches as a youth, Roger had a mixed Christian upbringing. In 1966 he converted to The Church of Jesus Christ of Latter-day Saints. At the time of the interview he was married with four children—two boys and two girls.

A Volkswagen Crash

Roger began to tell his story. "In the fall of 1966 I transferred to Brigham Young University in order to change majors. I wanted to get a degree in Russian.

"In February 1968, while still in college, I left Provo to visit my brother in Syracuse, Utah for his birthday. Returning to Provo on Sunday, February 4th, I had just passed the Lagoon interchange while driving south on US 89/91 in my little Volkswagen.

"There was a lot of snow piled alongside the highway, and it was a cold winter day. There were patches of ice on the highway and many chuck-holes from winter deterioration. Keeping up with traffic, I was traveling at 60 mph, but I got the feeling that I should slow down.

"For some reason I looked at my watch, and it was exactly 8:30 a.m. Looking at the speedometer, after slowing, I saw that my speed was 50 mph. At that instant I hit a chuck-hole, followed by a patch of black ice.

"The Volkswagen went into a skid, from which I recovered by steering into the skid. Unfortunately, the car was headed toward a steep railroad embankment. Although I had recovered from the first skid I knew that if I hit the railroad embankment head on it would be fatal, so I turned the wheel; that put the Volkswagen into another skid. Skidding along the road, the left rear wheel went into the dirt and mud just off the highway.

"People following me later told me that the car left the ground, flipped ten or fifteen feet into the air, landed on its roof, bounced a second time on its roof, and on the third bounce landed on its wheels. A highway patrol officer measured that the distance between where the car first left the ground and where it landed was 296 feet.

"My memory of the event was that as I looked at my watch and hit the chuck-hole I heard a voice. The voice said: 'Unfasten your seat-belt and lie down in the seat.' Never giving it a second thought, I did as the voice told me. After unfastening my belt I lay down with my head on the passenger side, and I pushed against the steering wheel to shove myself against the back of the seats.

"When the car came to rest with its wheels on the ground, the roof was pushed down nearly to the level of the arm-rests on the doors. In the older Volkswagens the battery was located under the rear seat. It had sprung loose and burst, thus scattering battery acid throughout the inside of the car—except where I was. It was as if a circle had been drawn around my body, and everything inside that circle was not touched."

Journey to Another World

"The interesting thing was what happened during the time that the car was airborne. Something happened to me that, at the time, I considered to be unique. My initial memory was of being surrounded by black darkness. There was no sound, and there was no sense of distance in the darkness, but there was a sense of rapid movement, as if I were being pulled somewhere.

"Somehow, while I was in this darkness, I could see what was happening to me in the car, but at the same time I was removed from it. And off in the distance, in the black void, I saw a tiny speck of light. My movement was toward the light.

"Getting closer to the light, it got larger and brighter. It was the whitest-white I had ever seen. The brightness was . . . I can't describe how it was. There is nothing on this earth that is that color. Wondering about the brightness as I got closer, I asked myself: *How can I stand to look at and be in this light? How is it that I can see?*

"By this time I was standing, enveloped in the light, and I could feel it. Permeating every cell of my body, it filled me with warmth, it filled me with love—it was an indescribable feeling. At the same time I became aware of music. It was music such as I had never heard before, and it was beautiful. The strains of music were soothing to my soul.

"Standing there in this light, and feeling wonderful, I became aware of a person, off to my right, descending a few stairs. Approaching me, he began to talk to me, and I knew who he was. He never told me his name, but I instantly recognized him, and I *wanted* to be with him. It was Jesus Christ."

A Visit With the Lord

"Knowing who the Savior was, and feeling of His love, I was interested in answering His questions. My focus was not on His appearance as much as it was on what He had to say. People have subsequently asked me what He looked like. Thinking back on it, He was slightly taller than I am (I am 5 feet 10 inches tall), of average stature, and He was dressed in a long flowing robe of the purest white I had seen. The robe was whiter, even, than the light. It was bright.

"Looking into the Savior's face, the light was astonishingly bright, bright enough that I couldn't see distinct details of his face. The light just glowed around him; it emanated from him. His eyes, filled with love, appeared to peer into the depths of my soul.

"I know the Savior talked to me, and it was a strange sensation. There was a hearing sensation, but it wasn't as if I were hearing with my ears. When He spoke, not into my ears, but into my mind, there was no possibility of misunderstanding. Everything He said gave me a sense of love.

"For many years I remembered, verbatim, what He said to me and what I responded. I thought I would never forget it, but I did. Now it is difficult to reconstruct exactly what our conversation was.

"Generally, I was asked some questions about being there, and if I understood what was happening. Answering as best I could about what I knew to be happening, I was asked if I were ready to come home.

"To the question, was I ready to come home, I answered something to the effect: 'Yes, I think so.' Even as I said it, though, I knew that I wouldn't be happy where I was going to end up.

"Interestingly, when I was there in the light I knew where I was, but I don't now know where it was—at the time I knew exactly. It seemed to be a room, bathed in white, but I don't remember any walls, ceiling, or windows. Everything in the background was a pure white.

"Remembering that room, or wherever it was, there were different kinds of white throughout. There was the room itself, the Savior's robes, the Savior himself, and each of the whites was different—and every one of them was prettier than anything I had seen on earth.

"Most of the questions the Savior asked me were short and to the point, although I've forgotten essentially all of what He asked. The one thing I remember, though, was when He asked me if I wanted to know for sure whether I was ready to come home. To that question I answered, yes."

A Detailed Life's Review

"Suddenly in front of me appeared . . . I don't know how to describe it. Something appeared that resembled a movie screen, yet it was sort of like a play—and I was the main actor. While I watched, astounded, I saw everything that ever happened to me from the second I was born until the accident—all twenty-four years.

"One of the scenes still sticks in my memory—when I was about five or six years old, and we were living in West Virginia. There was this little old table, approximately my height, and I remember walking up to it. My twin brother was standing on the other side of the table, and my little brother was next to him. We three boys were doing something to each other that I don't, now, recall.

"There wasn't a thing in my life that wasn't shown me. It was as if some super VCR were put on fast forward and I could recognize everything that I saw. The scenes were three-dimensional, and they were in color. What is more important, I understood everything that was happening as I watched my life unfold. Every emotion that was involved in each scene, I felt again. Not just my emotions, but the emotions of others involved in the scenes.

"Every sense that I had when I lived the event was sensed again by me, and I also sensed the feelings imposed on others by my actions. The last scene I remember seeing was the Volkswagen sitting on the ground after the crash.

"As the review was completed, He asked me something to the effect: 'How do you feel, now?' And, boy, I felt guilty. There were some good things in the review, of course, but the things that hit me the hardest were the ones that I was ashamed of, the ones where I had hurt people. . . ." Roger paused at this point as he sought to control his emotions.

"I remember, at that point, He told me not to dwell so much on the things that bothered me; rather, I should pay more attention to the events where I felt good about them. It seemed to me, though, that there were more of the bad ones than the good ones." Roger chuckled as he thought back.

"The Savior asked me some more questions, and then I was asked again if I wanted to stay or return to the earth. Obviously, since I am here, I said that I wanted to return. Instantly, upon making that decision, I was back in the Volkswagen."

Further Analysis of Roger's Experience

"While I was in the Savior's presence, I was told and shown many things besides my life's review. Enormous amounts of information flowed into my mind—information that I have since forgotten. When I first arrived in the room, for example, He asked me if I had any questions. I did, and the moment the question was formulated, the answer was in my mind. It was an amazing process.

"Pure knowledge seemed to pour into me from Him. The knowledge was transmitted by . . . energy. Energy flowed into me and with it was knowledge. It was as if my entire being was a receptor of knowledge. And it was knowledge that I seemed to have known before. Everything that was communicated to me made sense.

"Just before He asked me the last question, I was told firmly, but in a loving way, that much of what I had seen and heard I would not remember if I came back. He let me know that some of the things that would be taken from me I would again be allowed to remember, as they were needed to help me in some part of my future life.

"Shortly after my life's review ended, I noticed some other people in the room. They were known to me, but I don't remember now who they were. They were dressed in white, but their clothing was different from the Savior's. The men and women were dressed differently, also. Their garments were loose fitting, they all had long sleeves, and they were high at the neck. I remember four people in particular; others may have been there, but they are hazy in my memory.

"When the Savior asked me if I wanted to return, and I told Him yes, I also told Him that I wanted to try and do better. I wanted another chance."

Return to Life

"When I found myself back in the Volkswagen, I was trapped on the seats under the crushed roof. My only injury was caused by the right seat-back coming forward, knocking my glasses off, and putting a bruise on my right ear. People came rushing up to the car, and they asked me through what was left of the window if I could get out. I told them that I didn't think so.

"Two men pulled on one of the doors, and I braced myself and pushed against it with my feet. After about five minutes we got the door open. They escorted me across the road to another car, and my knees were shaking so badly that they had to half-carry me.

"For many years I never told anyone about my experience. My roommates in college were aware that I totalled my car, but I didn't tell them what happened during the accident. Nor did I tell my family until much later (in 1991)."

Other Strange Experiences

"On October 1, 1973, I went elk hunting with my twin brother and some other friends. At one o'clock in the morning, sleeping in this large tent with my brother, I was awakened by a voice. It called me by my first name three times.

"Looking around the tent to see where the voice was coming from, the tent began to fill with light, the same light I had seen during my accident. I pinched myself, hard, on the right arm to be sure I was awake. The pinch-marks were still there at 6:00 a.m.

"After calling me by my first name three times, the voice then spoke to me for thirty minutes, until 1:30 a.m. The precise words that were used, I don't remember now, but it was a repeated message.

"The voice was not the voice of Christ that I had heard during my previous experience, but it was from the same place. And its message was a message of warning. I had previously broken my engagement to a young lady I had been dating, and the voice was warning me not to reestablish the relationship with her no matter what the circumstances. The voice explained why I should not resume a relationship with her.

"After delivering this message for one-half hour, the light diminished and the voice ceased. It was a uniquely strange experience, apparently tailored to my needs. I did as the voice told me, and later I found out that it was good advice.

"The light that was in the tent was very bright, and the voice that spoke to me was loud. I later asked my brother if he had heard the voice or seen the light—they seemed so obvious that I was sure they would have wakened him—but he professed complete ignorance concerning them.

"Other, equally peculiar messages have been delivered to me over the years since my accident. They have all been very personal, and they have been oriented to my particular needs—or they have directed me to respond to some kind of life's mission that I sense from time to time. Mostly, they are too private, or too sacred, to be related here."

Carol asked Roger if there were any messages he would like to leave. He responded: "The most important message is one of love. And we should do things for the right reasons. My life's review taught me that many of the things I did were done for the wrong reasons, and they had a very negative effect on others. I learned that every little word we utter should be words that will build up, not tear down, those we interact with. Our words will later be recalled in vivid detail, and we will be accountable for them. Words are verbal expressions, or examples, that show the amount of love that we have and use as we communicate and interact with others."

Part II

The Meaning

Truth is knowledge of things as they are, and as they were, and as they are to come . . . .

Doctrine and Covenants 93:23.

Chapter 19

ARE THE STORIES TRUE?

Commonly Asked Questions

But Arvin, how do you know they were telling you the truth? Maybe they thought it was a real experience, but couldn't it have been some type of dream or hallucination? Couldn't their experience have been from the effects of the medication they were taking? Why in the world would anyone tell you a story like that—what was their motivation? Did you offer to pay them money for their stories? Do you really believe all of these stories? Aren't there a lot of nuts who call you with screwy stories—how do you separate them from the authentic experiences? Why do some people have near-death out-of-body experiences, and others with equally serious injuries or illnesses, do not? Why do individuals have such varied experiences—doesn't that prove that they are just figments of the mind? Do you think that these experiences prove that there is a life after death? Could reincarnation explain some of the experiences?

These are some of the questions I am repeatedly asked. Interestingly, they are most often asked by people who have not taken the trouble to read much, if anything, on the subject of near-death experiences. Those who have read extensively on the subject are equally curious, but their questions are centered more on what our research findings show. It is clear from these, and other questions, that the subject has created substantial interest with the public. Although a comprehensive review of all of these questions is beyond the scope of this book, I will attempt to respond to the most commonly asked ones.

225

Authenticity of the Experiences

Research by Others

The question of whether the experiences are truly out-of-body, and not some psychological or other phenomenon is of considerable interest to the research community as well as the public. Many studies have been done in an attempt to explain the NDE as some phenomenon other than a spiritual out-of-body experience. Dr. Kenneth Ring, a professor of psychology at the University of Connecticut, and one of the founders of the International Association for Near Death Studies (IANDS), has studied a number of possible explanations, including: depersonalization, wishful thinking, psychological expectations, dreams or hallucinations, anesthetics, other drugs, temporal lobe involvement, cerebral anoxia, and other physiological or neurological explanations. He concludes that none of these possibilities can satisfactorily account for all of the NDEs that he has researched.[1]

Dr. Melvin Morse, a physician involved in pediatrics in Seattle, and one who has done extensive research on NDEs for children, examined the following possible explanations that others had proposed: Lysergic Acid (LSD) induced hallucinations, morphine and heroin hallucinations, "recreational drug" hallucinations, anesthetic agents, ketamine, transient depersonalization, memories of birth (as suggested by Dr. Carl Sagan), autoscopic hallucinations, endorphin induced hallucinations, and hypoxia. He concludes from the research in his book that: "None of these mimics the powerful experiences revealed in this book."[2]

Dr. Raymond Moody, a psychiatrist whose classic book *Life After Life*[3] started much of the research in NDEs, said in his book *The Light Beyond:*

> For more than twenty years I have been working on the cutting edge of NDE research. In the course of my studies, I have listened to thousands of people tell about their deeply personal journeys into. . . what? The world beyond? The heaven they learned about from their religion? A region of the brain that reveals itself only in times of desperation?
>
> I have talked to almost every NDE researcher in the world about his or her work. I know that most of them believe in their hearts that NDEs are a glimpse of life after life. But as scientists and people of medicine, they still haven't come up with 'scientific proof' that a part

of us goes on living after our physical being is dead. This lack of proof keeps them from going public with their true feelings. . . .

I don't think science can ever answer the question. It can be pondered from almost every side, but the resulting answer will never be complete. . . .

In the absence of firm scientific proof, people frequently ask me what I believe: Do NDEs provide evidence of life after life? My answer is 'Yes.'[4]

No Scientific Proof for Life after Death

In the process of performing the research for the book *Glimpses of Eternity*, and for this book, Carol and I have interviewed approximately one-hundred people who have undergone NDEs or analogous spiritual experiences. In addition to that first-hand research work, I have read essentially all of the available literature on NDEs, and I am actively involved in a local chapter of IANDS.

As to the question, Can science provide proof of life after death?, I share Dr. Moody's skepticism. As I explained in *Glimpses of Eternity:*

Most near-death researchers argue that the NDE does not prove the existence of life-after-death. I agree with that position. If it were possible to prove life-after-death through the near-death experience then the Plan of Salvation would be compromised.

When we were born, we lost our memory of a previous life, and we lost our knowledge of a life to come. This forgetfulness was for a purpose—so that our free will might be more complete—to choose between right and wrong. It is a necessary part of our development that we move through this life with faith, faith in the ultimate goodness of our Father in Heaven, faith in the Lord Jesus Christ, faith that there is a life after death, faith that it does matter how we live.[5]

Patterns of Evidence Discerned

Despite the inability through scientific methods to *prove* the existence of a life after this life, the NDE does offer substantial evidence that there *could* be something beyond this life. The evidence comes in several forms.

One of the most fascinating forms of evidence is that provided by the witnesses themselves. Most of those who have had an NDE, when they tell of their experience (especially if they have not told it frequently before), are extremely moved by the experience. There is an awe about them that is obvious to anyone observing them. In many instances they tend to relive the experience, their emotions overcome them, and they are unable to continue with their discussion for a time. This is true whether or not the experience was negative or positive, whether or not they are male or female, and independent of their cultural and educational background. The only exceptions that Carol and I observed seemed to be small children. They simply told their experiences in a matter of fact manner, as if to say: *Of course I saw Jesus—doesn't everybody?*

Another form of evidence involves patterns of behavior by those being interviewed. Although the stories, by their very nature, are anecdotal and therefore not subject to the rigor of repeatability that characterizes most scientific research, there are certain aspects that are repeatable. In *Glimpses of Eternity*, for example, I pointed out how certain words were used by the respondents repeatedly, almost as if the respondents were programmed to use them.[6] Words such as *peace, warmth, love,* and *light* were used with such frequency—and with a scriptural context or meaning— that they clearly represented a significantly high pattern of usage. And that pattern of usage was extended into the research for this book.

A subtle form of evidence derives from the method I used to create the final written version of the experiences. After each experience was taped and transcribed into a computerized printed version, I forwarded that version to the respondents for their corrections. Invariably, they would return the copy with what to me were trivial corrections that had nothing to do with the substance of their stories. Yet, the respondents were adamant that the changes needed to be made in order for the stories to be correct. Typical of these changes was a recent one by a lady who said: "When I told you the story, I got the order of two events wrong. That wasn't the way it was. The first thing that happened was . . ." These kinds of small corrections, and the insistence of the respondents that I make the changes, gave further evidence that they, at least, had a sense of the reality and order of the events.

Other Significant Forms of Evidence

Many of the experiences, because of the circumstances involved, offered opportunities for partial corroboration. Julie's story in Chapter 4 of this book, for example, had many witnesses to the fact that she told the details of having seen Allen return from being killed in Vietnam, *before* the event was reported by the military. I interviewed two of those witnesses, and they confirmed what Julie said.

The two little children I interviewed (reported in Chapter 8) told their stories with complete candor and innocence. And their mothers related—with awe and reverence—their memories of the same events. I was fascinated to listen to Berta explain how her son—five-year-old Rocky, as he began to recover—described his experience on the other side by quoting scriptures from the King James version of the Bible, scriptures that he had not previously been taught.

When Bill told of his two-stage experience (Chapter 6), he explained how one of his cousins gave him a special blessing, while Bill was comatose, which Bill witnessed from out of his body. The physical details of what he saw were later confirmed by his cousin, and I obtained a written account of the record from the cousin as it was recorded shortly after the event.

In the books *In Search of Angels*, and *Glimpses of Eternity*, I described an NDE and subsequent miraculous healing by DeAnne Anderson Shelley.[7,8] Some years after DeAnne's experience I met the physician who attended her, Doctor Parkinson, and heard him explain that there was no medical explanation for why DeAnne was alive, nor for the healing that subsequently happened to her. The only explanation he could offer was her own account of the experience.

Three of the individuals I interviewed for this book suffered grievous gunshot wounds. In each case they showed me the scars from the wounds. It was obvious from these scars, and from the scars of the subsequent operations, that they had suffered immense damage to their persons. Although such evidence does not confirm the NDE, it does confirm that something significant happened to the individuals.

Several individuals told of visiting, during their out-of-body events, locations where they were later able to confirm physical evidences that could not have been seen from the location of their physical selves. Renee Zamora (Chapter 17), for example, later verified the presence of the frail old man in a hospital bed whom she saw while out of her body in an adjacent room; a location that could not have been seen from where she was being treated. There were several such instances in both books. Some individuals were able to later discuss with medical personnel the details of their treatment—details they should not have been able to see while they were under anesthetic.

A fascinating experience was reported by Professor Kimberly Clark of the University of Washington, Seattle, concerning a patient called Maria who suffered a cardiac arrest. Maria described an out-of-body experience that was typical of many undergoing an NDE. She saw the medical personnel working on her, and as is often the case, she floated out of the hospital. While in this spirit body state, she happened to observe an object on the third floor ledge on the north wall of the hospital. The object was a tennis shoe. During her recovery she described her NDE and told Professor Clark what she had seen. She asked Professor Clark to search for the tennis shoe—she wanted to satisfy herself that she had really seen it.

Professor Clark said of the event:

> With mixed emotions I went outside and looked up at the ledges but could not see much at all. I went up to the third floor and began going in and out of patients' rooms and looking out their windows, which were so narrow that I had to press my face to the screen just to see the ledge at all. Finally, I found a room where I pressed my face to the glass and saw the tennis shoe! My vantage point was very different from what Maria's had to have been for her to notice that the little toe had worn a place in the shoe and that the lace was stuck under the heel and other details about the side of the shoe not visible to me. The only way she would have had such a perspective was if she had been floating right outside and at very close range to the tennis shoe. I retrieved the shoe and brought it back to Maria; it was very concrete evidence for me.[9]

The Varied Nature of the Experiences

Which People Have NDEs?

A frequently asked question is why do some people have NDEs and others do not. There is no really good answer to that question, but there have been studies that examine which people, and what percentage of the population, are likely to have NDEs.

Kenneth Ring summarized the pertinent research with these words:

> Taking into account all the relevant research so far published then, and allowing for the possibility that Gallup's own figure may reflect a minimum value for the population, I would propose that somewhere between 35 and 40 percent of those who come close to death would report NDEs.[10]

In summarizing the research about whether one group of people is more likely to have an NDE than another, at least in western societies, Dr. Ring said the following:

> Demographic characteristics such as age, sex, race, social class, educational level, occupation, and the like seem to have no particular relationship to NDE incidence. . . . I found no relationship for such demographic variables as social class, race, marital status, or religious affiliation.
>
> . . . There is, in fact, no difference in either the type or incidence of NDEs as a function of one's religious orientation—or lack of it. To be sure, an agnostic or an atheist might—and actually appear to—have a more difficult time coming to terms with the experience and may be less likely to interpret it in conventional terms than a believer, but the form and content of the NDE will not be distinctive.[11]

Why Such Varied Experiences?

A recent article in the *Journal of Near-Death Studies* (an IANDS publication), by Professor John Wren-Lewis of the University of Sydney, argued that the varied nature of the NDE was proof that the experiences were not real. Professor Wren-Lewis said:

> But even among those NDE reports that do involve visions, the great majority could not be literal glimpses of the undiscovered country beyond the grave for the simple reason that they contradict each other in significant ways. Some, for example, depict the heavenly landscape as a pastoral scene, others as an insubstantial cloudy space, others as a science-fiction-style Celestial City, and still others as human scenes almost justifying the Monty Python spoof. The long-dead relatives encountered in certain much-publicized experiences sometimes appear the age they were when they themselves died, sometimes as the age they would have been had they lived on, sometimes miraculously rejuvenated, and sometimes totally transfigured into shining angelic forms that are somehow recognizable.[12]

In the book *Glimpses of Eternity* I wrote broadly on this subject, quoting my own findings and those of Howard Storm, an individual who had an extensive experience. My perspective was just the opposite from that of Professor Wren-Lewis. To quote from a portion of that work:

Why, then, does one person who has an out-of-body experience view a world with a beautiful garden, another views a city with beautiful buildings, another sees her mother in a prefabricated building with nasturtiums, and still another sees a gigantic geometric shape in the sky?

Why does one person see little children playing, another sees children who died presented in form as adults, another sees relatives in their earthly clothes, and still another sees them in white robes? Why does one person see the light, or have a life's review, and another not?

These different experiences stem from the Lord's knowledge of us, and his understanding of our needs. John Stirling commented after his experience that we see through a glass darkly in this life, but in the next we are known by Jesus Christ, and we know him. John said it was a comfortable feeling, one which he was familiar with. He was amazed at the review of his life, and at the complete knowledge of him shown in the review—in the presence of himself and his God.

Thus we are known by Jesus Christ far better than we know ourselves. When individuals leave this earth, even temporarily from some sort of trauma, the Lord understands them. He is able to tailor a view of the spirit world according to their particular needs. What to one person might be complete nonsense, to another is a tremendous spiritual experience.

And these experiences, in my view, are real. It is a real world that those having NDEs are visiting, albeit a spiritual one. Many whom we interviewed said that the other world was more real to them than this one.

We understand from latter-day scriptures that the Lord created this world and everything in it spiritually before he created it physically. It is, surely, a small matter for him to create—or allow us to view—a portion of a spiritual world tailored to the needs of each of us. Those privileged to view this world see that which will give them the greatest growth. Many feel of the great love and compassion of the Savior. They also get a glimpse of his power and glory.[13]

Motivation of Those Telling Their Stories

People responded to our advertisements and came to see us for several reasons, but none of the reasons had anything to do with money. Of the hundred or so people we interviewed, only three or four asked if there were a fee involved. When I explained to those few that such a fee would make the story itself suspect, they understood and dropped the subject.

The reasons that most people came were: to talk to someone who was sympathetic to what they had to say; to find out about others who had had similar experiences; and to help others by sharing what the respondent knew about death. Many of them, after the interview was completed, questioned Carol and me for an hour or more about others we had interviewed. They were thrilled that we accepted their stories for what they were—a profound spiritual experience—and they were extremely curious about others. Equally important to those we interviewed was the possibility of having their stories published in a manner that would help others. In many instances they felt an obligation to bear witness to what they had seen and heard.

With regard to whether or not some people might fabricate stories for a variety of reasons, that possibility exists, of course. In a research study of the size that Carol and I performed, there were a few individuals who professed to have had experiences that were quite possibly untrue. One man attempted to explain the details of his encounter with a UFO. The number of such instances, however, was remarkably small, perhaps three percent of the total. Those few individuals were identified within the first few minutes of the conversation, usually while the contact was still in the telephone stage. Upon being identified, I thanked them for their trouble and excused them from further discussion.

Although there is no absolute assurance that a fabricated story could not have found its way into this book, I believe that all included accounts are true and valid for the reasons discussed in the previous material. The evidences were overwhelmingly in favor of those telling their experiences, even those stories that fell somewhat out of the norm. In addition to the types of evidence already discussed, Carol and I also relied on the witness of the Spirit. Where the Holy Spirit bore witness that the story was real and true, then we accepted that as a final confirmation that it should be included in the book.

What About Reincarnation?

Surprisingly, questions about reincarnation continue to come up. In *Glimpses of Eternity* I explained some of the pitfalls for this point of view, and why certain groups continued to be enamored with it.[14] Since completing *Glimpses* I have discussed the issue with two clinical psychologists, both of whom have used hypnotherapy in their work.

Doctor Lynn Johnson discussed three cases that he was personally familiar with, where the patients who were subjected to hypnosis were regressed into presumably previous lives. He was able to show that the one patient claiming to speak in Spanish and German, from her previous lives, was in fact "producing random combinations of consonants mixed with the vowels O and E." His conclusion, based on his own and other research work, was: "It would appear that the specific cases which 'prove' reincarnation can be explained as confabulation [made-up stories], especially when a desire to believe that is combined with hypnosis which allows for vivid fantasies to be experienced as reality."[15]

Marian Bergin is a clinical psychologist who has engaged in hypnotherapy in her own practice. She is convinced that work which reveals previous lives in hypnotized subjects is false. She has given me a number of papers, of the type discussed below, in which researchers show the extreme culpability of the patients to suggestions by the hypnotherapists. Hypnotherapy may be used, with care, for treatment of specific psychic disorders, but not for accurately reclaiming historic information.

Marian sent me the paper: *Secondary Identity Enactments During Hypnotic Past Life Regression: A Sociocognitive Perspective.* Despite its ponderous title, it is an excellent work. It relates to the reincarnation hypothesis that is so popular among New Age adherents and some near-death researchers.

Researchers for this study, led by Nicholas Spanos of Carleton University in Ottawa, Canada, conducted a series of controlled experiments on 175 subjects at the university. The subjects were selected for their hypnotizability and separated into three control groups. The groups differed in the specificity of suggestions made before and during hypnosis by the hypnotist. Individuals in all groups were led by the hypnotist back in time to presumably earlier lives.

Results of the study showed that subjects in all three groups were significantly affected by what they thought was wanted of them by the hypnotist. The more information that was transmitted to them by the hypnotist, the more detailed their past life regressions became. The researchers also showed that the subjects confabulated, or made-up, their previous lives' histories from books they had read, plays they had seen, newspapers they had read, or travels they had taken. Where information was lacking about a topic the researcher was asking about the subjects' imagined fictitious stories and represented them as real. Some of the subjects were, in fact, convinced that their stories were real.

The researchers deliberately led the subjects into increasing detail about the geopolitical history from their so-called previous lives. These histories were checked later and found, universally, to be faulty.[16]

Perhaps the best argument against reincarnation, however, is that it is contrary to the scriptures. Paul, in the New Testament, said: "It is appointed unto men once to die . . . ."[17] Reincarnation doctrine is, of course, that we die many times; each time that we are reincarnated. In the Book of Mormon, Amulek, in speaking of the resurrection said "that they can die no more; their spirits uniting with their bodies, never to be divided; thus the whole becoming spiritual and immortal, that they can no more see corruption."[18] Many other scriptures attest to the fallacy of the doctrine of reincarnation.

What Do Carol and Arvin Gibson Believe About NDEs?

Carol said of her part in interviewing the people: "I saw tears running down the face of a man, as he relived the experience of a life's review, who told me his family thought he was not an emotional man. Another lady we interviewed was angry about returning to life. She knew that no one could love her like the love she felt in Christ's presence—and she wanted that love again. Yes, I believe the people were telling the truth, and they were describing real experiences from beyond the veil of this earthly life."

Do I believe that they were telling us the truth about real experiences, and do I believe that these experiences are evidence of life after death? The answer is unequivocally, *yes*. I further believe that the lessons learned from these experiences can aid us in this life, just as the scriptures and teachings of the Prophets can aid us. These stories provide windows, in today's language, of a spiritual realm where a loving God reigns supreme.

Chapter 20

FREEDOM OF CHOICE

The Plan of Salvation

When Elane Durham asked her guide in the other world why wars occur, he told her that wars were not in God's *plan*, but because she *chose* to go there (he pointed off in space and she saw the earth), she had subjected herself to an environment where wars could occur.

DeLynn, who was plagued by cystic fibrosis and wondered why, said this about his NDE:

That was the end of the scene, and it changed forever my perspective of the disease that I previously felt was a plague on my life. No longer did I consider myself a victim. Rather, I was a privileged participant, by *choice*, in an eternal *plan*. That *plan*, if I measured up to the potential of my *choice*, would allow me to advance in mortal life in the fastest way possible.

Dallas, who shot himself in the heart, said that the Lord told him he had done a foolish thing by attempting suicide. He had made the wrong *choice*. By committing suicide, Dallas would not be able to accomplish what the Lord had in mind for him to do.

These, and other analogous experiences, reveal that the Lord has a plan for us, and our ultimate destiny is determined by the choices we make. To understand how this works it is useful to know about the Plan of Salvation.

In *Glimpses of Eternity* I pointed out that fundamental to The Church of Jesus Christ of Latter-day Saints is the belief that Jesus Christ and his Father developed a Plan of Salvation for all humans. I noted that in order to understand the Plan it is important to know that, in LDS doctrine, people have existed in one form or another forever, and they will continue to exist throughout eternity. They started as individual intelligences and at some point were born as spirit children of our Father in Heaven. They continued in that form until they were born into this life, on earth, as mortal beings with both a physical body and a spirit.[1]

The basic elements of the Plan of Salvation, as detailed in LDS scriptures, are as follows:

1. An earth would be created upon which we could have a variety of experiences.[2] This earth would be filled with life, including humans, beginning with Adam and Eve. Adam, after being tempted by Satan, would fall from a sinless, childless, paradisiacal state in order that other humans might be born and die.[3]

2. We would take upon ourselves physical bodies by being born, and we would live a physical life on this earth. These bodies would be after the image of Jesus Christ and our Heavenly Father.[4] We would have children and be responsible for their physical and spiritual welfare.[5]

3. All memory of our previous existence would be removed from us while we were mortal and on this earth. This forgetfulness, or lack of complete knowledge of a previous life, would enhance our ability to make free choices.[6]

4. We would be allowed to choose the kind of life we lived within the constraints of physical mortality.[7] Freedom of choice would be guaranteed by providing for opposition in all things. That opposition would include suffering from illnesses, accidents and other events, some of our making and some not.[8] Our relationship with others, how we reacted to and how we treated our fellow humans would be tested.[9]

5. We would be given information about good and evil, through prophets speaking for Jesus Christ, by both the written word and by oral instruction.[10] Satan would be allowed to tempt us to do evil.[11] We would benefit by gaining knowledge while in this world.[12]

6. A Savior, Jesus Christ, would be provided who would atone for our sins, and who would make it possible for the resurrection of all individuals.[13] All would ultimately live again as resurrected beings, with their body and their spirit reunited—a gift from Jesus Christ.[14]

7. Means would be provided for saving ordinances to be performed on this earth for *all* persons, living or dead.[15]

8. At the end of mortal life we would die: our spirit and our body would separate, with the spirit continuing to live and the body being

temporarily discarded into the tomb. The spirit would pass to another sphere, the spirit world, and would reside there until the time of the resurrection. In this spiritual sphere, those who had not been taught the gospel during earth life would be given the opportunity to hear it.[16]

9. At some future time there would be a general resurrection, and we would again obtain a body which would never be lost nor destroyed.[17]

10. There would be a final judgment; and, depending upon how we lived and whether we repented of our sins or not, we would live eternally with our Father in Heaven and his son Jesus Christ.[18] In this state we would live with our families and would have immense knowledge. We would participate with our Father in Heaven in the creation of new worlds. We would experience eternal growth and happiness.[19]

11. Even those who do not live a very good life would find the new life rewarding and one which provides for growth. It would be much superior to the previous life on earth.[20]

These, then, are the main elements of the Plan of Salvation. All listed elements are not necessary for discussion in this chapter; some of them will be referred to in later chapters.

Some Aspects of Choice

A key element of the Plan of Salvation is the element of choice. The plan was structured so that, above all else, our freedom of choice would be protected, and thus our potential for growth would be maximized.

Forgetfulness of Our Previous Life

It is a fascinating experience to listen to people who have undergone an NDE describe some aspect of the Plan of Salvation, such as the freedom of choice, without realizing what they were doing. As I heard repeated explanations of their forgetfulness concerning certain portions of their NDEs, but not others, I couldn't help but reflect on that aspect of the Plan. Tracie, a fourteen-year-old girl whose experience is described in *Glimpses*, couldn't remember a portion of her NDE. My comment, as she told her story, was that it was too bad she couldn't remember. She responded: "It's sort of like I'm not supposed to remember it. I just get the feeling that I'm not supposed to recall what went on there. It was sort of withheld from my memory."

Roger Smith, who reported conversing with the Savior, said this of his experience: "Just before He asked me the last question, I was told firmly, but in a loving way, that much of what I had seen and heard I would not remember if I came back. He let me know that some of the things that would be taken from me I would again be allowed to remember, as they were needed to help me in some part of my future life."

Results of Improper Choices

The Plan protects our freedom of choice by allowing us to make improper choices. Guidance over the ages is given by Prophets, and from the scriptures, to help us make correct choices, but the ultimate freedom to choose is ours. Recognition of the inappropriate nature of some of our choices may be slow in coming, but come it will. Many who have had an NDE have been priviledged to have those improper choices displayed in dramatic ways.

The Choices of Elizabeth Marie

One of the most interesting cases was that of Elizabeth Marie. As a teenager, she went out of her body from smoking marijuana and opium. She found herself in a room full of people dressed in white, and she was embarrassed. The cause of her embarrassment was her white robe, which had black spots on its side—spots that represented things that she had done wrong. The people in the room were amused because Elizabeth tried to hide the spots, but she couldn't.

Later, Elizabeth met, and was loved by, the Savior. She said of that experience:

He put his arms around me and asked me if I had known that what I did was wrong. I told Him that yes, I had known it was wrong.

The amount of remorse I had, I'd never felt before. It was remorse over what I had done. I felt so sorry; there was a deep disappointment over my previous activities. The feelings of remorse and disappointment were pure feelings that permeated my body.

I was asked if I had known what was right and wrong—and I had. My knowledge, in the presence of Him, was that I couldn't progress from the place I had positioned myself. Knowing that I was stopped in my progression, and feeling great remorse, I asked if I could return and help others to come back to Him. There was an intense desire within me to amend for the pain and suffering that I had caused others.

The love I felt from Him during this period was extremely intense. Love traveled from my toes to my head, filling my entire body. There are no words that can adequately describe that love. It was a fatherly type of love, and I knew that He was pleased when I acknowledged my sins and asked if I could amend for them.

Life Reviews of John Stirling and Roger Smith

John Stirling, whose experience is given in *Glimpses*, and Roger Smith in this book had very similar experiences. Both John and Roger, when asked if they were through with life on earth, said that they were. Then, both were shown a detailed review of their life, and both described it in similar terms. John said it was the ultimate movie, in three-dimensions, in color, and with feeling.

Roger said of his experience:

Suddenly in front of me appeared . . . I don't know how to describe it. Something appeared that resembled a movie screen, yet it was sort of like a play—and I was the main actor. While I watched, astounded, I saw everything that ever happened to me from the second I was born until the accident—all twenty-four years. . . .

There wasn't a thing in my life that wasn't shown me. It was as if some super VCR were put on fast forward and I could recognize everything that I saw. The scenes were three-dimensional, and they were in color. What is more important, I understood everything that was happening as I watched my life unfold. *Every emotion that was involved in each scene, I felt again. Not just my emotions, but the emotions of others involved in the scenes.*

Every sense that I had when I lived the event was sensed again by me, and I also sensed the feelings imposed on others by my actions. The last scene I remember seeing was the Volkswagen sitting on the ground after the crash.

As the review was completed, He asked me something to the effect: 'How do you feel, now?' And, boy, I felt guilty. There were some good things in the review, of course, but the things that hit me the hardest were the ones that I was ashamed of, the ones where I had hurt people. . . .

Both John and Roger changed their minds and decided to return to earth after having seen their lifes' reviews. They both felt that there was more they had to accomplish, and in Roger's case he wanted a chance to make some different choices.

Premortal Choice

LDS Teachings

As noted above, basic LDS doctrine is that we have existed as individual beings for eternity. We know from the scriptures that agency existed in the premortal world, else there would have been no war in Heaven.[21] We know, also, from latter-day scriptures that Abraham was selected before he was born for his particular mission.[22]

Elder James E. Talmage, in his masterful book *Jesus the Christ*, comments on the important principle of premortal choice. A couple of quotations are given below:

> We have heretofore shown that the entire human race existed as spirit-beings in the primeval world, and that for the purpose of making possible to them the experiences of mortality this earth was created. They were endowed with the powers of agency or choice while yet but spirits; and the divine plan provided that they be free-born in the flesh, heirs to the inalienable birthright of liberty to choose and to act for themselves in mortality.[23]

> At Jerusalem Jesus mercifully gave sight to a man who had been blind from his birth. The miracle is an instance of Sabbath-day healing, of more than ordinary interest because of its attendant incidents. It is recorded by John alone, and, as usual with that writer, his narrative is given with descriptive detail. Jesus and His disciples saw the sightless one upon the street. The poor man lived by begging. The disciples, eager to learn, asked: 'Master, who did sin, this man, or his parents, that he was born blind?' The Lord's reply was: 'Neither hath this man sinned, nor his parents: but that the works of God should be made manifest in him.' The disciples' question implied their belief in a state of moral agency and choice antedating mortality; else, how could they have thought of the man having sinned so as to bring upon himself congenital blindness? We are expressly told that he was born blind. That he might have been a sufferer from the sins

of his parents was conceivable. The disciples evidently had been taught the great truth of an antemortal existence. It is further to be seen that they looked upon bodily affliction as the result of personal sin. Their generalization was too broad; for, while as shown by instances heretofore cited, individual wickedness may and does bring physical ills in its train, man is liable to err in his judgment as to the ultimate cause of affliction. The Lord's reply was sufficing; the man's blindness would be turned to account in bringing about a manifestation of divine power. As Jesus explained respecting His own ministry, it was necessary that He do the Father's work in the season appointed, for His time was short. With impressive pertinency as relating to the state of the man who had been in darkness all his days, our Lord repeated the affirmation before made in the temple, 'I am the light of the world.' [24]

These two references concerning premortal choice are particularly interesting. They further illustrate the doctrinal basis for this important concept.

DeLynn's Premortal Choice of Cystic Fibrosis

One of the surprising results of the research for this book was the number of people who, in their NDEs, spoke of premortal choices they had made. DeLynn, the individual who had cystic fibrosis and felt that he had been victimized by his disease, asked during his NDE why it was necessary for him to suffer so. The startling answer was: "You chose your disease and the amount of pain you would be willing to suffer before this life—when you were in a premortal state. *It was your choice.*"

To DeLynn's amazement, he was next transported to a premortal time and place, and he was able to see himself making choices for his future life on earth. Viewing a room with people in it, including himself, he saw an instructor teaching the people about accountability and responsibility—and about pain. The instructor told the spirit people in the room how they could learn the lessons of life through different choices, and DeLynn saw himself choose to suffer cystic fibrosis—in order to learn his lessons the quickest way possible.

Elane Durham's Premortal Choices

In her extensive NDE, Elane also saw herself in a premortal setting. She said, of that portion of her experience:

While he was teaching me about the importance of children he asked me if I would like to see myself before I was born—before I came to earth. I told him I would, and it was as if I were looking in a bathroom mirror that was fogged over. I could see myself, but I couldn't distinguish how my hair was done or my facial characteristics. Seated in what seemed to be a waiting area, I observed that there were five beings around me. Two of them were in a teaching capacity and were strong spiritual beings, and three of them were lesser spiritual beings. They were guardian angels, or whatever, and the three lesser ones were there to learn—sort of angels in training.

In this premortal environment I saw that I was making all the decisions for my life, the things that I chose to go through. These were things that I wanted to accomplish in order to learn various lessons. There were different choices available to me. I knew, for example, that I was going to be the oldest of the children in my family. There was a choice between three fathers and two mothers; I would have learned equal lessons from all of them. I knew that I would have a physical crisis and would be miraculously healed; and I would have a second health crisis which I would survive.

My life on earth could be prolonged, I understood, by living so as to be in a helping capacity—helping others. That might not sound like such a good deal here and now, but over there it was just understood that helping others is a primary purpose.

As I was making these different choices concerning my life one of the lesser spiritual beings remarked that the consequence of some of these choices would be that I would have a difficult life. He wondered if I were sure that was what I wanted to go through. One of the more advanced beings responded that I could advance faster by making such choices.

Julie's Experience
Julie's vision of herself in a premortal environment was similar to that of both DeLynn and Elane. She saw men who were authority figures whom she understood would give approval as to when she was to come to earth. She remembers thinking, in that premortal waiting room:
It is going to be so strange to go to earth and forget home. I can't comprehend that. I understand exactly what I'm getting into and what

I have to do. But I cannot comprehend forgetting home. Please let me remember this experience and this room.

Betty Eadie's Premortal Choices

In her book *Embraced by the Light*, Betty Eadie explains how, during her NDE, she was taught about premortal choices.[25] What she learned was remarkably similar to what DeLynn and Elane learned under similar circumstances.

> I saw that in the premortal world we knew about and even chose our missions in life. I understood that our stations in life are based upon the objectives of those missions. Through divine knowledge we knew what many of our tests and experiences would be, and we prepared accordingly. We bonded with others—family members and friends—to help us complete our missions. We needed their help. We came as volunteers, each eager to learn and experience all that God had created for us. . . .
>
> To my surprise I saw that most of us had selected illnesses we would suffer, and for some, the illness that would end our lives.

Some Teachings and Some Speculations—Summary

Teachings

The Church of Jesus Christ of Latter-day Saints is unique among religions in teaching that we lived forever in a premortal environment, with God, and that we were able to exercise choice in that environment. Elder Bruce R. McConkie, in his book *Mormon Doctrine* said about these two subjects:

> Pre-existence is the term commonly used to describe the pre-mortal existence of the spirit children of God the Father. Speaking of this prior existence in a spirit sphere, the First Presidency of the Church (Joseph F. Smith, John R. Winder, and Anthon H. Lund) said: 'All men and women are in the similitude of the universal Father and Mother and are literally the sons and daughters of Deity'; as spirits they were the 'offspring of celestial parentage.' (*Man: His Origin and Destiny*, pp. 351, 355.) These spirit beings, the offspring of exalted parents, were men and women, appearing in all respects as mortal persons do, excepting only that their spirit bodies were made of a

more pure and refined substance than the elements from which mortal bodies are made. (Ether 3:16; D. & C. 131:7-8.)[26]

Agency is the ability and freedom to choose good or evil. It is an eternal principle which has existed with God from all eternity. The spirit offspring of the Father had agency in pre-existence and were thereby empowered to follow Christ or Lucifer according to their choice. (Moses 4:3; D. & C. 29:36-37.) It is by virtue of the exercise of agency in this life that men are enabled to undergo the testing which is an essential part of mortality. (Moses 3:17; 4:3; 7:32; Abra. 3:25-28.)[27]

These beliefs of a premortal life extending back into infinity, and of agency to choose good or evil, have always been a part of the doctrine of The Church of Jesus Christ of Latter-day Saints. They are fundamental portions of the Plan of Salvation. Without agency, and its twin brother, opposition, growth in this life and beyond would be impossible. As Lehi, an ancient American prophet said to his son, Jacob, about opposition:

> For it must needs be, that there is an opposition in all things. If not so, my first-born in the wilderness, righteousness could not be brought to pass, neither wickedness, neither holiness nor misery, neither good nor bad. Wherefore, all things must needs be a compound in one; wherefore, if it should be one body it must needs remain as dead, having no life neither death, nor corruption or incorruption, happiness nor misery, neither sense nor insensibility.[28]

NDE Evidence, and Speculations

Although premortal existence, agency, and opposition have long been recognized as unique LDS doctrines, the linking evidence from NDEs concerning premortal choice has been missing until recently. The experiences of DeLynn, Elane Durham, Betty Eadie, and Julie are, therefore, most welcome. They suggest a freedom of choice that extends more broadly into the premortal sphere than had previously been supposed.

Many other NDE accounts have hinted at the idea of premortal choice by reason of the ubiquitous statement: "Your time is not up—your mission has not yet been accomplished." I heard that comment so often from those who have had an NDE that I came to expect it. The implication behind the statement, of course, is that an earthly mission was assigned to the individual before this life. What the recent evidence suggests is that the mission was largely self-selected. According to this idea, many individuals (perhaps all) in the premortal sphere chose many of the details of their future life, including their parents, difficulties they would encounter, illnesses, and specific life's tasks. The LDS scriptural reference to Abraham being chosen before he was born,[22] therefore, would be extended broadly to many others. Joseph Smith, the latter-day prophet of the LDS Church, said: "Every man who has a calling to minister to the inhabitants of the world was ordained to that very purpose in the Grand Council of heaven before this world was."[29]

Both Betty Eadie, and DeLynn, said something that is a natural extension of the idea of broad premortal choices. Betty said: "There are far fewer accidents here than we imagine, especially in things that affect us eternally. The hand of God, and the path we chose before we came here, guide many of our decisions and even many of the seemingly random experiences we have. It's fruitless to try to identify them all, but they do happen, and for a purpose."[30]

DeLynn, as I conducted his interview, put it more strongly. He said: "There are no accidents!" My response was: "Come on DeLynn, you don't mean that there are *no* accidents, do you? Do you also, then, believe in predestination?" He rebutted with: "Even though God knows, in His omniscience, my eventual destiny, it in no way precludes my right to make choices of my own free will. The path I choose, replete with obstacles, blessings, and consequences, is *my* responsibility and accountability. Consequently, I do not enjoy the luxury of blaming my outcome on God, which the theory of predestination would have me foolishly believe."

My previously held belief, before conducting the research for these two books, was that life was largely a crap-shoot. In accepting the tenants of the Plan of Salvation, I assumed that the Lord set up a system by which chance events would test us in a free environment, and our response to those chance events would be a measure of our growth. The LDS doctrine of foreordination answered my questions of accidental happenings. Elder McConkie's statement in *Mormon Doctrine* helped: "In all this there is not the slightest hint of compulsion; persons foreordained to fill special missions in mortality are as abundantly endowed with free agency as are any other persons. By their foreordination the Lord merely gives them the opportunity to serve him and his purposes if they will choose to measure up to the standard he knows they are capable of attaining."[31]

Truth, Uncertainty and Faith

My suspicion, now, is that Betty Eadie's statement, "there are far fewer accidents here than we imagine," is close to the truth. Admittedly, this suspicion, and much of the foregoing, is pure speculation on my part. The only real foundation for truth is to be found in the scriptures, in prayer and in the witness of the Holy Ghost. Until we enter again those dominions where Jesus and our Heavenly Father dwell, and know, even as we are known, we must struggle in uncertainty, having faith in a loving God. My faith is that if we live the commandments of God—according to the potential that is in us as spirit children of God—we will obtain a reward beyond our dreams. That reward will be consistent with the final accounting of our achievements measured against those choices which we may have made in a premortal environment concerning our own life's plan.

Chapter 21

NEGATIVE EXPERIENCES

The Nature of Negative Experiences

Most NDEs reported in the literature are positive in nature. Individuals who have had them report feelings of peace, bliss, joy, love and euphoria. Many are reluctant to return to this life because of the wonderful feelings they had in the other world.

That is not universally true, however. Increasingly, researchers are reporting different types of negative, or hell-like experiences.[1,2] My own research has divulged a number of negative experiences. The first encounter I had with this type of experience was when Carol and I interviewed Dee for the book *Glimpses of Eternity*. Dee had two out-of-body experiences: the first one was pleasant, the second experience was horrifying. Both were apparently triggered by an emotional trauma.

Dee's Encounter With an Evil Spirit
In Dee's second experience she reported leaving her body and traveling around the countryside while attached to her physical body by a silver thread. Dee's description of what happened during her journey is as follows:

> The next thing I knew was . . . there was something behind me, and I was afraid. I felt this awful presence—and I knew that it was after me. I looked back and I saw that my string, which I was hooked to, was getting tight. I was afraid, and I was thinking: *What is this thing behind me?* I started to circle, because I knew I had to get back to the house.

248

The thing was coming after me fast, and I had the feeling it could kill me. I was moving through the tops of the trees, and I was thinking that I couldn't break my string, and I had to get back quick.

This . . . this thing, this awful, this terrifying thing—I could feel it on me. It was pushing me away from the house, and I could see the string getting tighter. I was sure I was going to die. I was frantic for Sara, frantic over the idea that if I died she would be stuck with my husband. I felt I had to get back, but the thing kept trying to push me away from the house.

Every time I would circle and try to get back to the house the thing would come up behind and push me. I knew I was going to die. I could feel the tug at my string. I was being chased by something that was the personification of evil. And it wanted me. It wanted to destroy me. I was terrified and I was crying, and I remember thinking: *Oh God, help me, help me God.* I got all my strength to go as fast as I could—I could actually feel this thing on the back of my neck.[3]

As Dee described what had happened to her she was visibly distressed. With shaking hands and fearful features, she tried to explain how terrifying it was. She later read our typed version of what she had recorded on tape, and she insisted that we make several changes to the account to try and capture the awful nature of what had happened to her. We made the changes she suggested, but she was never satisfied that we had completely depicted the horror of the experience.

Since the encounter with Dee, I have interviewed a number of people who have had negative experiences. Most of these have not been exclusively negative. They may start out in a negative manner, and then finish with a very positive experience—sufficiently positive that the individual thinks of their NDE as positive. Others may have a strongly negative aspect, but they may be considered positive by the individuals experiencing them because of the instructive nature of the experience.

Kathleen Martinez's Feelings of Negativity

One individual we interviewed, Kathleen Pratt Martinez, had an experience that I initially considered positive—because she saw many of her deceased relatives. During her NDE, Kathy witnessed a trial conducted by her relatives to decide whether she would be allowed to return to life.[4] In a meeting of a local IANDS chapter in which Kathy was asked how she felt about her experience, she said: "I was terrified. I didn't understand what was going on, except that I knew I might not be allowed to return to life. There was nothing pleasant about my experience. It took me years to come to terms with it." She went on to observe that she knew that a condition for her return to this life would be that she change the way she was living to bring her life more in conformance with the teachings of her church—which she did.

Negative Experiences Tailored to Needs of Individual

As with positive NDEs, negative experiences seem to be tailored to the specific needs of the individual. One could expect, therefore, that there would be as wide a variety of experiences as there are individuals. Although research into the negative experiences is still limited, it does appear that there is a considerable variation in what happens to those undergoing negative NDEs.

Some Negative Examples

Karen's Suicide Attempt

The research I have performed has convinced me that suicide attempts can lead to either positive or negative NDEs. The only constant in them is the fact that the people return with no desire to repeat their suicide attempt—they recognize it as a mistake, no matter what the provocation.

One who learned her lesson in a negative setting was Karen. She had been depressed and contemplating suicide for some weeks when she had an unusual experience. She reported the following:

One night as I was lying in bed, asleep, I was awakened by a male voice saying: *I'm going to get you. Sooner or later, I'm going to get you.* The event frightened me and I sat up, wide awake. I told my roommate, and she said it was just a dream, and not to worry about it.

About a week later, everything seemed so hopeless that I took the bottle of tranquilizers. My full intention was to kill me. It seemed the best way to handle my problems, just go to sleep.

It didn't work out the way I wanted, though, because I fell out of bed and woke my roommate. She called the ambulance at about one o'clock in the morning. At the hospital, I found out later, they pumped my stomach and put charcoal in it. They didn't think I was going to make it. My heart had stopped, and they used defibrillator paddles to restart it.

During this period I became aware that I was conscious, but I was enveloped in total darkness. It was pitch-black all around, yet there was a feeling of movement. My conscious self assured me that I was in the form of a spiritual body.

A male voice spoke to me, a different voice than the one I heard a week before. This voice said: *You have a choice. You can stay here, or you can go back. If you stay here, your punishment will be just as it is, right now. You will not have a body, you will not be able to see, touch, or have other sensations. You will only have this darkness and your thoughts, for eternity.*

Terrified because of the experience, and because of what I had heard, I understood that this would be my private hell. There would be no contact with other life or with the sensations of life, for eternity. Yet I would remain conscious with my thoughts in total blackness.

Frantically scared, I knew immediately that I had made a terrible mistake. Telling the voice that I had made a mistake, I asked to go back, to return to life. The voice said, *All right, you may return.*

Patricia's Experience

Patricia had two experiences, one the result of sniffing gasoline and going out of her body, and the second some years later when she was suffering from severe depression. She described the second experience in this manner:

One night, as I sat in bed reading, a strange feeling came over me. It was as if someone, or something, had come into my room. And whatever it was felt evil.

In my bed, while I was wide-awake, I was suddenly pinned down—I couldn't move. It felt as though some evil presence were trying to get into my mind. There was pressure so that I couldn't breathe, and my hands were immobile. I wanted to reach for the phone and call for help, but I couldn't.

Something seemed determined to get into my mind or body. I was terrified. It felt like a see-through dark cloud that was overwhelming me. The only means I had of fighting the force was by thinking. My grandmother had earlier tried to teach me that if an evil presence ever came around I should command it to depart in the name of Jesus Christ.

As I thought of my grandmother's words, the force pulled off of me. . . .

Visions of Hell

Jack's View of Hell
In his description of his descent into hell with a woman he was having a seance with, Jack said:

While she was doing the seance, I went out of my body with the woman, and we descended into hell together. We went down this huge red shaft. We could see people as silhouettes on different levels. As we passed the people I could feel their agony; they seemed to be hopelessly trapped in their levels. Stark terror gripped me as I felt of their despair.

Returning from the shaft, through some transition I didn't understand, we came to an immense area that I recognized as the earth.

The Fires of Hell
Maurice Rawlings, in his book *Beyond Death's Door*, describes several individuals who had visions of hell. One individual whose experience he described had an NDE after falling from a trestle into a river. The account of what the individual saw during his NDE follows:

The next thing I knew I was standing near a shoreline of a great ocean of fire. It happened to be what the Bible says it is in Revelation 21:8: . . .*the lake which burneth with fire and brimstone*. . . .

I remember more clearly than any other thing that has ever happened to me in my lifetime every detail of every moment, what I saw and what happened during that hour I was gone from this world. I was standing some distance from this burning, turbulent, rolling mass of blue fire. As far as my eyes could see it was just the same. A lake of fire and brimstone. . . .

The scene was so awesome that words simply fail. There is no way to describe it except to say we were eye witnesses now to the final judgment. There is no way to escape, no way out. You don't even look for one. This is the prison out of which no one can escape except by Divine intervention.[5]

Evil Spirits

Dee's encounter with an evil spirit is a particularly vivid description of the types of negative experiences that can occur. She said of her experience that hate for an abusive husband and fear were causing her emotional destruction, and these emotions created the atmosphere that allowed her experience to happen. An even more graphic description of an encounter with evil spirits is given in Professor Howard Storm's extensive NDE. He describes a multitude of vicious beings whose pleasure was to attempt to destroy his spirit in a black void. He was rescued only when he called to Jesus for help.[6]

Mike's Encounter in a Black Void

When he was nine years old, Mike went on a hunting trip with some friends and fell off a cliff. Recalling the incident, Mike said he saw himself looking at his body, then he went on a trip to the stars until he came to a black void. There was no light at all. Of that portion of his experience, Mike said:

> While I was in this black void, there was a noise in the background. The noise was from the whispering of many others in the void, and I could feel their presence. I kept asking: *Who is there? Who is there?* but I got no response. Whispering noises continued, so I put my hand out to see what was there, and I touched something. Whatever it was that I touched let out an awful noise. It sounded as if it were a snarl or roar from some wild cat. I was very frightened by the noise.

Mike then left the dark void and traveled into the light where he met the Savior.

Nyk Fry's Encounter in a Black Void

Mike's encounter with a being that sounded like a snarl or a roar was similar to that of Nyk Fry, who said of his experience:

> . . . The car park was incredibly dark, I couldn't see the ground. It kept getting darker, and at that point . . . I realized I wasn't dreaming any more. Everything was really black and I felt myself . . . I felt like

I was going down. I was sinking—I struggled—it was total unpleasantness.

I knew I had to stop this, whatever it was, and the only words . . . it was hard to speak or do anything. I didn't know what to do, but the only words I could summon in my mind were: *Heavenly Father*. At that very moment I heard this sound of . . . the only way I can describe it was a mixture between a wolf and a horse. It was a horrible sound. And then I 'woke up.' [7]

Lori's Account of Unpleasant Experiences

Lori had several out-of-body experiences. When asked if they were all pleasant, she said:

No. The one where I found my boyfriend with another girl wasn't pleasant. Also, when I was under stress, sometimes, I felt an evil presence. Pressure on my chest accompanied this evil feeling, and it was as if someone or something were trying to get me out of my body. These events were very frightening. During one of these episodes I remember that my mother couldn't wake me for a long time. On another one I heard a terrible growling noise.

Trapped Souls

Doctor George Ritchie, whose extensive NDE caused Raymond Moody to start much of his near-death research, saw many beings confined to a state that can only be described as hell. He describes this in considerable detail in *Return from Tomorrow*,[8] and in his more recent book *My Life After Dying*.[9] Both are good books and show the presence of evil beings, and the hopeless state of those who cannot escape from this evil realm.

Elane Durham's View of Confused Spirits

In Elane Durham's NDE, she had a view of spirit persons trapped in a less-than-heavenly sphere, similar to some of those described by George Ritchie. She described them this way:

When I got close to the light, something on the side of my vision distracted me. I looked down and to the side and saw a host of people. Rays from the light were shining over the tops of the heads of the people, but they didn't seem to notice. They appeared to be shuffling around, and I could feel anger and confusion coming from them. It was as if they were all lost, and they were agonizing over the pain that they felt. They seemed to be earth-bound and unable to see the light that was over them.

As I looked at the people I thought to myself: *You can go to the same place, all you have to do is, look at the light.*

Instructions to Betty Eadie Concerning Earth-Bound Spirits

During her NDE, Betty Eadie was instructed by spirit guides, and she said about a portion of those instructions:

They told me that it is important for us to acquire knowledge of the spirit while we are in the flesh. The more knowledge we acquire here, the further and faster we will progress there. Because of lack of knowledge or belief, some spirits are virtual prisoners of this earth. Some who die as atheists, or those who have bonded to the world through greed, bodily appetites, or other earthly commitments find it difficult to move on, and they become earth-bound. They often lack the faith and power to reach for, or in some cases even to recognize, the energy and light that pulls us toward God. These spirits stay on the earth until they learn to accept the greater power around them and to let go of the world.[10]

Why Not More Negative Experiences?

These examples should be sufficient to show that negative experiences do occur, as well as visions of a negative or hell-like world of spirits. The question remains, however, why are they not a larger fraction of the reported NDEs?

Doctor Maurice Rawlings, doing NDE research as a side issue to his medical practice as a heart specialist, came to the conclusion that there are as many negative NDEs as there are positive ones, but the positive ones get reported and the negative ones don't. The negative experiences are not reported for two reasons: the people are afraid to tell others about them, or they forget them quickly because the events are too horrible to remember. Some of his findings are reported in his book *Beyond Death's Door* published by Bantam Books. Quoting from a summary of his findings:

Let me tell you how I began my study of after-death experiences. I began following published reports of Elizabeth Kubler-Ross and Dr.

Raymond Moody. Except for cases of attempted suicide, all of their
published reports represented unbelievably good experiences.   I
couldn't believe this!   Their case reports were too pleasant, too
euphoric to be true, I thought. As a youth I had been taught there was
a *good place* and a *bad place*, a heaven and a hell. After the experience of resuscitating a man who said he was in hell and my subsequent
belief in scriptural truth, I assumed that some would go to the bad
place.

. . . I have found that most of the bad experiences are soon
suppressed deeply into the patient's subliminal or subconscious mind.
These bad experiences seem to be so painful and disturbing that they
are removed from conscious recall so that only the pleasant experiences—or no experiences at all—are recollected.[11]

My own findings in doing the research for these books showed that
some people are, indeed, afraid to tell of their negative NDEs. Dee was
reluctant, initially, to tell her story. During the work on this book, two
individuals called me and reported on their very negative NDEs. Both
seemed to be fairly extensive experiences, and both individuals backed off
when I asked to visit with them and tape their stories. I promised them
anonymity, but they still would not allow me to do more than hear, on the
telephone, a brief accounting of what happened to them. Their primary
interest seemed to be to find out about others who had undergone a
similarly negative NDE.

There is another reason why there are not more negative experiences,
in my opinion. Most researchers, including myself, obtained interview
candidates through advertisements and other means, from the cultural
mainstream. The participants selected by this means were basically law-
abiding, family-loving, patriotic citizens. Some, by their own admission,
broke some of the laws of God (they sinned), but in general they were
"good" people. No researcher to my knowledge has deliberately interviewed a cross-section of murderers, rapists, gun-runners, narcotics-deal-
ers, child-abusers, wife-beaters, or thieves, to see what kind of NDEs they
have. It would be an interesting research project to visit the prisons,
interview those claiming to have had NDEs, and tabulate the results.

LDS Teachings and Scriptures Concerning Evil

The Role of Satan

Part of the Plan of Salvation was that Satan (and his followers) would be allowed to tempt us to do evil. This is recorded in the Pearl of Great Price, as follows:

Wherefore, because that Satan rebelled against me, and sought to destroy the agency of man, which I, the Lord God, had given him, and also, that I should give unto him mine own power; by the power of mine Only Begotten, I caused that he should be cast down;

And he became Satan, yea, even the devil, the father of all lies, to deceive and to blind men, and to lead them captive at his will, even as many as would not hearken unto my voice.[12]

A primary objective of Satan, then, is to destroy the agency of man by trapping him in a web of deceit and lies. That Satan and his dominions have been fairly successful in that effort is clear by looking at a TV screen and observing what passes for entertainment or news.

Satan's greatest effort is often against those who provide a threat to him. Thus, in the New Testament, we read of Satan trying to tempt the Lord: "Then was Jesus led up of the Spirit into the wilderness to be tempted of the devil." Matthew describes how the devil offered the Lord food, power, and glory, but the Lord cast him out.[13]

Joseph Smith's Experience with an Evil Power

Joseph Smith, in his first vision, describes how Satan attempted to bind him:

After I had retired to the place where I had previously designed to go, having looked around me, and finding myself alone, I kneeled down and began to offer up the desire of my heart to God. I had scarcely done so, when immediately I was seized upon by some power which entirely overcame me, and had such an astonishing influence over me as to bind my tongue so that I could not speak. Thick darkness gathered around me, and it seemed to me for a time as if I were doomed to sudden destruction.

But, exerting all my powers to call upon God to deliver me out of the power of this enemy which had seized upon me, and at the very moment when I was ready to sink into despair and abandon myself to destruction—not to an imaginary ruin, but to the power of some actual being from the unseen world, who had such marvelous power as I had never before felt in any being—just at this moment of great alarm, I saw a pillar of light exactly over my head, above the brightness of the sun, which descended gradually until it fell upon me.

It no sooner appeared than I found myself delivered from the enemy which held me bound.[14]

Several of the NDEs in this book and *Glimpses of Eternity* include elements that are remarkably similar to Joseph Smith's account. Howard Storm's description of surrendering himself to destruction by the evil spirits, then calling upon the Lord and seeing a Light approach him, is one such example. Both Nyk Fry and Patricia described an evil presence that bound them so that they couldn't move until they called upon the Lord. Patricia even had difficulty breathing while under the evil influence.

The Fate of Good and Evil Spirits

In *Glimpses of Eternity,* I reviewed in some detail the LDS teachings concerning the fate of the spirits of good and bad people when they leave this life. Joseph Fielding Smith, the sixth President of The Church of Jesus Christ of Latter-day Saints, had this to say about these two classes of spirits:

This knowledge is one of the greatest incentives that we have to live right in this life, to pass through mortality, doing and feeling and accomplishing good. The spirits of all men, as soon as they depart from this mortal body, whether they are good or evil, we are told in the Book of Mormon, are taken home to that God who gave them life, where there is a separation, a partial judgment, and the spirits of those who are righteous are received into a state of happiness which is called paradise, a state of rest, a state of peace, where they expand in wisdom, where they have respite from all their troubles, and where care and sorrow do not annoy. The wicked, on the contrary, have no part nor portion in the Spirit of the Lord, and they are cast into outer darkness, being led captive, because of their own iniquity, by the evil one. And in this space between death and the resurrection of the body, the two classes of souls remain, in happiness or in misery, until the time which is appointed of God that the dead shall come forth and be reunited both spirit and body, and be brought to stand before God, and be judged according to their works. This is the final judgment.[15]

It is interesting, in reading this information, that those spirits confined to outer darkness are not left in this state forever, as understood by Karen, but only until the final judgment. It is also interesting, that President Smith refers to a partial judgment that occurs at the time the spirit leaves the body. Many who have had a life's review understand the nature of this partial judgment. The judgment is largely rendered by the person undergoing the review—a self-judgment—and it is a judgment tempered by the mercy of the Lord.

Further information concerning the length of time spirits must be punished is given by Elder Bruce R. McConkie in *Mormon Doctrine:*

Eternal damnation is used further to specify the torment and anguish to which the spirits of the wicked are heir in the spirit prison as they await the day of their resurrection. This type of eternal damnation ceases when the offender has finally come forth in the resurrection. In this sense, eternal damnation is the type, kind, and quality of torment, punishment, or damnation involved rather than the duration of that damnation. In other words, *eternal* is the name of the kind of punishment involved, just as it is the name of the kind of life referred to in the expression *eternal life*. Eternal punishment is, thus, the kind of punishment imposed by God who is *Eternal*, and those subject to it may suffer therefrom for either a short or a long period. After their buffetings and trials cause them to repent, they are freed from this type of eternal damnation.[16]

Anguish of Evil Spirits

The scriptures give ample evidence of the tortured existence of wicked spirits, and of their desire to enter the bodies of susceptible beings. One of the best-known stories involves Christ's encounter with the man who could not be bound with chains, and who cut himself with stones. When challenged by Christ, evil spirits in the man identified themselves as "Legion." Christ ordered them to leave the man and they entered a herd of two thousand swine nearby. The swine then ran off a cliff into the sea.[17]

An interesting parallel is contained in the autobiography of Levi Hancock, who witnessed the Prophet Joseph Smith casting out devils:

Joseph put his hands on Harvey Whitlock and ordained him to the high priesthood. He turned as black as Lyman was white. His fingers were set like claws. He went around the room and showed his hands and tried to speak; his eyes were in the shape of oval O's.

Hyrum Smith said, 'Joseph, that is not of God.' Joseph said, 'Do not speak against this.' 'I will not believe,' said Hyrum, 'unless you inquire of God and he owns it.' Joseph bowed his head, and in a short time got up and commanded Satan to leave Harvey, laying his hands upon his head at the same time. At that very instant an old man said to weigh two hundred and fourteen pounds sitting in the window turned a complete somersault in the house and came his back across a bench and lay helpless. Joseph told Lyman to cast Satan out. He did. The man's name was Leanon [Leman] Coply [Copley], formally a Quaker [Shaker]. The evil spirit left him and as quick lightning Harvey Green fell bound and *screamed like a panther*. Satan was cast out of him.[18]

This account is useful because of its parallelism to the earlier scripture, but also because of the reference to the individual who "screamed like a panther." Nyk Fry, Mike, and Lori, in their experiences, all said they heard a frightening cry that resembled that of an animal.

Dr. George Ritchie described several instances of seeing evil spirits while he was out of his body and being led by a being-of-light to various places on this earth. In one instance he described entering a bar with many service men and, as individuals drank themselves into a stupor, seeing evil spirits enter the bodies of those who became unconscious.[19]

Summary Concerning Negative Experiences

The Plan of Salvation makes clear that Satan and his dominions will have certain powers to lead us astray during our mortal lifetimes. That he is active in using these powers is clearly shown by scriptures, LDS teachings, and by the NDEs of many individuals. Additional research needs to be done to learn more concerning negative NDEs, but sufficient information exists in the present literature to understand that negative NDEs do exist.

I shall end this chapter by quoting from Elder Delbert L. Stapley in the April 1968 Conference Report:

Satan is a formidable opponent, and it will take extraordinary toughness to subdue him and his agents. The Lord has never promised that the overcoming of evil would be easy, but everyone can, if he wills, win the battle against the power of Satan.

The gospel of Christ is a lamp in our hands to guide us in righteous paths. Light can always dissipate darkness, but darkness can never replace light. It is only when the light of the Spirit within us is dimmed or goes out that the darkness of temptation and sin enters in, and Satan takes over. . . .

There are two powerful forces operative in the world today: one is the powerful influence of God; the other emanates from Satan. Even though evil is in constant competition with the good, the noble, and the beautiful in life, we should remember Joshua's declaration: '. . . but as for me and my house, we will serve the Lord.' (Josh. 24:15.)[20]

Chapter 22

PATTERNS AND PARALLELS

Statistical Summary

Introduction

While performing the research for the book *Glimpses of Eternity*, it became apparent that certain patterns were appearing. Particular words kept showing up in the vocabulary of the subjects being interviewed, for example, and the people were unaware that they were repeating words used by others. The word *peace* was used so often that I began to look for it in the vocabulary of the candidates. It was almost as if they were programmed to repeat the word.

I asked one fourteen-year-old girl, Tracie, why she used the word *peace* in describing how she felt during her NDE. Her response was: "I don't know. It just seems like the right word."

Most of those using the word peace did not think of it in the normal sense of the word (lack of conflict); rather, they thought of it in the scriptural sense, the sense that Christ used it as reported in the New Testament: "Peace I leave with you, my peace I give unto you: Not as the world giveth, give I unto you. Let not your heart be troubled, neither let it be afraid."[1]

Paul described the Lord's peace in this manner: "And the peace of God, which passeth all understanding, shall keep your hearts and minds through Christ Jesus."[2]

Other interesting patterns and parallels developed as the interviewing process continued. Some of these patterns and parallels related to the Plan of Salvation and other latter-day scriptures and teachings. The description of the bright light seen and felt by many during their NDE, for example, was best explained by passages from the 88th Section of the Doctrine and Covenants. The scriptural parallels were so striking, in this case, that I wrote an entire chapter entitled: *The Light*.

As the research continued for the present book, previous patterns continued to develop, and new unsuspected patterns also became apparent. The most surprising new pattern was the recognition by three candidates I interviewed, and by Betty Eadie in her book *Embraced by the Light*, of themselves in a premortal environment (See Chapter 20 for discussion).

Tabular Data

In order to systematically examine some of the patterns and parallels that were becoming apparent I decided to tabulate certain repeating characteristics that the subjects spoke of in their experiences. All of the tabulated data for each person interviewed for the books *Glimpses of Eternity* and *Echoes From Eternity* are given in the Appendix. A summary of a portion of that data is shown in the following table.

TWO BOOK STATISTICAL SUMMARY

	Total People	Religion at Experience	Religion at Interview	One or Multiple Experiences	Out of Body	Saw Body
Totals	68	39 LDS	43 LDS	83	71	44
Percent	58.8 Female	57.0 LDS	63.2 LDS	20.5	85.5	53.0

	Spirit Had Form	Tunnel	Light	Landscape	People	Knew People
Totals	49	18	50	18	46	33
Percent	59.0	21.6	60.2	21.1	55.4	39.0

TWO BOOK STATISTICAL SUMMARY, CONT'D.

	Rela-tives	Voice	Deity	Saw Deity	Life's Re-view	Build-ings
Totals	23	53	22	15	9	6
Per-cent	27.7	63.8	26.5	18.1	10.8	7.2
	Know-ledge	Ener-gy	Peace	Love	Warm	Pure
Totals	28	6	38	39	17	4
Per-cent	33.7	7.2	45.7	47.0	20.5	4.8
	Re-morse	Fear	Music	Sense of Mis-sion	2nd Heal-ing	Saw Pre-mor-tal
Totals	5	10	9	52	10	3
Per-cent	6.0	12.0	9.6	62.6	12.0	3.6

Multiple Experiences by People

It is seen from the table that several subjects had more than one experi-ence. There was a total of 68 people interviewed (58.8 % female), and 20.5 % of them had multiple experiences.

A large fraction of the experiences were out-of-body (85.5%), and in 53 % of the experiences the people saw their physical bodies lying beneath them. Most (59%) felt that their spirit-bodies had form—or they were able to see those forms, sometimes as energy fields, shaped similarly to their physical bodies.

Light, Color and Landscapes

The NDE literature is filled with descriptions of people who went through a tunnel and saw a light. A relatively modest 21.6% of the experiences tabulated here included a tunnel, but 60.2 % involved some aspect of the bright light. The bright light dominated much of the discussion concerning what the subjects saw and felt during their NDEs.

Twenty-one percent of the experiences involved some type of landscape feature. In most of these cases the people said that they saw plants, trees, shrubs, flowers and gardens with colors that were more vivid and alive than anything they had seen on earth. In a few cases animals were also seen.

Spirit People and Communication

A large fraction of the experiences (55.4%) involved other spirit people, and in 39% of the cases the individuals undergoing the NDEs understood that they knew the spirit people whom they saw. Often, however, unless the other spirit people were relatives, the subjects could no longer recall who the people were that they saw. They just knew that at the time of their NDE the other people were known to them. If the spirit people were relatives (27.7% of the time), then the subjects were able to recall many details about the people they saw. In most cases the relatives were delivering a particular message to the subjects involved.

It was interesting to hear the people discuss the voices that they heard. Sixty-three percent of the experiences included some memory of voice communication. In some instances the subjects said that communication was as it is on earth, by voice in a person-to-person manner. These were the minority of the cases, though. Most felt that the *voice* was transmitted into their mind without the benefit of vocal cords. Usually, the voice could be recognized as male, female, or from a particular person. In a few instances the subjects actually heard their own voices delivering a message to themselves. Where deity was involved, they recognized the voice as coming from Heavenly Father or from Jesus Christ, and, often with great emotion, they said that it was a familiar voice—one that they had known from before.

Deity (God the Father, or His son, Jesus Christ) was involved in a surprising twenty-six percent of the cases, and in eighteen percent of the experiences Deity was actually seen. In these instances the subjects were emphatic about whom and what they saw. A later chapter will be devoted to this subject.

Life's Reviews—Buildings

A life's review occurred in only eleven percent of the cases, but when it did it was usually under dramatic circumstances. Four of the nine cases, for example, happened while the subjects were in space and just after they had been traveling through the stars. Their stellar journeys were interrupted so that they could learn something about themselves through a review of their lives. In these particular cases they were able, after the reviews, to decide whether or not they wanted to continue with their lives on earth.

Few, only seven percent of the experiences tabulated, involved people who saw buildings. In some of these, little detail was seen of the buildings. Others, such as Jean's view of the "Libraries" (recorded in *Glimpses*), included detailed descriptions of exterior and interior features.

Knowledge

One-third of the experiences included people who said that unusual knowledge was theirs while they were undergoing the NDEs. After the NDE they forgot most of what they had known, but they still remembered the remarkable feeling they got when the mere hint of a question resulted in a fountain of information flowing into them. Elane described it this way: "At that point the light spoke to me—only not in language as here on earth. It spoke to me from everything that it was into everything that I was. I not only heard it, but I understood it with every fiber of my being. There was total communication between that being and my being."

DeLynn said of the experience:

It was astonishing, the speed with which I was learning. Knowledge that had somehow slumbered deep in my soul was released, and I was extremely exhilarated by this reawakened knowledge. Light and knowledge were flowing into me from every direction. I could feel it. Every part of my body was reverberating with the light gushing in. Even my fingertips were receptors of light and knowledge. It was as if I were drinking from a fully engaged fire hydrant.

Another person who spoke of his entire being acting as a receptor of knowledge was Roger Smith. He said:

Pure knowledge seemed to pour into me from Him. The knowledge was transmitted by . . . energy. Energy flowed into me and with it was knowledge. It was as if my entire being was a receptor of knowledge. And it was knowledge that I seemed to have known before. Everything that was communicated to me made sense.

Words Concerning Feelings During the Experiences

Several words were repeated often enough in the interviews that they attracted my attention. These were words that the candidates used in their attempts to describe what they felt. The words were: *Energy* (7.2%), *Peace* (45.7%), *Love* (47.0%), *Warmth* (20.5%), and *Pure* (4.8%). In many instances, as with the word *love*, the individuals said that this was an improper word to describe what they felt. DeLynn put it this way: "We don't have a word that would describe what I felt from Him toward me. The closest word we have is *love*, but it doesn't begin to describe the feeling. There is not an appropriate description in mortal tongue that can explain the feeling—you have to feel it."

Remorse and Fear

Remorse and fear were two emotions suffered by those whose experience included some negative features. It was not necessary for the entire experience to be negative, as with Howard Storm's extensive experience which included both positive and negative aspects, or as with Jack's view of Hell. In some cases, as with Dee's bout with an evil spirit, it was terrifying. Remorse played a part in most cases where an individual had a life's review. Sometimes remorse was a major factor in helping the individuals decide that they needed to come back for a second try at life.

Music

Music was mentioned as a factor in only 9.6% of the cases, but where it was mentioned, it was a major factor. Katrina, in *Glimpses*, told how she spent months listening to various classical pieces in an attempt to find what she had heard in the other world. She finally settled on Daniel Kobialka's version of "Pachelbel's Kanon" as a poor (too loud) substitute for what she had heard. Elane Durham said:

There was a sound in the air that completely defies description. It was as if there were a multitude of voices, and a multitude of instruments, blended and playing soft music. The twittering of birds, and other beautiful sounds, were all melodically instrumented into the music which wafted through the air. The sounds just flowed into me in a soft, soft manner.

Derald Evans, in *Glimpses*, said this about the sights and sounds that he witnessed:

> I was absorbed in watching the light—the beautiful bright white light. It gave me a feeling like . . . almost like soft music, or something that was one-hundred percent pure. It's hard to describe in words. I had never seen nor heard anything like it before. It was not frightening, though. More softening.

Sense of Mission

An amazingly high (62.6%) returned from the other world with a strong sense of mission. In most of those instances they were not aware of exactly what they were supposed to accomplish, just that it was an important part of their lives from thenceforth forward. Elizabeth Marie, for example, remembered that she was told she should help others who had lost their way to Christ. She forgot the details, however, and she said this about it:

> Since my experience, though, I haven't known who it was that I was supposed to help. I've wondered if it was one person, or many persons. I understood that it was to help someone, or several people, who had lost their way, to return to His presence, but I still don't know who they are.

David Chevalier, who was shot in the lower abdomen by a drunken uncle, when I asked him if he had any sense about why he was allowed to come back, said:

> That question has plagued me since I was shot. Initially I thought it might be to help my wife and my two sons. Then, after I completed my education and started teaching, I thought it might be because I am able to express myself and to teach others well. Recently, when my daughter was born, I suspected it might be to help nurture and raise her. Maybe it's all of those things.

Dallas, who shot himself in a suicide attempt, said this:

> The Lord called me by name and told me that I had done a foolish thing, and it was not my time to be there. He said that there was a lot of work on the earth that I must do for Him. There were certain things I must accomplish with my family before I would be

allowed to return to the Lord. If I did what he asked, he said that my life would be great—not great in an earthly sense, but great in a spiritual sense, and I would be richly rewarded on the other side.

Dallas was still puzzling over exactly what it was he was supposed to do when I interviewed him.

This sense of mission, but not necessarily an exact sureness of what the mission was to be, was fascinating to observe. It speaks to the portions of the Plan of Salvation (Chapter 20) that deal with freedom of choice and of a premortal existence. I have already observed in Chapter 20 that, if we accept the premise of a preassigned mission, then we must also accept the fact of having existed in a premortal environment where the mission was first assigned.

The Plan requires that we not remember much—except what we are told by the Prophets—of our premortal life, or of a life to come, so that our free agency may be protected. This explains the lack of memory of exactly what it was the subjects were to accomplish for their missions. Indeed, it appears that the missions are largely self-chosen, as evidenced by those who saw themselves in a premortal environment. The Plan also requires that we make our own choices in as free a milieu as possible. Howard Storm, in his extensive experience, related that when he asked the angels how he would know which choices he should make, they said:

> We want you to do what *you* want to do. That means making choices—and there isn't necessarily any right choice. There are a spectrum of possibilities, and you should make the best choice you can from those possibilities. If you do that, we will be there helping you.

Second Healings

In *Glimpses* I observed: "A totally unexpected pattern concerned healings. I expected to find people who had returned to this life after an NDE more-or-less healed after their bout with death. And this was the case. Indeed, with several, in addition to the miracle of the NDE, there was a miraculous healing upon their return to this life."

There were four individuals who went through this particular pattern of experiences as recorded in *Glimpses*. Each of the experiences was spectacular in its own right and involved a second, serious, life-threatening event that was miraculously removed. I watched with interest, during the research period for the present book, therefore, to see if there were repeats of the pattern. And repeats there were—six more. The percentage of these unusual healings totalled at twelve percent of all experiences.

As a result of the original work (four cases), I suggested a tentative model and hypothesis. Quoting from that work:

"The pattern that became evident from these experiences was the following:

● The individuals were good people, who, as the result of an illness or an accident had an out-of-body experience.

● They came back to this life with an even firmer resolve to live a righteous life. They were more spiritually attuned than they previously had been. They had a sense of purpose about life.

● An illness or injury developed (or lingered) which threatened their ability to carry out their perceived purpose.

● A healing occurred which defied medical knowledge. . . ."

From the observed experiences I reached a tentative conclusion—or hypothesis. The hypothesis was:

When an individual undergoes an NDE and returns to this life, that return is for a purpose. If the individual, after return, has some illness or injury that threatens to thwart the person's life purpose, then the Lord intervenes and removes the threat.

I said, at the time, that "this hypothesis should be tested by further research of persons having NDEs." Additional tests have now been made that tend to confirm the hypothesis—usually in a dramatic manner. Further work should be done to establish the statistical correlations. To be useful, this work should also attempt to identify individuals who do not meet the conditions of the hypothesis. That is, were there those who—after experiencing an NDE and returning *with a sense of mission*—then promptly died? None of the sixty-eight persons I interviewed for the two books (including follow-up studies on those in the first book) failed to comply with the hypothesis.

The very fact that a person has an out-of-body experience and comes back gives evidence of the Lord's interest in the person. I have already discussed how the majority of the people felt that they came back for a purpose. To allow the person to return to this life and then not be able to fulfill his or her purpose would seem a fruitless exercise.

This is not to suggest that all persons return with a strong and healthy body. Just the opposite is often true—and the people having had an NDE understand that they may have to live under difficult circumstances when they return.

Conclusions Concerning the Tabulated Data

These were the only data that I tabulated, but they are sufficient to show the existence of some interesting patterns and parallels. It was exciting to interview a person and witness that person attempting to explain a situation with the same stumbling words, and with the same surging emotions, as another individual who had been through a similar situation. Even more exciting was to discover patterns that linked to scriptural passages or other teachings from the Prophets. I still marvel at the correspondence between the descriptions of The Light, as given by those witnessing it, and the description given in the 88th Section of the Doctrine and Covenants.

Other Patterns and Parallels

There were many other patterns and parallels that became obvious while Carol and I were doing the research for these two books. Some of them related to the findings of others in the literature, and others did not seem to lend themselves to the tabular mode of accounting. I will now review a few of these other patterns.

Instructions Repeated Three Times

I first became aware of an unusual circumstance in John Stirling's account of his flight to the stars, described in *Glimpses*, when he said:

And the voice . . . the voice asked me if I were done. . . .

I said: 'Yes, I'm done. I don't want to go back there. I don't ever want to go back there.' The voice asked me a second time: 'Are you done?' And I said: 'Yes, I'm done. I don't want to go back.' The voice asked me a third time if I were done, and again I said that I was.

Then the voice said: 'Well, let's look at your life.'

What attracted my attention when I was doing the research for *Glimpses*, was the similarity between the thrice repeated question, and some latter-day scriptural events where the Lord, or one of his messengers, repeated certain messages three times. I was alerted, therefore, to watch for more of the same in research for *Echoes From Eternity*. I was not disappointed.

One of the more striking accounts of a message repeated three times was that given by Vern Swanson. Vern's wife, Elaine, and his small son Brett had been killed in a car accident, and Vern was unable, emotionally, to accept the death of his son. Vern described an experience in which his deceased wife appeared with their dead son in this manner:

"Then I looked down and I saw my son. Elaine was holding Brett in her arms. When I touched my son it was as if I had touched something that had been frozen, similar to cold clay. He looked dead.

"I kissed my son, and he felt cold and dead. Elaine sternly said: 'Vern, he is dead.' And I said: 'No, no, it can't be,' and I kissed him again. Elaine repeated a second time that he was dead.

"During this episode Elaine was very serious. She was most dedicated to delivering a message. There was no funny business about her; rather she seemed intent solely on the message. I kept telling her no, and I was crying.

"Repeating the message that he couldn't be dead, I said things like: 'No, no, he's okay. He'll be okay.' And I was crying.

"Then she said the third time, very emphatically: 'Vern, he is dead.'

"By the third time, similar to hitting a boxer with a one-two-three punch, it penetrated and I understood. I still didn't want to accept it, but I knew it was true."

Following this experience, Vern was able accept the death of his son and resume life. He became a happy person again.

DeLynn had a similar experience to that of John Sterling, when he was asked if he wanted to return to earth. His account of the event was as follows:

"When I finished asking questions about returning or staying, I again analyzed the risks and rewards of staying or returning. After I was satisfied that I understood the options, I said: 'I choose to return.'

"The Voice asked me: 'Are you sure?'

"My response was: 'Yes, I'm sure.

"He asked, again: 'Are you sure?'

"My answer, this time, was: 'Yes, I think so.'

"A third time the Voice asked: 'Are you sure?'

"This time it hit me. My answer must be certain—I must not lie to myself or try to conceal my real intent from Him. I looked again at my family. I thought about it, and I said: 'Yes, I choose to return.'"

Scriptural Accounts of Triple Messages

Joseph Smith, the latter-day Prophet, gave an account of the angel Moroni's visit to him one night after he prayed. It is a remarkable account from many points of view. The appearance of the angel, and the Prophet's description of the event, are so similar to other descriptions of many having gone through an NDE that I included much of what he said in *Glimpses* (in the Chapter on The Light). The pertinence of the event to the present discussion is given in a few passages from Joseph's account:

> After this communication, I saw the light in the room begin to gather immediately around the person of him who had been speaking to me, and it continued to do so until the room was again left dark, except just around him; . . . he entirely disappeared, and the room was left as it had been . . . .

> I lay musing on the singularity of the scene, and marveling greatly at what had been told to me by this extraordinary messenger; when, in the midst of my meditation, I suddenly discovered that my room was again beginning to get lighted, and in an instant, as it were, the same heavenly messenger was again by my bedside.

> He commenced, and again related the very same things which he had done at his first visit, without the least variation; . . . Having related these things, he again ascended as he had done before.

> By this time, so deep were the impressions made on my mind, that sleep had fled from my eyes, and I lay overwhelmed in astonishment at what I had both seen and heard. But what was my surprise when again I beheld the same messenger at my bedside, and heard him rehearse or repeat over again to me the same things as before; . . .[3]

After this third visit by Moroni, Joseph was exhausted, but he was able to later recall, in detail, particular passages of scripture that were quoted to him by Moroni. He also was able to write a detailed account of Moroni's visit.

Another important passage is the account given in the Book of Mormon of Christ's visit to the Nephites on the American Continent. After His crucifixion in the old world, many devastating events happened to the Nephites—earthquakes, floods, darkness, and other destruction by the elements—and the people were in a state of shock. Upon the Savior's resurrection He appeared to these residents of the American Continent. The description of His appearance is recorded thus:

And it came to pass that while they were thus conversing one with another, they heard a voice as if it came out of heaven; and they cast their eyes round about, for they understood not the voice which they heard; and it was not a harsh voice, neither was it a loud voice; nevertheless, and notwithstanding it being a small voice it did pierce them that did hear to the center, insomuch that there was no part of their frame that did not cause to quake; yea it did pierce them to the very soul, and did cause their hearts to burn.

And it came to pass that again they heard the voice, and they understood it not.

And again the third time they did hear the voice, and did open their ears to hear it; and their eyes were towards the sound thereof; and they did look steadfastly towards heaven, from whence the sound came.

And behold, the third time they did understand the voice which they heard; and it said unto them:

Behold my Beloved Son, in whom I am well pleased, in whom I have glorified my name—hear ye him.[4]

It is apparent from the NDE accounts cited above, and from the scriptural references, that when God wants to make a point he does so with emphasis. That emphasis includes repeating the desired message, or question, three times. This seems to be sufficient to get the attention of us preoccupied mortals.

Time

There are innumerable references in the NDE literature to the fact that time is different in the spiritual realm than it is on earth. Many of those I interviewed confirmed that fact. Barry Kirk said of his experience: "It seemed to be a long time, and yet it probably was not a long time—I do not know how long it was." I asked Dallas, in his experience, how much time elapsed between the time he left his body and when he returned. He responded: "I have no idea. I cannot comprehend how time worked there." Elizabeth Marie, when asked by me how long her experience took, said: "I don't know. I didn't really have a sense of time."

An example of time passing slower than on earth was given by Renee Zamora, who, during her illness, went out of her body several times. She said of that experience: "There were many trips that I made between my hospital room and the park area. Whenever a nurse came into my room, I came back. It occurred over a period of three days, yet a puzzling aspect of the experience was the fact that time didn't seem to pass as fast for the people in the park area as it did for me. My three days were like five minutes to them, and I wondered how that could be."

An example of NDE time passing faster than on earth was given by Roger Smith, who in the few seconds that his Volkswagen was airborne, had a complete life's review. The only sure thing from these experiences is that time, as we know it on earth, is vastly different on the other side. Julie, in her out-of-body experience in which she saw her deceased cousin, Allen, remembers telling him: "You are going to a place where there is no time." She said that she has no idea where she got the concept that there would be no time in the spirit world. She was a teenager at the time of her experience and had not been taught such ideas—the knowledge seemed to come from within her, she said.

LDS scriptures teach that time is different in the Lord's realm than it is on earth. In Abraham we are told that one day of the Lord's time is as one-thousand years of our time.[5] In the Doctrine and Covenants, it speaks of a period during the millennial reign of the Savior, when "there shall be time no longer" on the earth.[6]

Right Hand Raised to the Square

The Elders of the LDS Church have long had a practice of raising their right arm to the square for particular ordinances or important prayers. In the baptismal prayer, for example, before the candidate for baptism is immersed, the officiator raises his arm to the square and pronounces the prayer.

Two of those I interviewed gave examples of a spirit person raising his right arm to the square. Jean, whose deceased husband appeared to her when she was pregnant and ill, described the event this way:

At that moment, I was wide awake, and I became aware of two people standing in the corner of my room. One was my husband. The other was a personage, a male, wearing a long white robe. I couldn't see the face of this personage—I wasn't allowed to see his face. They were about two feet off the ground, and they were standing there looking at me.

My husband turned to him and said: 'Does she have to suffer like that?' The personage in the robe raised his right arm to the square. Then they disappeared and I lay down. The next thing I knew it was morning and I felt wonderful.

My interview with Dallas, who saw the Lord in his NDE, went like this: "So the Lord then told you that you had to go back?"

"Yes. It's interesting how he did it. At the time I was not an active member of the Church and I didn't understand some of the things I saw. When we were finished talking, the Lord raised his right arm to the square and commanded me to return to my body."

NDE Parallels in The Book of Mormon

My wife, Carol, first called my attention to Alma's account of a visit by an Angel and his follow-on experiences that paralleled many of the elements of an NDE. Subsequently I read an account by Kevin Christensen entitled: *"Nigh unto Death": NDE Research and the Book of Mormon.*[7] The article proceeds to document many of the comparable experiences of Alma and those of the classic NDE. Mr. Christensen says: "The clearest and most concentrated descriptions of the afterlife experience in the Book of Mormon come from the books of Mosiah and Alma. Appropriately, Alma's conversion appears to have occurred through an NDE."

Symbolism

Many of the NDEs reported in the literature, and several of the subjects I interviewed, depicted events that could best be described as symbolic. In many cases the symbolism might not be clear, but the fact that it was a symbolic representation seemed apparent.

Forrest Hansen, in his experience (recorded in *Glimpses*), first described a scene that seemed to be a symbolic representation. Forrest saw a giant double-cone-shaped object in the sky which he understood to represent the spectrum of possibilities in the past, present and future for the universe. This unusual experience, I thought was unique, until I read Phyllis Atwater's account[8] of a similar experience—with almost identical meaning to that assigned by Forrest.

Research for the present book discovered additional symbolic type experiences. Jack, in his out-of-body experiences, saw several events that seemed symbolic in nature. In his trip to hell and back, he explained part of his experience as follows:

> Returning from the shaft, through some transition I didn't understand, we came to an immense area that I recognized as the earth.

Enormous numbers of people were leaving the earth to a place where a giant bearded angel was holding a door open for them. I understood these people to be the dead who had died in the love and grace of God, and He was calling them up from the earth. The people were illuminated, and they were passing through the door into heaven.

. . . It [the field] was flat, and it seemed to extend out in every direction. It was strange, the whole experience seemed so symbolic, and yet there I was. This enormous bearded person, who was letting the people through the gate, was an angel, or . . . something I didn't understand.

An analogous experience was reported by Mike. He described what he saw in this manner:

The Being urged me to enter the light, and He said: 'Come, I want to show you something.' He took me up, and we went to another place, a different world bathed in light. Located in a large field was an enormous and beautiful gate. It had jewels on it and it was of a shining golden color. My guide pointed at it and said: 'That is the gate to heaven.' . . . There was a large wall that the gate was mounted on, and He let me know that heaven was beyond the gate.

Rocks and other things were there. All around the gate there was a large field. . . . Mostly the colors were associated with the gate. It sparkled with many jewels and with the golden material that it was made of.

The scriptures speak of pearly gates. One account is from John's vision of the celestial earth where he saw "the holy Jerusalem, descending out of heaven from God. . . . And the twelve gates were twelve pearls: every several gate was of one pearl."[9]

In the 137th Section of the Doctrine and Covenants, Joseph Smith described the vision of the Celestial Kingdom that he had. He said:

The heavens were opened upon us, and I beheld the celestial kingdom of God, and the glory thereof, whether in the body or out I cannot tell.

I saw the transcendent beauty of the gate through which the heirs of that kingdom will enter, which was like unto circling flames of fire;[10]

Chapter 23

FAMILIES

Examples of Family Ties

In *Glimpses of Eternity* I observed that there was an obvious pattern of family affiliation that extended beyond the grave. In the last chapter it was seen that 27.7% of the experiences involved family members. Some of these family-oriented experiences were under dramatic circumstances.

Eloise and Dave Weaver Say Goodbye

One of the most unusual NDEs occurred when Eloise Weaver and her husband, Dave, crashed in their car. She broke her neck, and he was fatally injured. Eloise explained it this way:

"The paramedics got my daughter out first. Then they began to pry on the door where my husband was. Dave kept saying how badly he hurt, and they were afraid he was dying. He turned toward me, and that's when everything in the car got really bright, very warm, and very quiet. I didn't hear my daughter screaming anymore, and I didn't hear any voices coming from outside the car.

"I felt Dave's presence very close to me, and suddenly we were above our bodies. He held me really tight, and he said: 'Hang in there babe; I love you.' That's what he always called me. Then he said: 'I'm being called home, and you need to go back and raise our girls.'

"I remember telling Dave that I really didn't want to go back without him, but he told me I had to return. Then the warm feeling left, and I was hit with pain—immense pain. The pain was more horrible than when the car first hit us.

"I could hear the people again, and I saw Dave as they were pulling him out of the car. He winked at me. Then they began doing CPR on him;

278

I knew he was gone. I could feel his presence near me. He had a habit of brushing my hair off my forehead—I could feel him doing that, and I felt very calm.

"Dave lived as long as he did, I think, (three hours before they got him out) so that he could encourage me to live. I wouldn't have struggled to live as much as I did without him there to help me."

Vern Swanson is Visited by his Deceased Wife

The visit to Vern Swanson by his wife Elaine, in his desperate state after the death of his wife and son, was spectacular. Vern described the circumstances as follows:

"One night, about six months after Elaine and our son had died, I was lying restlessly in bed. Suddenly I looked up and I saw a light. Standing there in the light was my wife.

"As I remember, it seems as if I were instantly out of bed—just thuung! . . . and I was up next to her. It was the most interesting situation you could imagine, because she looked exactly like Elaine, yet she didn't. It's hard to explain.

"My wife, the woman, the angel in front of me was so peaceful, so beautiful. There was a light that came from within her so that she glowed. It wasn't reflected light; it was almost as if there were a bright candle inside of her.

"I had always thought that Grace Kelly, the movie star, was the most beautiful woman in the world. Elaine, standing before me, would have put Grace Kelly to shame. She was very white with that inner glow, and she was absolutely the most beautiful person I had ever seen. To this day I can remember how she looked, and I marvel at what I saw. Elaine, in life, was a good-looking woman, working as a model during college, but her earthly body was a poor shadow, an impoverished copy, when compared with that beautiful person before me—yet it *was* Elaine.

"As she stood before me I began to embrace and kiss her; I smothered her with kisses. When I touched Elaine, I was filled with joy from her white radiance—not a cold white, but a warm white."

These two examples speak eloquently and poignantly of the loving ties between a husband and wife. They illustrate the point that those ties can extend beyond the grave. Apparently the love shared by husband and wife are not destroyed by death.

Bill Meets His Deceased Father

The accident on an all-terrain-vehicle left Bill paralyzed from the chest down, and led him to question whether he should continue to live. During his NDE he said the following things happened:

"As I walked along the path in the meadow I came to a stone archway. It seemed almost as if I were called, or drawn, to the archway. I walked through it and entered a courtyard where I saw my father. He was dressed all in white, and he was bathed in sort of an iridescent white light.

"We approached each other, and I remember telling him that I was feeling lost and confused. I realized at that point that I was either in the process of dying, or I had already died. My confusion centered on my earthly life. I was feeling a great loss because of my children, and I was sharing that feeling with my father. Additionally, I wasn't sure that I wanted to live in the paralyzed state that the doctors said I would live in.

"My father said to me: 'You aren't going to be lost or confused any longer. Everything will be fine. It's not time for you to be here, now, but when it is I will be here.' Then he embraced me—there was an enormous outpouring of peace—and he took me back to the archway. As I entered the archway, I had the feeling that everything would be okay. That's the last thing I remember until I came out of the coma."

Jennifer and Rocky's View of Their Grandparents

Jennifer Pitcher, who had her NDE at age five when she was run over by a truck, saw her great-grandfather, whom she had never met before. He was dressed in a white robe, and he told her she would be all right. Later, Jennifer identified her grandfather from pictures that her grandmother had of him when he was a young man.

Rocky, who fell from a second-story window onto his head when he was four years old, met his grandfather who had died before Rocky was born. He described his grandfather as looking like himself.

In both of these cases the grandparents apparently visited with the children during their NDEs in order to reassure the children. The visits were an expression of concern and love.

Lavor Allen's Instructions from His Parents

When he suffered heart failure and had an NDE, Lavor Allen said he met his deceased parents. They told him to return to earth:

"Then I became aware that I was moving, and I entered an area with beautiful grounds. It was outdoors, and everything seemed white—or a pretty color. There was a shine about everything, as if bushes and flowers had been waxed.

"A trail went through the grounds, and I followed it, not walking, but sort of floating over it. Ahead of me on the trail I saw a couple of people. Getting close to the couple, I saw that it was my dad and my mother, both of whom had died. My mother had died when I was just a child. . . . They were dressed in white, and my mother's red hair showed. In terms of age, they looked as I remembered them.

"It seemed as though I said: 'I'm here to meet you.' My dad responded: 'You've got more work back there. Now, be sure and go back.'

"There was something else he told me concerning an uncle of mine, named Percy. It's not clear in my memory what he said about Percy, I just remember that Dad said something about him. He also told me, again, that there were some things that I had to do."

Elane Durham's View of Her Relatives

As part of her extensive NDE, Elane Durham saw several of her relatives. She described the encounter in this way:

"In the distance by the river there were six or seven people standing by some trees, and I could tell that they were waiting for me. It was as if they knew I was coming; one of them looked up and said: 'There she is!' A man leaning against a tree motioned with his arm and said: 'Hurry, Elane, everyone's waiting.' . . .

"Two women broke away from the group and began running toward me. When they got within about twenty feet, I recognized one as my grandmother. She had been dead since I was about nine years old. The man against the tree was my mother's step-dad, and he had been dead since I was sixteen or seventeen. The lady immediately behind my grandmother was Aunt Virginia, my husband's aunt, who had died the previous February.

"All of them were dressed in white, a white which radiated light. Their hair and faces were not the same as on earth, but I recognized them quickly. They were about thirty years of age in appearance, much younger than when I had seen them last. Aunt Virginia was badly crippled when I knew her in life with one leg shorter than the other. Here, she was completely restored to normal function.

"As I saw my relatives and felt of their joy, I had the thought: *Man, if my kids could only see this; if they could only see Aunt Virginia now.* I no sooner had the thought, than: WHAM. It was a heavy duty body slam, and I was back in my body at the hospital."

Genealogy Experiences

Introduction

Most of those I interviewed who had encounters with relatives, described relatively straightforward visits by the deceased. All but one of the examples given above fall in that category. The exception was Lavor Allen's case, where he was told to do something about Uncle Percy, but he wasn't sure what. He said that he thought it might have something to do with the genealogy and temple ordinance work for Percy, but he had been unsuccessful in finding the necessary information.

In two other cases there was a marked departure from the usual pattern of a straightforward visit. In each case, a major purpose of the visit was to communicate genealogical information. One account was that of DeLynn, who said that his deceased father visited him and "told me several things, including why he had to go, what I should be doing, and what my mother should do regarding our genealogy. . . ." The most extraordinary account concerning genealogy, though, was that of Renee Zamora.

Renee Zamora's Experience

There are too many important parts of Renee's experience, and the text is too long, to duplicate it here. Instead, I will summarize, then discuss, the important points. For the complete text, please refer again to Chapter Seventeen. The main points are as follows:

- When Renee was desperately ill, and wanted to be alone, she saw people enter her hospital room and began to play checkers. The people were dressed in clothes styled for the late 1800s or early 1900s. She became aware that the people were all related. Renee was angry that the people ignored her and continued to chat with each other and play their game.
- This scene, with variations as described below, kept repeating itself, perhaps as many as twenty times over the next two or three days. Despite Renee's annoyance, the people returned whenever the nurse left

her hospital room. Her intense headache continued throughout the initial visits by the people. She wanted to ignore the people, but seemed forced to know their names and relationships to each other.

- After several times of being visited in her room, Renee found herself floating through the hospital walls and joining the people as they traversed to a park area, which Renee understood to be overlaid over the city of Provo. More and more people became a part of the initial family group. They were all related, and Renee always was aware of their names and relationships to each other. The people continued to be oblivious to Renee's presence. Her intense headache was still with her.

- Some people in the park were playing croquet, and others were having a picnic near a large tree. There were many people, all dressed in period clothes, and all related. Renee wondered why some of them could be engaged in such a trivial pursuit as playing croquet. When she went near the picnic area, Rence found to her relief that her headache disappeared. When she thought about the relief, though, she found herself back in her hospital bed with the same intense headache.

- Renee learned that if she concentrated on the people and their relationships, and if she went to the picnic area, her headache would be removed. She therefore continued to join the people in the park and to study them. On one such trip she saw a striking man near the tree. When she looked at him, she was instantly conscious that, unlike the other people in the park, he was aware of her presence and he knew her. Feeling fear, she was repelled by the man, and she knew that she didn't want to be anywhere near his presence.

- Later, after her NDE, Renee became aware of why she was repelled by the man. She understood that he was Satan. She also knew that in order to comprehend her experience, which she understood to be partly symbolic, she should read and study Section 138 of the Doctrine and Covenants, and she should attend the LDS temple.

Ordinances Which Tie Families Together

Baptism—For Whom?

If it is true that, as those having NDEs observed, there is a continuation of family ties after death, then there must be some way—guaranteed by the power of God—that marriage vows and family affiliations can be sustained in the next life. God must arrange for earthly ordinances to be binding in the next life as well as this one. But what are those ordinances and how do they work?

Chapter 20 outlined the main elements of the Plan of Salvation. Element 7 stated that: "Means would be provided for saving ordinances to be performed on this earth for all persons, living or dead." There are several ordinances that allow families to be tied together. One of those ordinances is baptism, which Christ himself set the example for. In Mark we are told: "He that believeth and is baptized shall be saved; but he that believeth not shall be damned."[1]

The Book of Mormon makes clear that little children, under the age of eight, are automatically saved in the Celestial Kingdom if they die—there is no necessity for baptism.[2] All others—being accountable for their sins—must repent and be baptized.

Baptism for the Dead

But what about those who have died and never heard of baptism, how are they saved? Are they damned simply because they never had the opportunity to be baptized?

In First Corinthians, Paul, in making an argument that there is a resurrection, asks, "Else what shall they do which are baptized for the dead, if the dead rise not at all? why are they then baptized for the dead?"[3] Apparently there was an ordinance in which baptism for the dead was practiced during Paul's time. This practice, about which more will be said in a moment, is one of those ordinances which are vital for the salvation of those who never had the opportunity during life. Baptism is required before individuals can be tied together as families.

The Authority to Act for God

In May 1829, John the Baptist appeared to Joseph Smith and bestowed upon Joseph Smith and Oliver Cowdery the Aaronic Priesthood with its authority to baptize. Later, Peter, James and John restored the Melchizedek Priesthood to Joseph and Oliver with its increased authority.[4] These two priesthoods, again, gave man the ability to act in the name of, and with the power and authority of God.

Elijah—Ties That Bind

In the last two verses of Malachi, the Lord tells us: "Behold, I will send you Elijah the prophet before the coming of the great and dreadful day of the Lord: And he shall turn the heart of the fathers to the children, and the heart of the children to their fathers, lest I come and smite the earth with a curse."

On April 3, 1836, in the Kirtland, Ohio Temple, Joseph Smith, the Prophet, and Oliver Cowdery were visited by a series of heavenly beings, including Elijah, who restored the heavenly keys necessary to bind families for eternity—in short, to turn the heart of the fathers to the children, and the heart of the children to their fathers. These heavenly keys made it possible for all individuals to have an equal opportunity to partake of saving ordinances and to be bound as eternal family units.

The Doctrine and Covenants sheds further light on the scripture from Malachi:[5]

> It is sufficient to know, in this case, that the earth will be smitten with a curse unless there is a welding link of some kind or other between the fathers and the children, upon some subject or other—and behold what is that subject? It is the baptism for the dead. For we without them cannot be made perfect; neither can they without us be made perfect. Neither can they nor we be made perfect without those who have died in the gospel also; for it is necessary in the ushering in of the dispensation of the fulness of times, which dispensation is now beginning to usher in, that a whole and complete and perfect union, and welding together of dispensations, and keys, and powers, and glories should take place, and be revealed from the days of Adam even to the present time.

In LDS temples, baptism for the dead is performed where living persons, acting as proxy for the dead, are baptized for individuals who never had that opportunity during life. Individuals for whom the vicarious baptism has been performed will have the gospel taught to them in the spirit world, and will be able to either accept or reject their baptism. Similarly, husbands and wives (both living and dead) are sealed together for eternity, with their children bound to them in family units.

Genealogy With a Purpose

The LDS Church has the largest genealogical effort in the world. The purpose of this work is to identify family ties as far back as possible, and to perform the vicarious ordinance work for those individuals which will tie them together. In order for that work to be efficacious, though, the individuals must accept it. They still have their free agency in the spirit world and can either accept or reject the work being performed for them.

Thoughts on Renee's Experience

Section 138 of the Doctrine and Covenants
Renee understood that in order to comprehend her experience she should study the 138th Section of the Doctrine and Covenants. This Section documents the vision received by President Joseph F. Smith, which he received on October 3, 1918. That vision, which came in response to questions President Smith had about the writings of Peter and of the Lord's visit to the spirit world, unfolded a marvelous view of the spirit world. It provided knowledge, previously lost to the world, of what happens to righteous and unrighteous spirits when they depart from this life. Chapter 21, under the subtitle *The Fate of Good and Evil Spirits* documents some of what President Smith had to say about what happens to good and evil spirits when they leave this life.

From this remarkable vision we know the following:
- When we die, our spirits leave our bodies and return to that God who gave us life.
- In the spirit world, there is a partial judgment and a separation. The righteous spirits are received into a state of happiness which is called paradise. It is a place of peace where the righteous expand in wisdom and where they have respite from all their troubles, and where care and sorrow do not annoy. They dwell in the presence of the Lord.
- The wicked have no part nor portion of the Spirit of the Lord. They are cast into outer darkness, or prison, being led captive, because of their own iniquity, by the evil one. Satan continues to have power in this realm.
- In the space between death and the resurrection of the body, the two classes of souls remain, in happiness or in misery, until the time which is appointed of God that the dead shall come forth and be reunited both spirit and body. They shall then be brought to stand before God, and judged according to their works. This is the final judgment.
- From among the righteous spirits, the Lord organized his forces and appointed messengers, clothed with power and authority, and commissioned them to go forth and carry the light of the gospel to them that

were in darkness. Thus, *all* individuals, have an opportunity to accept or reject the truths of the Gospel of Jesus Christ.

Brigham Young's Teachings Concerning the Spirit World

Concerning the spirit world, Brigham Young said this:

When you lay down this tabernacle, where are you going? Into the spiritual world? It is right here. Do the good and evil spirits go together? Yes they do. . . . Do they go beyond the boundaries of the organized earth? No, they do not. . . . Can you see it with your natural eyes? No. Can you see spirits in this room? No. Suppose the Lord should touch your eyes that you might see, could you then see the spirits? Yes, as plainly as you now see bodies.[6]

Teachings of the Prophet, Joseph Smith, About Spirits

Regarding the righteous spirits, Joseph Smith taught this:

The spirits of the just are exalted to a greater and more glorious work; hence they are blessed in their departure to the world of spirits. Enveloped in flaming fire, they are not far from us, and know and understand our thoughts, feelings and motions, and are often pained therewith.[7]

Of the unrighteous spirits, he said:

The great misery of departed spirits in the world of spirits, where they go after death, is to know that they come short of the glory that others enjoy and that they might have enjoyed themselves, and they are their own accusers.[8]

Teachings of the Prophet Joseph Smith About Records

. . . I want you to remember that John the Revelator was contemplating this very subject in relation to the dead when he declared, as you will find recorded in Revelation 20:12—'And I saw the dead, small and great, stand before God; and the books were opened; and another book was opened, which is the book of life; and the dead were judged out of those things which were written in the books, according to their works.'

You will discover in this quotation that the books were opened; and another book was opened, which was the book of life; but the dead were judged out of those things which were written in the books, according to their works; consequently, the books spoken of must be the books which contained the record of their works, and refer to the records which are kept on the earth. And the book which was the book of life is the record which is kept in heaven; the principle agreeing precisely with the doctrine which is commanded you in the revelation contained in the letter which I wrote to you previous to my leaving my place—that in all your recordings it may be recorded in heaven.

Now, the nature of this ordinance consists in the power of the priesthood, by the revelation of Jesus Christ, wherein it is granted that whatsoever you bind on earth shall be bound in heaven, and whatsoever you loose on earth shall be loosed in heaven. Or, in other words, . . . whatsoever you record on earth shall be recorded in heaven, and whatsoever you do not record on earth shall not be recorded in heaven; for out of the books shall your dead be judged, according to their own works; . . .[9]

Discussion of Renee's Experience

From these scriptures and teachings, we may deduce some speculative thoughts concerning the meaning of Renee's experience. The people that she saw, apparently, were spirits from deceased people, all related, who lived in the late 1800s and early 1900s. These were people who had not received the fullness of the Gospel of Jesus Christ, while here on the earth, and were confined to a state of no progress, and one where Satan still had power.

The repeated visits, by Renee, to the park area where the people were located forced her to concentrate on what she was seeing. She understood that it was, in part, symbolic, but the reality of the scenes still impressed her. Implicitly, the message was that something needed to be done for the people she saw—something concerning the relationships of the people to each other. She later understood this to mean that she should work to find and record the detailed genealogies of the people involved. In that manner, the records of the people could be completed here on earth so that ordinances could be performed that would be binding in heaven.

Families are Forever

I observed in *Glimpses* that balladeers often sing of a love that persists forever. I further observed that the singers were more correct than they knew. The NDE literature, and my research findings, all validate the continuation of loving ties beyond the grave.

This idea of "forever-families" is confirmed by LDS teachings and scriptures. Under the Lord's fabulous Plan of Salvation, Eloise and Dave Weaver will be reunited with their girls; Vern Swanson will see again Elaine and his beloved son, Brett; Bill will meet his father and understand that his father's statement, concerning no more confusion, was correct; Jennifer Pitcher and Rocky will feel again the love they felt from their grandfathers; Lavor Allen will see his mother's red hair and feel of the love of his father; Elane Durham will have another joyous reunion with her relatives, and this time she will be able to talk to Aunt Virginia.

That death should destroy these family ties is inconceivable with a loving God. If that were so, then "the things that matter most [would] ultimately be at the mercy of the things that matter least."[10] God, in his mercy, has provided a way—through the Plan of Salvation—for us to live again with those that we loved and cherished while we traveled together through the adventure of life.

Vern Swanson said, about the Plan of Salvation:

. . . My belief is that the Mormon doctrine of the eternities is a doctrine of peace. I would urge all to familiarize themselves with the Plan of Salvation as taught in the LDS Church.

Knowledge about the Plan of Salvation is ultimately what saved me from the despair I felt after the death of my wife and son. It prepared me so that when I had the unique experience of seeing my wife after her death the whole thing made sense. It gave me the perspective I needed to put my life back together again.

The doctrine of salvation is a gentle doctrine of peace. The LDS Church, for example, is the only Christian church I know of that provides salvation for people like my father who professes to be an atheist. He may not reach the highest kingdom in heaven—as others may who profess Christ and who live according to Christ's teachings—but it will be a kingdom, and it will be in heaven. This gentle doctrine can buffer the problems of life, reduce pain, and energize us to be better people.

Chapter 24

APPEARANCES OF DEITY

NDE Accounts of Deity

Previous Descriptions

One of the issues that initially attracted my attention to the subject of near-death experiences was my father's description (Marshall Gibson) of his extensive experience following a heart attack in 1920. In that experience he told of being taken by a guide to a beautiful world of light, peace and love. While traveling on a beautiful path, in that world, he came upon the Savior, and he was overwhelmed by the love he found in the Savior's presence. He said of that experience:

. . . I noticed someone on the path ahead of us. As we got closer to the individual I could see and feel that he was a magnificent person. I felt overwhelmed as I looked at him. He was bathed in light. [My guide] asked if I knew who that was, and I answered yes. It was Jesus Christ.

When we got close to the Savior, I felt a tremendous love emanating from Him. It's hard to describe, but you could feel it all around Him. And I felt a similar enormous love for Him. I fell at His feet—not because I thought about it, but I couldn't stand. I felt an overpowering urge to fall at His feet and worship Him.

. . . As I knelt there at the feet of this marvelous being I became conscious of my past life being reviewed for me. It seemed to occur in a short period, and I felt the Savior's love during the entire process. That love was . . . well, it was everywhere. And it was as if we could communicate with each other without speaking. After a period the Savior reached down and I knew I should stand. As soon as I stood, He left.[1]

290

During the research for the book *Glimpses of Eternity* four other individuals said that during their NDE they saw the Savior. Some of the descriptions, such as Ann's, were just as dramatic and emotion filled as was the event described by my father. Anticipating repeat descriptions when I commenced the research for the present book, I watched carefully for similar experiences. I was not surprised when the first individuals told of seeing Jesus, therefore, but I *was* surprised at the total number of them—ten more after the first book. Eighteen percent of those interviewed for the two books said that they saw Jesus. It is useful to consider some of these accounts.

Eloise Weaver (as a child) Sees Jesus

When Eloise was nine or ten years old, and was seriously ill with rheumatic fever, her parents left her alone one night. She explained what happened next:

My parents told me to keep the door locked and to stay in bed. I was scared and crying, and I remember praying for help. All of a sudden a great light filled the room. Standing there by me in the light was Jesus. He put His hands on my head and I felt this enormous outpouring of love.

Jesus was all dressed in white, and He was very handsome. His eyes were the most wonderful blue, and there was the most warm, wonderful feeling emanating from Him. I don't remember Him saying anything—just His hands on my head. It seemed that He was there for a long time, and the room was very bright. Then He left, and the room was dark again.

Cynthia Prueitt (as a child) Sees Jesus

Cynthia was seven years old when she had her NDE. She said this about her experience:

My mind kept dwelling on my problems, wondering why it was happening to me, and I prayed to God for help. The next thing I remember was being introduced into a room that was completely and brilliantly white. There was a man sitting on a chair that resembled a chair-type throne.

Seeing this man with a beard sitting there, I ran up to Him and climbed on His knees. He gathered me in his arms and began to . . . He just began to comfort me. He gave me such a warm, warm feeling of love, and . . . I've never felt anything like it. It was warm, it was love, it was joy—I didn't want it to end. It was the most thrilling feeling I had ever experienced before or since.

This wonderful being wrapped me in His arms and held me close. I began to sob and tell Him my problems. He comforted me with words of comfort. Then He began to talk to me about my life. He told me that I had certain things in this life that I had to do. He began to tell me what they were and how I was to accomplish these things. As He outlined what I was to do he asked me if I would try to accomplish what He had described, and I promised that I would.

Then He said that it was time for me to leave. I began to bawl, and I told Him that I didn't want to go. Crying helplessly, I pled that I might stay in his presence. . . .

I began to cry again as I returned. Crying for some time, I again made the promises I had previously made to Jesus Christ when I was on His lap. I promised that I would do the things He told me—no matter what it took to do them. And I stopped crying.

Dallas Sees Jesus in a Garden

In his suicide attempt Dallas found that he had made a mistake. During his experience he described having seen Jesus in a garden:

Standing in the garden was the Lord Jesus Christ. The feeling I had was beyond description. As wonderful as the garden had been, it was no longer my center of attention. My whole being focused on this magnificent personage standing before me. . . .

The robe He was clothed in was white beyond any description, with a beautiful sash in the middle—it was gorgeous. His hair was long and it was a golden-brown color, and he had a beard. Actually, in terms of describing Christ himself, the closest I can come to it is the print of a painting I saw in Deseret Book Store some years later.

The painting is entitled *The Second Coming*, and the original painting was done by the artist Harry Anderson. I purchased a print that I hang in my bedroom, because it is the best representation of what I remember seeing when I stood at Christ's feet. When I first saw the picture it brought back the memory of my experience, and I stood in front of the picture crying. As good as that painting is, though, it is a poor representation of the magnificent being I saw before me.

Debbie is Cradled by Christ

When Debbie was nineteen years old, and in the military service, she had an operation that resulted in her NDE, which she described thus:

"While the doctors were having these problems I suddenly felt warmth all around me, and I knew that somebody was holding me. The area I was in was surrounded by light.

"It felt as though I were being cradled by someone, and when I saw all this light, I looked around to see what was happening. As I lifted my head I found myself looking into the eyes of Christ. He was carrying me, as a child would be carried, in a cradling fashion.

"There were no fear and no pain, just a feeling of lightness and security—and I kept staring at Him. He was walking with me; then, strangely, He carried me through a wall, or something, and we went from the light into darkness.

"Christ's lips never moved, but He communicated with me, . . .

"Having a sense that I would have to return to my body, I asked Him repeatedly, 'Why? Why?'

"In a soothing way He told me that it was not my time yet. While He stood there holding me, I could see my body plainly. But at the same time, I knew I had a semblance of a body, or a spirit body, that Christ was holding. And I could feel His strength while He held me.

"When He went to lay me down into my body, I tried to resist by grabbing at Him. Crying desperately, I kept repeating: 'Please don't. I don't want to go back.'

"Struggling with my emotions, and crying continuously, I asked Him what I must do. He smiled at me and responded: 'Shhh, everything will be all right.' My gaze was riveted on Him, and he began backing away.

". . . His hair was long and sandy-blonde, with a nice wave in it. He was bearded with a smooth face, and His eyes . . . His eyes were the bluest blue I had ever seen; they were a clear see-through blue. There was warmth, there was love, there was compassion in His eyes. I couldn't look away from Him . . . . There was light all around Him; it actually stood off of Him. It was an energy."

Common Elements

There is insufficient room in the book to repeat all of the accounts of those who saw Christ. These should be sufficient to identify some of the common elements of the experiences, though. The most common elements were: seeing a being who transmitted light, or energy; seeing brilliantly bright white clothes in the form of a robe that covered Him from his neck to his ankles and wrists, usually with a sash; having a feeling of love, peace and joy that emanated from Him; noticing His long hair and beard, colored either sandy-brown, or sandy-blonde (and in one case, white); looking into His penetrating blue eyes; receiving intense knowledge communicated from Him without its being spoken; observing a muscular feeling of strength coming from Him (other accounts); and having innate knowledge that it was Him.

Concerning the last element, I asked several people how they knew it was Christ. Their responses were engrossing. The conversation David Chevalier and I had went in this manner:

"How did you know it was your Savior?"

"I know Jesus Christ when I see Him."

"How did you know?"

David chuckled as he thought. Then he said: "Probably it was the sense of goodwill and the sense of comfort that I felt—together with the other events that I witnessed. The fact is, *I just knew. I knew!*"

Mike's account was especially interesting:

"The figure was a man; he was in a white robe, he was transparent, and he was very bright. Instantly, upon His touching my hand, I knew it was the Lord. I was filled with peace, I felt calm, and there was an assurance that the peace would stay with me. There was an overpowering love coming from Him to me—I could feel it. The warmth I felt . . . There is no experience in life that can duplicate what I experienced there in His presence."

"How did you know it was the Lord?" I asked.

"There were the love and the comfort that He gave. He was radiantly beautiful, dressed in a white robe, and he had long brown hair. His dress and appearance were that of the Lord—He showed me the nail prints in his hands."

"Where were the nail prints?"

"They were on his wrists."

When I asked Mike if there were any final messages he would like to leave for others, this is what he said:

"My message to others is that when they see the Lord they will know who He is. There will be no question about whom it is when they see

Him—if there is the slightest doubt then it is not the Lord. Doubt will flee when He appears; *He will know you and you will know Him.*"

When I asked Eloise Weaver how she knew it was Jesus, she said:

"*Oh, I knew it was Jesus.* His beautiful face, His countenance, His hair, it was . . . it was a beautiful brownish-golden color. And those wonderful big blue eyes. He had a little beard—and when He put his hands on my head I felt His strength. It was a strength that I felt through my whole body. I'll never forget the feelings that I had in His presence."

"What were His clothes like?" I asked.

"They were white; they covered His arms down to His wrists, and they were open at His neck a little way. They were flowing, and white; and the room was gold and blue and pink. It was radiant—it was just wonderful."

"Did He glow too?"

"Oh yes, there was just a . . . it was like an aurora coming off of Him. And the feeling. I'll never forget the feeling of His hands on my head.

Other NDE Accounts of Encounters with Deity

In addition to those who said they saw Deity in the research for these two books, there were those who felt the presence of Deity or heard a voice ascribed to Deity. There were an additional seven experiences (in addition to the fifteen who said they saw Christ) that involved either a feeling of the presence of Deity or heard a voice.

DeLynn, in his extensive experience, recognized the voice of Heavenly Father. In that regard, he was similar to David Herard, the Vietnam veteran in *Glimpses of Eternity* who said the he felt the hand of God on his shoulder. All of the individuals who were interviewed were certain that it was Deity they encountered, and not some lesser being. Where there were lesser beings involved, such as angels or deceased relatives, then they were clearly identified.

Scriptural Descriptions of Christ and Heavenly Father

There are numerous references to Christ during his earthly ministry in the old world. I shall select a few pertinent references to his appearance to people before and after his earthly ministry.

Christ Seen Before His Earthly Ministry

In Ether in the Book of Mormon, the Brother of Jared, because of his great faith, was permitted to see Jesus Christ before the Lord had been born on this earth and before his resurrection. Christ said to the Brother of Jared:[2]

> . . . Seest thou that ye are created after mine own image? Yea, even all men were created in the beginning after mine own image.
>
> Behold, this body, which ye now behold, is the body of my spirit; and man have I created after the body of my spirit; and even as I appear unto thee to be in the spirit will I appear unto my people in the flesh.

The Lord thus appeared in the form of a man while still in his Spirit body, and he indicated that he would, at a later date, take upon himself a physical body. Moreover, he told the Brother of Jared that men, also, were created in a form like Him.

Christ Seen by the Eleven

Luke records the visit of the resurrected Christ to the eleven Apostles in this manner:[3]

> And as they thus spake, Jesus himself stood in the midst of them, and saith unto them, Peace be unto you.
>
> But they were terrified and affrighted, and supposed that they had seen a spirit.
>
> And he said unto them, Why are ye troubled? and why do thoughts arise in your hearts?
>
> Behold my hands and my feet, that it is I myself: handle me, and see; for a spirit hath not flesh and bones, as ye see me have.

Other New Testament Accounts

There are many other examples given in the New Testament where the resurrected Christ visited different individuals. Thomas, the doubting Apostle, would not believe until he personally saw and felt the risen Christ.[4] Stephen, the first martyr for the testimony of the resurrected Savior, just prior to being stoned to death, saw Jesus standing on the right hand of God.[5] Saul (later Paul), on the road to Damascus, saw in a vision a bright light, and heard a voice declaring that it was Jesus of Nazareth whom Saul had persecuted.[6]

Christ Appears on the American Continent

In Chapter 22 I discussed the account given in The Book of Mormon of Christ's initial appearance to the Nephites on the American Continent. After the people heard the voice of God the Father, repeated three times, they saw Christ descending. It is recorded in this way:[7]

And it came to pass, as they understood they cast their eyes up again towards heaven; and behold, they saw a Man descending out of heaven; and he was clothed in a white robe; and he came down and stood in the midst of them; and the eyes of the whole multitude were turned upon him, and they durst not open their mouths, even one to another, and wist not what it meant, for they thought it was an angel that had appeared unto them.

And it came to pass that he stretched forth his hand and spake unto the people, saying:

Behold, I am Jesus Christ, whom the prophets testified shall come into the world.

And behold, I am the light and the life of the world; and I have drunk out of that bitter cup which the Father hath given me, and have glorified the Father in taking upon me the sins of the world, in the which I have suffered the will of the Father in all things from the beginning.

Later Accounts of Christ's Appearance

Joseph Smith Sees the Father and the Son

In Chapter 21, the account of Joseph Smith's prayer and initial encounter with an evil spirit is given. Immediately after the evil spirit released its hold on the young prophet, he described what happened next, as follows:[8]

. . . Just at this moment of great alarm, I saw a pillar of light exactly over my head, above the brightness of the sun, which descended gradually until it fell upon me.

It no sooner appeared than I found myself delivered from the enemy which held me bound. When the light rested upon me I saw two Personages, whose brightness and glory defy all description, standing above me in the air. One of them spake unto me, calling me by name and said, pointing to the other—'This is My Beloved Son. Hear Him!'

The Lord Appears in the Kirtland Temple

In April 1836, after the Church had been established, and when the majority of the Saints were living in Ohio, a temple had been built in Kirtland. In the afternoon of April 3, the Prophet and Oliver Cowdery retired to the pulpit in the temple and began to pray. The account of what they saw is given in the Doctrine and Covenants:[9]

> The veil was taken from our minds, and the eyes of our understanding were opened.
>
> We saw the Lord standing upon the breastwork of the pulpit, before us; and under his feet was a paved work of pure gold, in color like amber.
>
> His eyes were as a flame of fire; the hair of his head was white like the pure snow; his countenance shone above the brightness of the sun; and his voice was as the sound of the rushing of great waters, even the voice of Jehovah, saying:
>
> I am the first and the last; I am he who liveth, I am he who was slain; I am your advocate with the Father. . . .
>
> For behold, I have accepted this house, and my name shall be here; and I will manifest myself to my people in mercy in this house.

Vision of Christ by Newel Knight

On June 9, 1830, the first conference of the newly organized Church of Jesus Christ of Latter-day Saints was held in New York. Many manifestations of the Spirit were described by those present. Joseph Smith recorded one event that happened to Newel Knight who was present at the meeting:[10]

> . . . Much exhortation and instruction was given, and the Holy Ghost was poured out upon us in a miraculous manner—many of our number prophesied, whilst others had the heavens opened to their view, and were so overcome that we had to lay them on beds or other convenient places; among the rest was Brother Newel Knight, who had to be placed on a bed, being unable to help himself. By his own account of the transaction, he could not understand why we should lay him on the bed, as he felt no sense of weakness. He felt his heart filled with love, with glory, and pleasure unspeakable, and could discern all that was going on in the room; when all of a sudden a vision of the future burst upon him. He saw there represented the great work which through my instrumentality was yet to be accomplished. He saw heaven

opened, and beheld the Lord Jesus Christ, seated at the right hand of the majesty on high, and had it made plain to his understanding that the time would come when he would be admitted into His presence to enjoy His society for ever and ever. When their bodily strength was restored to these brethren, they shouted hosannas to God and the Lamb, and rehearsed the glorious things which they had seen and felt, whilst they were yet in the spirit.

Summary

From these NDE accounts, and from the scriptural passages pertaining to visitations by the Lord, it appears that the Savior and His Father are vitally interested in this earth. More to the point, they are vitally interested in each of us who live here. Both the scriptural passages and the NDE descriptions seem tailored to the specific needs of the individuals to whom the Lord appears (or speaks to), and the events are tailored to help others of us when we hear the testimonies of those who saw Christ.

Thus, the Lord appeared to the old-world Apostles to verify the reality of the resurrection. Appearing to the Brother of Jared before His earthly ministry, Jesus showed the type of body He would appear in, and He taught the efficacy of premortal life. He taught Thomas, and the rest of us, the value of belief through faith. Stephen's vision showed that God the Father and Jesus Christ were two separate entities. Paul had his vision so that he could become the greatest missionary of all time—the Lord understood Paul's potential. Joseph Smith reestablished the truth that God the Father and Jesus Christ were separate individuals—and he restored the Lord's Church. Oliver Cowdery and Joseph Smith needed to understand that the Lord had accepted His house in Kirtland. Newell Knight was another witness of the glory and separateness of God the Father and the Son.

In an analogous manner, my father saw Christ, and in the process, Dad fortified his own testimony of the enormous unconditional love of the Savior. For the rest of his life Dad exemplified that love, and he was instrumental in establishing initial branches of The Church of Jesus Christ of Latter-day Saints in small Northern California towns.

Eloise Weaver and Cynthia Prueitt, with the faith of children, saw their Master and understood that He was healing them and helping them to know their missions. Cynthia, in a later Patriarchal Blessing, recognized the same personal mission goals that the Lord had previously given her.

Dallas learned that he had made an enormous mistake in attempting suicide, and in the process became a witness of that fact. He learned that he had a mission to perform that could make him great in the eyes of the Lord—not in a worldly sense.

Debbie, as she was cradled by Jesus, learned of the healing love that the Savior has for each of His children. She was later able to tell others of the peace and unconditional love she found in His arms.

David Chevalier and Mike both bore testimony of the reality of Jesus as the Savior of the world. Mike was privileged to see the nail prints in the Lord's wrists, and both Mike and David stated that Jesus was known by them and would be known by each of us.

One question that might be asked from some of the NDE descriptions given of Christ, is: "Why weren't the descriptions all identical?" Dallas and Eloise Weaver described the Lord's hair color as golden-brown. Mike said it was brown, and Cynthia remembered it as white. Rocky said that Jesus had dark hair. Aside from questions associated with the witnesses' memory of the event or variations in the lighting, a possible explanation involves how the Savior chose to appear to each individual. In some cases, for example, witnesses described the Savior as a bright light—without form that they could see—yet they knew it was the Savior.

Analogous questions may be asked concerning the appearance of deceased relatives to those undergoing an NDE. In some instances the relatives appeared as younger than when they died, and in other cases they were aged. Duane Crowther in his book *Life Everlasting* describes the experience of Bishop Hunter whose small child died. The child later appeared to his father *in the stature of full-grown manhood*, and said: "I am your son."[11]

The Lord apparently reveals himself in a manner best suited to the needs of the individual. In all of these accounts, scriptural or from NDEs, it is clear that the Lord knows us intimately—better than we know ourselves—and He loves us unconditionally. His understanding of us extends into the everyday details of our lives. The experiences of those who saw and felt Him thus become personal revelations tailored to the needs of the individuals—and the experiences bear witness to the rest of us that Jesus is the Christ, the Savior of us all. Joe Swick, in *Glimpses of Eternity*, said this about his experience:

I haven't shared this experience with many people. It is too sacred to me. But whenever I have shared it, I have always told people that the experience has taught me that God is willing to reach out and talk with us. I'm nobody special, I don't have a . . . all I do is translate languages. Nobody knows my name—but I do know that God knows my name. And that He was willing to reach out and talk with me. If He would talk to somebody like me, then He would do it for anybody.

That was a realization that profoundly influenced my joining the Church. God didn't just talk to Joseph Smith, a farm boy in New York. He talked to me too. *And He would talk to anybody, it seems to me, if He would talk to somebody like me.*

Chapter 25

SOME FINAL THOUGHTS

Finding the Truth

Incomplete Knowledge

I began this book by observing that Carol and I, in our search for the truth, had drunk briefly from the river of knowledge that we found. I noted that our drink, though refreshing, had not quenched our thirst for knowledge. Light had illuminated some truths—truths that we had dimly understood—but ultimate knowledge eluded us. Sir Isaac Newton said it better when he stated: "I do not know what I may appear to the world, but to myself I seem to have been only like a boy playing on the seashore, and diverting myself in now and then finding a smoother pebble or a prettier shell than ordinary, whilst the great ocean of truth lay all undiscovered before me."[1]

As with those we interviewed, it was thrilling when we recognized some bit of knowledge that had previously been buried from our sight, but it was frustrating to recognize the incomplete nature of that knowledge. It appears that we, like Paul, can in this life only see through a glass darkly, abiding in faith, hope and charity.[2]

The Plan of Salvation

The Plan of Salvation, which the Lord in his wisdom established, provides that we can move through this life grasping those truths given by Him through the prophets. Complete knowledge of our premortal existence, and of the miracle of our earthly birth—and later rebirth into a spiritual realm—is withheld so that we might have free agency. Our agency to choose good or evil is a sacred right, and the Lord has protected that right with many safeguards, including our failed memory of a previous existence. In order to be truly free, and to grow and develop as a consequence of that freedom, we must have the freedom to fail as well as the freedom to succeed.

Faith

A major part of the Gospel plan, then, is to move through life with faith—faith in the love, goodness, power and mercy of the Lord Jesus Christ. And faith in the words of the prophets. An ancient prophet, Alma, put it this way:[3]

> Now, as I said concerning faith—that it was not a perfect knowledge—even so it is with my words. Ye cannot know of their surety at first, unto perfection, any more than faith is a perfect knowledge.

> But behold, if ye will awake and arouse your faculties, even to an experiment upon my words, and exercise a particle of faith, yea, even if ye can no more than desire to believe, let this desire work in you, even until ye believe in a manner that ye can give place for a portion of my words.

> Now, we will compare the word unto a seed. Now, if ye give place, that a seed may be planted in your heart, behold, if it be a true seed, or a good seed, if ye do not cast it out by your unbelief, that ye will resist the Spirit of the Lord, behold, it will begin to swell within your breasts; and when you feel these swelling motions, ye will begin to say within yourselves—It must needs be that this is a good seed, or that the word is good, for it beginneth to enlarge my soul; yea, it beginneth to enlighten my understanding, yea, it beginneth to be delicious to me.

The Ultimate Source of Truth

The great universities of the world are repositories of much knowledge, and a great deal can be learned by attending them. Their knowledge, though, is but as a firefly in a dark night compared with the light of Christ. That light is described in this manner:[4]

> He that ascended up on high, as also he descended below all things, in that he comprehended all things, that he might be in all and through all things, the light of truth;

Which truth shineth. This is the light of Christ. As also he is in the sun, and the light of the sun, and the power thereof by which it was made. . . .

And the light which shineth, which giveth you light, is through him who enlighteneth your eyes, which is the same light that quickeneth your understandings;

Which light proceedeth forth from the presence of God to fill the immensity of space—

The light which is in all things, which giveth life to all things, which is the law by which all things are governed, even the power of God who sitteth upon his throne, who is in the bosom of eternity, who is in the midst of all things.

The prophets through the ages have felt of the light of Christ, and they have used it to enlighten us. Many individuals Carol and I interviewed also felt of that light. Roger Smith explained the light in this way:

Getting closer to the light, it got larger and brighter. It was the whitest-white I had ever seen. The brightness was . . . I can't describe how it was. There is nothing on this earth that is that color. Wondering about the brightness as I got closer, I asked myself: 'How can I stand to look at and be in this light? How is it that I can see?'

By this time I was standing, enveloped in the light, and I could feel it. Permeating every cell of my body, it filled me with warmth, it filled me with love—it was an indescribable feeling.

The Lord's Church

The Church of Jesus Christ of Latter-day Saints

It should be clear to the reader by this point that I am a dedicated believer in the doctrines and practices of The Church of Jesus Christ of Latter-day Saints. I, like Vern Swanson, believe that the Plan of Salvation as taught in the LDS Church is a gentle doctrine of peace. The unrestricted love of God for His children, as felt by those who had NDEs, is guaranteed under the Plan of Salvation. *All* who live on the earth will have an equal opportunity to reach their fullest potential.

I further believe that Joseph Smith was a prophet of the Lord in the same sense that Jeremiah, Moses and Mormon were prophets. Joseph, the boy prophet, was the instrument used by the Lord to reestablish His church in these latter days.

In the year 1820, in order to know which church he should join, Joseph appealed to the Lord in prayer. In response to that prayer, God the Father and the Son appeared to him. Joseph described what happened next in these terms:[5]

My object in going to inquire of the Lord was to know which of all the sects was right, that I might know which to join. No sooner, therefore, did I get possession of myself, so as to be able to speak, than I asked the Personages who stood above me in the light, which of all the sects was right—and which I should join.

I was answered that I must join none of them, for they were all wrong; and the Personage who addressed me said that all their creeds were an abomination in his sight; that those professors were all corrupt; that: 'they draw near to me with their lips, but their hearts are far from me, they teach for doctrines the commandments of men, having a form of godliness, but they deny the power thereof.'

Joseph was later told that he would receive a record of a people, on gold plates, that had lived anciently on the American Continent. The record would describe God's dealings with that people, just as the Bible described God's dealings with the people in the old world. After translating the plates, the record would become The Book of Mormon and would constitute another witness for Christ. Joseph would also restore The Church of Jesus Christ with all of its ordinances, rights, powers and authority that were held at the time of the Lord in the old world.

Questions About the Lord's Church by Those Having NDEs
Howard Storm

Howard Storm, the atheistic professor who changed his mind about God after his extensive experience, asked his angel guides many questions. One of the questions was about the Lord's Church. He described that portion of his experience in this manner:[6]

. . . I asked them, for example, which was the best religion. I was looking for an answer which was like: 'Presbyterians.' I figured these guys were all Christians. The answer I got back was: 'The best religion is the religion that brings you closest to God.'

Subsequent to his experience, Howard became a pastor in the United Church of Christ.

Dallas

Dallas, who attempted suicide and then saw the Lord, was a member of the LDS Church at the time of his experience. He said, of a portion of his experience:

Taking the initiative, I asked Him about the Church. I don't know why I asked Him about the Church, but I did. The response was: 'You are where you need to be for what you have to do. You are in the right place.' That's what He said.

Elane Durham

Elane Durham, who had attended many protestant denominations when she had her extensive experience, asked her teacher-guide about the Bible and the Church. She explained what happened next:

I wondered which was the correct version [of the Bible], and I asked my teacher.

In his response he didn't use the word Bible to describe it. He used the term, a history of a people. I don't remember the exact words, but that was the sense of it. At any rate, he told me that our Bible was only a small portion of the history of the people and the King James version was the most accurate. He said that more records had been found, and there were still more records to be found.

A corollary question which I asked in conjunction with the question about the Bible was which church was true. As I told you earlier I had investigated a number of churches and I was still searching for the correct church.

My instructor said that The Church was created in heaven, but that we, as individuals, had divided that church with our fears and with our groping for power and control. The word, pagan, wasn't used, but the sense of it was that humans had divided the original church in mankind's quest to rule.

He let me know that when I found the church here on earth that believed in the history of the people (as described in the King James version of the Bible) and believed that there was additional history that had been found—and that there was still more to be revealed—I would recognize that church by the same spirit I felt there with him. He also told me that The Church had Apostles and Prophets but that they weren't accepted any more today than they had been in ancient times when Christ was here.

Elane searched for sixteen years to find a church that matched the description given by her teacher. She ultimately joined The Church of Jesus Christ of Latter-day Saints.

Gary Gillum

Gary Gillum, in *Glimpses of Eternity*, said that he was in college studying to be a Lutheran minister when he prayed to know the truth of certain doctrine that was troubling him. He later took a trip, had a head-on crash with another automobile, and went through an NDE. He explained what happened in his NDE:

> Basically, I was given a choice to stay or to return to this life. Having prayed for some kind of experience, I sort of felt the question and the answer. It was: 'If I don't go back to earth and to my body, what am I going to miss out on?' And the answer was: 'If you go back, some day you will find the truth.'

While he was in the hospital, he had a second experience:

> It was even more strange than the first experience. I saw a building with tall spires, and I saw people in a room dressed in white clothing. The people were involved in a strange ceremony. I didn't understand any of it. It was totally foreign to my experience, and I didn't know what it symbolized, if anything.

Gary later joined the LDS Church, and some years afterwards, in the Manti Temple, he recognized the scene that he had viewed during his second experience in the hospital.

Some Speculation

There are other examples of those having NDEs and asking about the Lord's Church, but this should be adequate to make some observations. Unlike Joseph Smith who was given very specific instruction concerning which church he should join, those having NDEs were given only hints or clues. They were left to their own devices to decide what church, if any, to join. Sometimes, as in the case of Elane Durham, the clues were quite explicit. Still, each of the individuals was left to ferret out what truths they could from the many churches on earth.

It seems to me that this is perfectly consistent with the Lord's Plan of Salvation. In Joseph Smith's case, he was selected as a prophet to restore the Lord's Church on the earth. He was forbidden to join any of the sects he had been studying for the simple reason that the Lord wanted to use Joseph in reestablishing His Church on the earth.

Those having NDEs, by contrast, were to find their own way through life, exercising their free choices—with faith—according to the Plan of Salvation. They were not prophets working to help the Lord restore His Church. If the Lord had told them explicitly what they should do, then their free agency would have been abridged.

Does the Lord love an individual less who does not find and join His Church? Of course not. If there was any single issue that Carol and I learned doing research for these books it was that the Lord's love for His children is universal and unequivocal. His love is independent of our actions. Just as earthly parents want the best for their children, though, so too does the Lord want us to realize our full potential. If we do not reach our full potential His infinite love still embraces us. If we misbehave and break His laws, He may not say to us: "Behold my beloved child, in whom I am well pleased . . . ," as His Father said about Him—but love us He will.

As Christians we sometimes think that we have the inside track with the Lord. Sixty percent of the world's five billion people live in Asia, and the vast majority of that group are non-Christian. There are 750 million Muslims and 600 million Buddhists in the world. To assume that the Lord loves and cares for those people any less than he does us would be extreme arrogance on our part.

Human Destiny

Those Having an NDE Were Not in Heaven

None of the adults Carol and I interviewed for the two books felt that they had reached heaven (one of the children did). Two individuals described where they were as a sort of *way station*. Others said that if they had kept going they felt as if they would have reached an even more marvelous place than the wonderful world that they saw. Two individuals said that they saw the gates of heaven, but they did not pass through.

As discussed in Chapter 20, the Plan of Salvation provides that there will be a final judgment, and depending upon how we lived, we will be assigned to one of the three degrees of glory of our Heavenly Father. Even the least of these kingdoms, the Telestial glory, will be magnificent beyond imagining.

The Celestial Kingdom

For those righteous individuals who reach the Celestial Glory, the Doctrine and Covenants describe it in this manner:[7]

And again we bear record—for we saw and heard, and this is the testimony of the gospel of Christ concerning them who shall come forth in the resurrection of the just—

They are they who received the testimony of Jesus, and believed on his name and were baptized after the manner of his burial, being buried in the water in his name, and this according to the commandment which he has given—

That by keeping the commandments they might be washed and cleansed from all their sins, and receive the Holy Spirit by the laying on of the hands of him who is ordained and sealed unto his power;

And who overcome by faith, and are sealed by the Holy Spirit of promise, which the Father sheds forth upon all those who are just and true.

They are they who are the church of the Firstborn.

They are they into whose hands the Father has given all things—

They are they who are priests and kings, who have received of his fulness, and of his glory;

And are priests of the Most High, after the order of Melchizedek, which was after the order of Enoch, which was after the order of the Only Begotten Son.

Wherefore, as it is written, they are gods, even the sons of God—

Wherefore, all things ar theirs, whether life or death, or things present, or things to come, all are theirs and they are Christ's and Christ is God's.

And they shall overcome all things. . . .

And thus we saw the glory of the celestial, which excels in all things—where God, even the Father, reigns upon his throne forever and ever;

Before whose throne all things bow in humble reverence, and give him glory forever and ever.

They who dwell in this presence are the church of the Firstborn; and they see as they are seen, and know as they are known, having received of his fulness and of his grace;

And he makes them equal in power, and in might, and in dominion.

Destiny of the Righteous

From this scripture we may understand that human destiny, for the righteous, is to become as God is and to share in his power. We can become teachers of spirits, organizers of worlds, creators of living beings, in short—gods, heirs of God![8]

Will all share in this power and glory? Of course not—only those who kept the commandments, repented of their sins and "who received the testimony of Jesus, believed on his name and were baptized after the manner of his burial, being buried in the water in his name." But all will obtain a glory that is beyond what they expected, and one that is as much as they will feel comfortable with. And all will have had an equal *opportunity* to achieve the highest glory our Father has to offer.

Joseph Smith, as he saw and understood some of the glory that he had seen in vision concerning the fate of those dead who had languished in prison, recorded his thoughts in the Doctrine and Covenants. Under inspiration from the Lord, he said:[9]

> Let your hearts rejoice, and be exceedingly glad. Let the earth break forth into singing. Let the dead speak forth anthems of eternal praise to the King Immanuel, who hath ordained, before the world was, that which would enable us to redeem them out of their prison; for the prisoners shall go free.
>
> Let the mountains shout for joy, and all ye valleys cry aloud; and all ye seas and dry lands tell the wonders of your Eternal King! And ye rivers, and brooks, and rills, flow down with gladness. Let the woods and all the trees of the field praise the Lord; and ye solid rocks weep for joy! And let the sun, moon, and the morning stars sing together, and let all the sons of God shout for joy! And let the eternal creations declare his name forever and ever! And again I say, how glorious is the voice we hear from heaven, proclaiming in our ears, glory, and salvation, and honor, and immortality, and eternal life; kingdoms, principalities, and powers!

This, then, is the testimony that Carol and I leave with you. Our testimony is of a life beyond this one that is marvelous to behold. It is a life, if we live righteously now, where Jesus Christ and His Father will join us in an eternal adventure of growth, development, creation, joy, peace, love and happiness. It is a life where our righteous family and ancestors will be bound to us in an eternal tie.

The life to come will be a life of truth and knowledge, where uncertainty, doubt, fear and pain will evaporate as the morning dew. Memory of our premortal existence will be restored, and our present earthly life will seem but a short—but immensely important—interlude in the reality of forever. Earthly death will be presented for what it is; namely, birth back into the presence of our heavenly parents and our real home.

Let me end this book by quoting from Julie, when I asked her to tell me how she felt in the light:

"I guess why it's so hard to talk about the light is . . . ," Julie paused to wipe away tears, "because it makes me homesick."

"Is that because you have known it before?" I asked.

"Yes. When I was in the light it felt natural—as if I were home."

Appendix
Two Book Statistical Data

BookStats	A	B	C	D	E	F	G	H	I	J	K
1		Age at	Age at	Male or	Religion	Religion	Educa.	One or	Out of	Saw	Spirit
2	Name	Interview	Exper.	Female	at Exper.	at Interv.	at Exper.	Mult Exp.	Body	Body	Had Form
3	Gibson, Marshall	62	36	M	LDS	LDS	2.3	1	1	1	1
4	Evans, Derald	60	22	M	LDS	LDS	2.2	1	1	1	1
5	Muecke, Karl	72	59	M	LDS	LDS	2.3	1	1	0	1
6	McClellan, Janet	31	27	F	LDS	LDS	4	1	0	0	0
7	Ruth	63	36	F	Prot.	Prot.	3	1	1	0	1
8	Shelley, DeAnne	59	32	F	Prot.	LDS	2.4	1	1	0	0
9	Clark, Lois	57	31	F	LDS	LDS	2	1	1	1	1
10	Ann	42	4/28	F	LDS	LDS	0/2.5	2	1/1	1/1	1/1
11	Lucy	34	25	F	LDS	LDS	2.2	1	1	1	1
12	Jennette	49	46	F	Prot.	Prot.	2	1	1	1	1
13	Pauline	51	29/43	F	LDS	LDS	2.4	2	0/1	0/1	0/1
14	Hansen, Forrest	35	18/20	M	Atheist	Agnostic	2.2	2	1/1	1/0	0
15	Amodt, Bob	33	22	M	Catholic	Christian	2.4	1	?	0	0
16	Amodt, Margaret	29	20	F	LDS	LDS	2	1	1	0	1
17	Norma	37	26	F	Christian	LDS	2.3	1	1	1	1
18	Kerry	41	14	M	LDS	LDS	1.6	1	1	0	1
19	Herard, David	45	22	M	Catholic	Catholic	2.4	1	1	0	1
20	Walker, Chris	19	10	M	Catholic	Catholic	0.8	2	1/1	1/1	0
21	Kim	15	14	F	LDS	LDS	1.6	1	1	0	0
22	Niitsuma, James	26	21	M	Meditative	Meditative	2.3	1	1	1	1
23	Fry, Nyk	26	23	M	LDS	LDS	2.5	2	0	0	0
24	Vorwaller, Eliz.	30	25	F	LDS	LDS	2.4	1	1	0	1
25	LaRue, Stephanie	40	29	F	Catholic	Catholic	4	1	1	1	1
26	Melvin, Joy	31	27	F	LDS	LDS	2	1	1	0	1
27	Anderson, Marcia	42	29	F	LDS	LDS	3	1	1	1	1
28	Jones, Joanne	61	54	F	LDS	LDS	2	1	1	1	0
29	Jackie	32	22	F	Christian	Christian	2	1	1	1	0
30	Berg, Ray	51	26	M	LDS	LDS	2	1	0	0	0
31	Doris	70	22	M	LDS	LDS	2.4	1	1	1	0
32	Katrina	36	35	F	LDS	LDS	2	1	1	0	1
33	Dee	42	22/24	F	Catholic	Catholic	2	2	1/1	0/1	1/1
34	Tracie	16	15	F	LDS	LDS	1.8	1	1	1	1
35	Daniels, Maureen	31	23	F	Catholic	Catholic	2.5	1	1	0	0
36	James, Shirley	57	31	F	LDS	LDS	2	1	0	0	0
37	Martinez, Kathy	45	21	F	LDS	LDS	2	1	1	1	1
38	Jean	45	40	F	LDS	LDS	2.5	1	1	0	1
39	Stirling, John	38	25	M	LDS	LDS	2.4	1	1	1	1
40	Gillum, Gary	47	19	M	Lutheran	LDS	2.8	1	1	0	0
41	Swick, Joe	30	9	M	Prot.	LDS	0.3	1	1	0	1
42	Storm, Howard		45 (Est)	M	Atheist	Chc. Chrst	4	1	1	1	0
43	Weaver, Eloise	50	10/48	F	LDS	LDS	0.5/2	2	0/1	0/1	1/1
44	Prueitt, Cynthia	34	7	F	LDS	LDS	0.2	1	1	1	1
45	Kirk, Barry	42	23	M	LDS	LDS	2.8	1	1	1	1
46	Swanson, Vern	48	30	M	LDS	LDS	4	1	1	0	1
47	Julie	42	17/19	F	LDS	LDS	1.9/3.2	2	1/0	0	1/1
48	Durham, Elane	48	32	F	Prot.	LDS	2.4	1	1	1	1
49	Bill	42	41	M	Prot.	Prot.	3	1	1	1	1
50	Louise	36	24	F	LDS	LDS	3	1	1	1	0
51	Joyce	47	36	F	Christian	LDS	2	1	1	0	1
52	Pitcher, Jennifer	11	5	F	LDS	LDS	0	1	0	0	0
53	Rocky	13	4	M	Prot.	Prot.	0	1	1	1	1
54	Jack	40	5/21	M	Christian	Christian	0/2.6	2	1/1	1/1	0
55	DeLynn	42	37	M	LDS	LDS	3	1	1	1	1
56	Karen	37	20	F	Christian	Catholic	2.3	1	1	1	1
57	Dallas	54	40	M	LDS	LDS	2.3	1	1	0	0
58	Chuck	50	25	M	LDS	LDS	2.4	1	1	1	0
59	Mike	31	9	M	Christian	Christian	0.3	1	1	1	1
60	Allen, Lavor	81	56	M	LDS	LDS	1.5	1	1	1	1
61	Barbara	41	15	F	Christian	Christian	1.5	1	1	1	1
62	Patricia	37	13/25	F	Christian	Christian	1.3/2.5	2	1/0	1/0	1/0
63	Elizabeth Marie	29	14/28	F	LDS	LDS	1.3/2	2	1/1	1/0	1/0
64	Lori	29	16/25/29	F	Catholic	Catholic	1.8/2.5	3	1/1/1	1/0/0	1/1/1
65	Mary	59	34/52	F	Christian	Christian	1.8	2	1/1	0/1	0
66	Maria	78	41	F	LDS	LDS	2	1	1	0	0
67	Debbie	32	21	F	Prot.	Prot.	2.2	1	1	1	1
68	Chevalier, David	40	28	M	Christian	LDS	2.8	1	1	0	1
69	Zamora, Renee	32	31	F	LDS	LDS	2.1	1	1	1	1
70	Smith, Roger	49	24/29	M	LDS	LDS	2.5	2	1/0	0	0
71											
72	Totals			68	39 LDS	43 LDS		83	71	44	49
73				40F 28M							
74	Percentages			58.8F	57.0 LDS	63.2 LDS		20.5 Mult.	85.5	53	59

312

BookStats	A	L	M	N	O	P Knew	Q	R	S	T Saw	U Life's
1											
2	Name	Tunnel	Light	Landscp	People	People	Relatives	Voice	Deity	Deity	Review
3	Gibson, Marshall	0	1	1	1	1	0	1	1	1	1
4	Evans, Derald	0	1	0	1	1	0	1	0	0	0
5	Muecke, Karl	0	0	1	0	0	0	1	1	0	0
6	McClellan, Janet	0	0	0	0	1	0	1	0	0	0
7	Ruth	1	1	0	1	1	0	0	0	0	0
8	Shelley, DeAnne	0	1	0	0	0	1	1	0	0	0
9	Clark, Lois	0	1	0	1	0	0	1	0	0	0
10	Ann	1/1	1/1	1/0	1/0	0	0	1/1	0/1	0/1	0
11	Lucy	0	1	0	1	0	0	1	1	1	0
12	Jennette	1	1	0	0	0	0	1	1	1	0
13	Pauline	0	0	0	0	0	0	0	0	0	0
14	Hansen, Forrest	0/1	1/1	0	1/0	0	0	1/0	0	0	0/1
15	Amodt, Bob	0	0	0	0	0	0	0	0	0	0
16	Amodt, Margaret	0	1	0	0	0	0	0	0	0	0
17	Norma	0	1	0	0	0	0	0	0	0	0
18	Kerry	0	1	0	1	1	1	1	0	0	0
19	Herard, David	0	1	1	1	1	0	1	1	0	0
20	Walker, Chris	0	0	0	0	0	0	0	0	0	0
21	Kim	1	1	0	1	0	0	1	0	0	0
22	Niitsuma, James	0	1	0	1	0	0	1	0	0	1
23	Fry, Nyk	0	0/1	0	0	0	0	0	0	0	0
24	Vorwaller, Eliz.	0	0	0	1	1	0	1	0	0	0
25	LaRue, Stephanie	0	0	0	0	0	0	0	0	0	0
26	Melvin, Joy	0	1	1	1	1	1	1	0	0	0
27	Anderson, Marcia	0	1	0	1	0	0	0	0	0	0
28	Jones, Joanne	0	0	1	0	0	0	1	1	1	0
29	Jackie	0	1	0	0	0	0	0	0	0	0
30	Berg, Ray	0	0	0	0	0	0	0	0	0	1
31	Doris	0	0	0	0	0	0	0	0	0	0
32	Katrina	0	1	1	1	0	0	1	1	0	0
33	Dee	0	0	0	0	0	0	0	0	0	0
34	Tracie	1	1	0	1	1	0	1	0	0	0
35	Daniels, Maureen	0	1	0	1	1	1	1	0	0	0
36	James, Shirley	0	1	0	1	1	1	1	0	0	0
37	Martinez, Kathy	1	0	0	1	1	1	1	0	0	0
38	Jean	0	0	1	1	1	1	1	0	0	0
39	Stirling, John	0	0	0	0	0	0	1	1	0	1
40	Gillum, Gary	0	1	1	1	1	1	1	0	0	0
41	Swick, Joe	1	1	0	0	0	0	1	0	0	0
42	Storm, Howard	0	1	0	1	0	0	1	0	0	1
43	Weaver, Eloise	0	1/1	0	1/1	1/1	0/1	0/1	1/0	1/0	0
44	Prueitt, Cynthia	0	1	0	0	0	0	1	1	1	0
45	Kirk, Barry	1	1	0	1	1	1	0	0	0	0
46	Swanson, Vern	0	1	0	1	1	1	1	0	0	0
47	Julie	0	1/1	0	1/1	1/0	1/0	1/0	0	0	0
48	Durham, Elane	0	1	1	1	1	1	1	1	0	1
49	Bill	0	1	1	1	1	1	1	0	0	0
50	Louise	1	1	0	1	1	0	1	0	0	0
51	Joyce	1	1	0	0	0	0	1	0	0	0
52	Pitcher, Jennifer	0	0	0	1	1	1	1	0	0	0
53	Rocky	0	0	0	1	1	1	1	1	1	0
54	Jack	0	0/1	0/1	1/1	1/0	0	1/0	1/0	1/0	0
55	DeLynn	1	1	0	1	0	1	1	1	0	0
56	Karen	1	0	0	0	0	0	1	0	0	0
57	Dallas	1	1	1	0	0	0	1	1	1	0
58	Chuck	0	0	0	1	1	1	1	0	0	0
59	Mike	1	1	1	1	1	1	1	1	1	0
60	Allen, Lavor	0	1	1	1	1	1	1	0	0	0
61	Barbara	0	1	0	1	1	1	1	0	0	0
62	Patricia	0	0	0	0	0	0	0	0	0	0
63	Elizabeth Marie	1/0	1/0	0	1/1	0/1	0	1	1/0	0	1/0
64	Lori	0	0	0/0/1	1/0/0	0	0	0	0	0	0
65	Mary	1/0	1/0	0	0/1	0/1	0/1	0/1	0/1	0/1	0
66	Maria	0	0	0	0	0	0	1	0	0	0
67	Debbie	0	1	0	0	0	0	1	1	1	0
68	Chevalier, David	0	0	1	1	0	0	1	1	0	0
69	Zamora, Renee	0	0	1	1	1	1	0	0	0	0
70	Smith, Roger	0	1/1	0	0	1/0	0	1/1	1/0	1/0	1/0
71											
72	Totals	18	50	18	46	33	23	53	22	15	9
73											
74	Percentages	21.6	60.2	21.1	55.4	39.8	27.7	63.8	26.5	18.1	10.8

BookStats	A	V	W	X	Y	Z	AA	AB	AC	AD	AE
1											
2	Name	Buildings	Knowldg	Energy	Peace	Love	Warmth	Pure	Remorse	Fear	Music
3	Gibson, Marshall	1	1	0	1	1	0	0	0	0	0
4	Evans, Derald	0	1	0	0	0	0	1	0	0	0
5	Muecke, Karl	0	0	0	0	1	0	0	0	0	1
6	McClellan, Janet	0	0	0	0	0	0	0	0	0	0
7	Ruth	0	0	0	0	0	0	0	0	0	0
8	Shelley, DeAnne	0	0	0	1	1	0	1	0	0	0
9	Clark, Lois	0	0	0	1	0	0	0	0	0	1
10	Ann	0	0	0	1/1	1/1	0	0	0	0	0
11	Lucy	0	0	0	0	1	0	0	0	0	0
12	Jennette	0	1	0	1	1	0	0	0	0	0
13	Pauline	0	0	0	1/0	0	1/1	0	0	0	0
14	Hansen, Forrest	0	0	0	0	0	0	0	0	0	0
15	Amodt, Bob	0	0	0	0	0	0	0	0	0	0
16	Amodt, Margaret	0	0	1	1	0	0	0	0	0	0
17	Norma	0	0	0	1	0	0	0	0	0	0
18	Kerry	0	0	0	1	1	0	0	0	0	0
19	Herard, David	0	1	0	1	1	1	0	0	0	0
20	Walker, Chris	0	0	0	1/1	0	0	0	0	0	0
21	Kim	0	0	0	1	0	1	0	0	0	0
22	Niitsuma, James	0	0	0	0	0	1	0	0	0	0
23	Fry, Nyk	0	0	0	0/1	0	0	0	0	0	0
24	Vorwaller, Eliz.	0	0	0	0	0	0	0	0	1/0	0
25	LaRue, Stephanie	0	1	0	1	1	0	0	0	0	0
26	Melvin, Joy	0	0	0	0	1	1	0	0	0	1
27	Anderson, Marcia	0	1	0	1	1	0	0	0	0	0
28	Jones, Joanne	0	0	0	0	1	0	0	0	0	0
29	Jackie	0	0	0	0	0	0	0	0	0	0
30	Berg, Ray	0	0	0	0	0	0	0	0	0	0
31	Doris	0	0	0	0	0	0	0	0	0	0
32	Katrina	0	1	0	1	1	0	0	0	0	0
33	Dee	0	0	0	0	0	0	0	0	0/1	0
34	Tracie	1	1	0	1	1	1	0	0	0	0
35	Daniels, Maureen	0	1	0	1	1	0	0	0	0	1
36	James, Shirley	0	0	0	0	1	1	0	0	0	0
37	Martinez, Kathy	0	0	0	0	0	0	0	1	1	0
38	Jean	1	1	0	1	0	0	0	0	0	0
39	Stirling, John	0	1	1	1	1	0	0	0	0	0
40	Gillum, Gary	0	1	0	1	1	0	0	0	0	0
41	Swick, Joe	0	0	1	0	1	0	0	0	0	0
42	Storm, Howard	0	1	0	0	1	0	0	1	1	0
43	Weaver, Eloise	0	0	0	0/1	1/1	0/1	0	0	0	0/1
44	Prueitt, Cynthia	1	1	1	0	1	1	0	0	0	0
45	Kirk, Barry	0	0	0	1	0	1	0	0	0	0
46	Swanson, Vern	0	0	0	1	1	0	0	0	0	0
47	Julie	0	1/1	0	0	1/0	0	0	0	0	0
48	Durham, Elane	0	1	0	1	1	0	1	0	0	1
49	Bill	0	0	1	1	0	1	0	0	0	0
50	Louise	0	0	0	1	0	0	0	0	0	0
51	Joyce	0	0	0	0	1	0	0	0	0	0
52	Pitcher, Jennifer	0	0	0	0	0	0	0	0	0	0
53	Rocky	0	1	0	0	0	0	0	0	0	0
54	Jack	0	1/0	0	1	0	0	0	0	0/1	0/1
55	DeLynn	1	1	0	1	1	1	0	0	0	0
56	Karen	0	1	0	0	0	0	0	1	1	0
57	Dallas	0	1	0	0	1	1	0	1	0	0
58	Chuck	0	1	0	0	0	1	0	0	0	0
59	Mike	0	0	0	1	1	1	0	0	1	1
60	Allen, Lavor	0	0	0	1	0	0	0	0	0	0
61	Barbara	0	0	0	0	1	0	0	0	0	0
62	Patricia	0	0	0	0	0	0	0	1/0	1/1	0
63	Elizabeth Marie	0	1/0	0	0	1/1	0	1/0	1/0	0	0
64	Lori	0	0	0	1/0/0	0	0	0	0	0	0
65	Mary	1/0	0	0	1/1	1/1	1/0	0	0	0	0
66	Maria	1	0	0	1	1	0	0	0	0	1
67	Debbie	0	0	0	1	1	0	0	0	0	0
68	Chevalier, David	0	1	0	0	0	0	0	0	0	0
69	Zamora, Renee	0	1	0	0	0	0	0	0	1	0
70	Smith, Roger	0	1/1	1/0	0	1/0	0	0	1/0	0	0
71											
72	Totals	6	28	6	38	39	17	4	5	10	9
73											
74	Percentages	7.2	33.7	7.2	45.7	47	20.5	4.8	6	12	9.6

BookStats	A	AF	AG	AH	AI
1		Sense of	Second	Saw	
2	Name	Mission	Healing	Premortl	**Legend for Statistical Data**
3	Gibson, Marshall	1	0	0	Name: Those interviewed as they appear in the two books.
4	Evans, Derald	1	0	0	Age at Interview: Reported age at time of interview.
5	Muecke, Karl	1	0	0	Age at Experience: Calculated age at time of experience.
6	McClellan, Janet	1	0	0	Male or Female: As stated.
7	Ruth	1	1	0	Religion at Experience: Religions as given by people. Christian used where loose
8	Shelley, DeAnne	1	1	0	definition was given.
9	Clark, Lois	1	1	0	Religion at Interview: Same as above except at time of interview instead of at
10	Ann	0/1	1	0	time of experience.
11	Lucy	1	1	0	Education at Experience: Less than Grammar School=0; Grammar School=1;
12	Jennette	1	0	0	High School=2; BS or BA=3; Graduate Degree=4.
13	Pauline	0	0	0	One or Multiple Experiences: The number of experiences, on different days, for
14	Hansen, Forrest	0	0	0	the individual.
15	Amodt, Bob	0	0	0	Out of Body: 0 if not out of body; 1 if out of body.
16	Amodt, Margaret	1	0	0	Saw Body: 0 if individual did not see their own body; 1 if they did see their body.
17	Norma	1	0	0	Spirit had Form: 1 if individual had a sense that their body had form; 0 if they
18	Kerry	1	0	0	didn't know.
19	Herard, David	1	0	0	Tunnel: 1 if individual described something like a tunnel; 0 if they did not.
20	Walker, Chris	0	0	0	Light: 1 if individual saw an unusual bright light; 0 if they did not.
21	Kim	0	0	0	Landscape: 1 if individual saw landscape features in another world; 0 if they
22	Niitsuma, James	0	0	0	did not.
23	Fry, Nyk	1	0	0	People: 1 if individual saw people; 0 if they did not.
24	Vorwaller, Eliz.	1	0	0	Knew People: 1 if individual felt they knew people, even if they later forgot;
25	LaRue, Stephanie	1	0	0	otherwise 0.
26	Melvin, Joy	0	0	0	Relatives: 1 if individual knew the people as relatives; 0 if not.
27	Anderson, Marcia	1	0	0	Voice: 1 if individual heard or knew a voice was communicating; 0 if not.
28	Jones, Joanne	0	0	0	Deity: 1 if individual identified the presence of Deity; 0 if not.
29	Jackie	1	0	0	Saw Deity. 1 if individual said that they saw Deity; 0 if not.
30	Berg, Ray	0	0	0	Life's Review: 1 if individual had a life's review (or analogous event); 0 if not.
31	Doris	0	0	0	Buildings: 1 if individual spoke of being in or seeing buildings; 0 if not.
32	Katrina	1	0	0	Knowledge: 1 if individual spoke of receiving unusual knowledge, even if later
33	Dee	0	0	0	forgotten; 0 if not.
34	Tracie	1	0	0	Energy: 1 if individual spoke of energy as part of experience; 0 if not.
35	Daniels, Maureen	1	0	0	Peace: 1 if individual spoke of peace as part of experience; 0 if not.
36	James, Shirley	0	0	0	Love: 1 if individual spoke of love as part of experience; 0 if not.
37	Martinez, Kathy	1	0	0	Warmth: 1 if individual spoke of warmth as part of experience; 0 if not.
38	Jean	1	0	0	Pure: 1 if individual spoke of pure as part of experience; 0 if not.
39	Stirling, John	1	0	0	Remorse: 1 if individual appeared to have remorse related to what they were
40	Gillum, Gary	1	0	0	shown; 0 if not.
41	Swick, Joe	1	0	0	Fear: 1 if individual experienced fear at some part of experience; 0 if not.
42	Storm, Howard	1	0	0	Music: 1 if individual spoke of music or music-like sounds during experience;
43	Weaver, Eloise	0/1	0	0	0 if not.
44	Pruett, Cynthia	1	0	0	Sense of Mission: 1 if individual returned from experience with a sense of mission;
45	Kirk, Barry	1	0	0	0 if not.
46	Swanson, Vern	0	0	0	Second Healing: 1 if individual later had life-threatening illness that was
47	Julie	0	0	0/1	miraculously cured; 0 if not.
48	Durham, Elane	1	1	1	Saw Premortal: 1 if individual saw themselves in a premortal environment; 0 if not.
49	Bill	1	0	0	
50	Louise	0	0	0	
51	Joyce	1	0	0	
52	Pitcher, Jennifer	0	0	0	
53	Rocky	1	0	0	
54	Jack	1/1	0	0	
55	DeLynn	1	0	1	
56	Karen	1	1	0	
57	Dallas	1	1	0	
58	Chuck	1	1	0	
59	Mike	1	0	0	
60	Allen, Lavor	1	0	0	
61	Barbara	1	0	0	
62	Patricia	0	0	0	
63	Elizabeth Marie	1/1	0	0	
64	Lori	0	0	0	
65	Mary	0/1	1	0	
66	Maria	1	0	0	
67	Debbie	0	0	0	
68	Chevalier, David	1	0	0	
69	Zamora, Renee	1	0	0	
70	Smith, Roger	1/1	0	0	
71					
72	Totals	52	10	3	
73					
74	Percentages	62.6	12	3.6	

Notes

Introduction

1. Gibson, Arvin S., *Glimpses of Eternity*. Bountiful, Utah: Horizon Publishers and Distributors, Inc., 1992, pp. 52-54.
2. *The Bible*. 1 Corinthians 13:12.
3. Moody, Raymond A., Jr., *Life After Life*. New York, N.Y.: Bantam Books, 1988.
4. Crowther, Duane S., *Life Everlasting*. Salt Lake City, Utah: Bookcraft, Inc., 1967.

Chapter 19: Are the Stories True?

1. Ring, Kenneth, *Life at Death—A Scientific Investigation of the Near-death Experience*. New York, N.Y.: Quill, 1982, pp. 206-17.
2. Morse, Melvin, *Closer to the Light—Learning from the Near-Death Experiences of Children*. New York, N.Y.: Villard Books, 1990, pp. 183-93.
3. Moody, Raymond A., Jr., *Life After Life*. New York, N.Y.: Bantam Books, 1976.
4. Moody, Raymond A., Jr., *The Light Beyond*. New York, N.Y.: Bantam Books, 1988, pp. 151-54.
5. Gibson, Arvin S., *Glimpses of Eternity*. Bountiful, Utah: Horzon Publishers and Distributors, Inc., 1992, pp. 301-02.
6. Gibson, *op. cit.,* pp. 265-67.
7. Gibson, Arvin S., *In Search of Angels*. Bountiful, Utah: Horizon Publishers and Distributors, Inc., 1990, pp. 157-73.
8. Gibson, Arvin S., *Glimpses of Eternity*. Bountiful, Utah: Horizon Publishers and Distributors, Inc., 1992, pp. 44-47.
9. Wilson, Ian, *The After Death Experience—The Physics of the Non-Physical*. New York, N.Y.: William Morrow and Company, Inc., 1987, pp. 132-33.
10. Ring, Kenneth, *Heading Toward Omega—In Search of the Meaning of the Near-Death Experience*. New York, N.Y.: Quill, 1985, p. 35.
11. Ring, *op. cit.,* pp. 45-46.
12. Wren-Lewis, John, "Avoiding the Columbus Confusion: An Ockhamish View of Near-Death Research," *Journal of Near-Death Studies*, Vol. 11, No. 2, Winter 1992. 233 Spring St., New York, N.Y. 10013: Human Sciences Press, Inc., p. 78.

13. Gibson, *op. cit.,* p. 249.

14. Gibson, *op. cit.,* pp. 302-06.

15. Johnson, Lynn D., *Letter to Author*, February 7, 1993.

16. Spanos, Nicholas P.; Menary, Evelyn; Gabora, Natalie J.; DuBreuil, Susan C.; and Dewhirst, Bridget; "Secondary Identity Enactments During Hypnotic Past-Life Regression: A Sociocognitive Perspective," *Journal of Personality and Social Psychology*, 1991, Vol. 61, No. 2., pp. 308-20.

17. *The Bible.* Hebrews 9:27.

18. *The Book of Mormon.* Alma 11:45.

Chapter 20: Freedom of Choice

1. Gibson, *op. cit.,* p. 219.

2. *Pearl of Great Price.* Abraham 3:24, 25.

3. *The Book of Mormon.* 2 Nephi 2:25.

4. *Pearl of Great Price.* Moses 3:26-28; *The Book of Mormon.* Ether 3:15-17.

5. *Doctrine and Covenants* 68:25-28; 88:4.

6. *The Book of Mormon.* Alma 42:7-10.

7. *The Book of Mormon.* 2 Nephi 2:27.

8. *The Book of Mormon.* 2 Nephi 2:11-16.

9. *Doctrine and Covenants* 59:6.

10. *The Book of Mormon.* 1 Nephi 22:1,2. *The Bible.* Amos 3:7.

11. *The Book of Mormon.* 3 Nephi 18:17-20.

12. Doctrine and Covenants 130:18,19.

13. *The Book of Mormon.* Alma 22:14.

14. *The Book of Mormon.* 2 Nephi 9:21,22.

15. *The Book of Mormon.* Ether 4:18; *Doctrine and Covenants* 128:1-25.

16. *Doctrine and Covenants* 138:1-36.

17. *The Book of Mormon.* Mormon 9:13.

18. *The Book of Mormon.* Alma 41:1-7; 3 Nephi 26:4-5.

19. *Doctrine and Covenants* 76:54-70.

20. *Doctrine and Covenants* 76:81-90.

21. *The Bible.* Revelation 12:7-8; *Doctrine and Covenants* 29:36-38.

22. *Pearl of Great Price.* Abraham 3:23.

23. Talmage, James E., *Jesus the Christ.* Salt Lake City, Utah: Deseret Book Company, 1982, Chapter 3, p. 16.

24. Talmage, *op. cit.,* Chapter 25, pp. 383-84.

25. Eadie, Betty J., *Embraced by the Light*. Placerville, California: Gold Leaf Press, 1992, pp. 48, 49, 67.
26. McConkie, Bruce R., *Mormon Doctrine*. Salt Lake City, Utah: Bookcraft, Inc., 1958, p. 530.
27. McConkie, *op. cit.*, p. 25.
28. *The Book of Mormon*. 2 Nephi 2:11.
29. *Teachings of the Prophet Joseph Smith*. Compiled by Joseph Fielding Smith. Salt Lake City, Utah: Published by The Church of Jesus Christ of Latter-day Saints, 1938, Section 6, p. 365.
30. Eadie, *op. cit.*, pp. 68, 69.
31. McConkie, *op. cit.*, p. 269.

Chapter 21: Negative Experiences

1. Rawlings, Maurice, *Beyond Death's Door*. New York, N.Y.: Bantam Books, 1979.
2. Atwater, P.M.H., "Is There A Hell? Surprising Observations About the Near-Death Experience." *Journal of Near-Death Studies,* Vol. 10, No. 3, Spring 1992., pp. 149-60.
3. Gibson, Arvin S., *Glimpses of Eternity*. Bountiful, Utah: Horizon Publishers and Distributors, Inc., 1992, pp. 154-55.
4. Gibson, *op. cit.*, pp. 170-76.
5. Rawlings, *op. cit.*, pp. 86-87.
6. Gibson, *op. cit.*, pp. 253-56.
7. Gibson, *op. cit.*, pp. 109-10.
8. Ritchie, George G., *Return from Tomorrow*. Old Tappan, New Jersey: Spire Books, 1978.
9. Ritchie, George G., *My Life After Dying—Becoming Alive to Universal Love*. Norfolk, Virginia: Hampton Roads Publishing, 1991.
10. Eadie, Betty J., *Embraced by the Light*. Placerville, California: Gold Leaf Press, 1992, p. 84.
11. Rawlings, *op. cit.*, pp. 46-47.
12. *Pearl of Great Price*. Moses 4:3-4.
13. *The Bible*. Matthew 4:1-11.
14. *Pearl of Great Price*. Joseph Smith 2:15-17.
15. Smith, Joseph Fielding, "Gospel Doctrine," p. 448. *Gospel Library, Third Edition*. Computer CD from Folio Infobase, 1993.
16. McConkie, Bruce R., *Mormon Doctrine*. Salt Lake City, Utah: Bookcraft, Inc., 1958, p. 218.

17. *The Bible.* Mark 5:1-13.
18. "Levi Hancock Autobiography—Typescript BYU-S," p. 33. *LDS Historical Library, Second Edition.* Computer CD from Folio Infobase, 1993.
19. Ritchie, George G., *Return from Tomorrow.* Old Tappan, New Jersey: Spire Books, 1978, pp. 59-61.
20. Stapley, Elder Delbert L., *Conference Report,* April 1968, The Church of Jesus Christ of Latter-day Saints, pp. 28-29.

Chapter 22: Patterns and Parallels

1. *The Bible.* John 14:27.
2. *The Bible.* Philippians 4:7.
3. *Pearl of Great Price.* Joseph Smith 2:43-46.
4. *The Book of Mormon.* 3 Nephi 11:3-7.
5. *Pearl of Great Price.* Abraham 3:4.
6. *Doctrine and Covenants* 84:99; 88:110.
7. Christensen, Kevin, "'Nigh unto Death': NDE Research and the Book of Mormon." *Journal of Book of Mormon Studies,* Vol 2, No. 1, Spring 1993. Provo, Utah: Foundation for Ancient Research & Mormon Studies, pp. 1-20.
8. Atwater, P.M.H. *Coming Back to Life.* Ballantine Books, New York, N.Y., 1988, pp. 45-47.
9. *The Bible.* Revelation 21:10-27.
10. *Doctrine and Covenants* 137:1-2.

Chapter 23: Families

1. *The Bible.* Mark 16:16.
2. *The Book of Mormon.* Moroni 8:10-22.
3. *The Bible.* I Corinthians 15:29.
4. *Doctrine and Covenants* 27:12, 13.
5. *Doctrine and Covenants* 128:18.
6. Young, Brigham, *Discourses of Brigham Young.* Salt Lake City, Utah: Edited by John A. Widtsoe, 1946, pp. 376-81.
7. *Teachings of the Prophet Joseph Smith.* 1843-1844, p. 326.
8. *Teachings of the Prophet Joseph Smith.* 1843-1844, Section 6, pp. 310-11.
9. *Doctrine and Covenants* 128:5-8.

10. Madsen, Truman. *Eternal Man*. Salt Lake City, Utah: Deseret Book Company, 1966, p. 30.

Chapter 24: Appearances of Deity

1. Gibson, Arvin S., *Glimpses of Eternity*. Bountiful, Utah: Horion Publishers and Distributors, Inc., 1992, pp. 13-14.
2. *The Book of Mormon*. Ether 3:15-16.
3. *The Bible*. Luke 24:36-39.
4. *The Bible*. John 20:24-29.
5. *The Bible*. Acts 7:55-56.
6. *The Bible*. Acts 22:68.
7. *The Book of Mormon*. 3 Nephi 11:8-11.
8. *Pearl of Great Price*. Joseph Smith 2:16-17.
9. Doctrine and Covenants 110:1-4, 7.
10. *History of the Church*, Vol. 1, Salt Lake City, Utah: Deseret Book Company, 1971, p. 84.
11. Crowther, Duane S., *Life Everlasting*. Salt Lake City, Utah: Bookcraft, Inc., 1967, p. 83.

Chapter 25: Some Final Thoughts

1. Moore, L.T., *Isaac Newton*. 1934, p. 664.
2. *The Bible*. 1 Corinthians 13:12-13.
3. *The Book of Mormon*. Alma 32:26-28.
4. *Doctrine and Covenants* 88:6, 7, 11-13.
5. *Pearl of Great Price*. Joseph Smith 2:18-19.
6. Storm, Howard. Taped, and later transcribed, experience recorded in 1989 at The NDE Research Institute, Fort Thomas, Kentucky.
7. *Doctrine and Covenants* 76:50-60, 92-95.
8. *The Bible*. Galatians 4:7.
9. *Doctrine and Covenants* 128:22-23.

Selected Bibliography

Latter-day Saint Scriptures

The Book of Mormon—Another Testament of Jesus Christ. Translated by Joseph Smith, Junior. Salt Lake City, Utah: Published by The Church of Jesus Christ of Latter-day Saints, 1989.

The Doctrine and Covenants of The Church of Jesus Christ of Latter-day Saints. Salt Lake City, Utah: Published by The Church of Jesus Christ of Latter-day Saints, 1989.

The Holy Bible. Authorized King James Version. Salt Lake City, Utah: Published by The Church of Jesus Christ of Latter-day Saints, 1979.

The Pearl of Great Price. Salt Lake City, Utah: Published by The Church of Jesus Christ of Latter-day Saints, 1989.

Latter-day Saint Historical and Doctrinal Books and Periodicals

Crowther, Duane S., *Life Everlasting*. Salt Lake City, Utah: Bookcraft, Inc., 1967.

History of the Church of Jesus Christ of Latter-day Saints, 7 volumes plus Index. Salt Lake City, Utah: Deseret Book Company, 1970.

Journal of Discourses, 26 volumes. Los Angeles, CA: General Printing and Lithograph Co., 1961.

"Levi Hancock Autobiography—Typescript BYU-S," p. 33. *LDS Historical Library, Second Edition*. Computer CD from Folio Infobase, 1993.

Madsen, Truman G., *Eternal Man*. Salt Lake City, Utah: Deseret Book Company, 1966.

McConkie, Bruce R., *Mormon Doctrine*. Salt Lake City, Utah: Bookcraft, Inc., 1958.

Smith, Joseph Fielding, "Gospel Doctrine," *Gospel Library, Third Edition*. Computer CD from Folio Infobase, 1993.

Stapley, Elder Delbert L., *Conference Report*, April 1968, The Church of Jesus Christ of Latter-day Saints pp. 28-29.

Talmage, James E., *Jesus the Christ*. Salt Lake City, Utah: Deseret Book Company, 1982.

Teachings of the Prophet Joseph Smith. Compiled by Joseph Fielding Smith. Salt Lake City, Utah: Published by The Church of Jesus Christ of Latter-day Saints, 1938.

Young, Brigham, *Discourses of Brigham Young*. Salt Lake City, Utah: Edited by John A. Widtsoe, 1946.

Near-Death Literature

Almeder, Robert, *Beyond Death*. Springfield, Illinois: Publisher, Charles C. Thomas, 1987.

Atwater, P.M.H., *Coming Back to Life*. New York, N.Y.: Ballantine Books, 1988.

Atwater, P.M.H., "Is There A Hell? Surprising Observations About the Near-Death Experience." *Journal of Near-Death Studies*, Vol. 10, No. 3, Spring 1992.

Christensen, Kevin, "Nigh unto Death: NDE Research and the Book of Mormon." *Journal of Book of Mormon Studies*, Vol 2, No. 1, Spring 1993. Provo, Utah: Foundation for Ancient Research & Mormon Studies,

Crowther, Duane S., *Life Everlasting*. Salt Lake City, Utah: Bookcraft, Inc., 1967.

Eadie, Betty J., *Embraced by the Light*. Placerville, CA: Gold Leaf Press, 1992.

Flynn, Charles P., *After the Beyond—Human Transformation and the Near-Death Experience*. New York, N.Y.: Prentice Hall Press, 1986.

Gallup, G., Jr., *Adventures in Immortality*. N.Y.: McGraw Hill, 1982.

Gibson, Arvin S., *Glimpses of Eternity*. Bountiful, Utah: Horizon Publishers and Distributors, Inc., 1992.

Grey, Margot, *Return from Death*. London and New York: Arkana, 1987.

Grosso, Michael, *The Final Choice*. Walpose, New Hampshire: Stillpoint Publishing, 1985.

Harris, Barbara, *Full Circle*. Pocket Books, 1991.

Kübler-Ross, Elisabeth, *On Children and Death*. New York, N.Y.: Collier Books, MacMillan Publishing Company, 1983.

Kübler-Ross, Elisabeth, *Questions and Answers on Death and Dying*. New York, N.Y: Collier Books, MacMillan Publishing Company, 1974.

Lundahl, Craig R., *A Collection of Near-Death Research Readings*. Chicago, Ill.: Nelson-Hall Publishers, 1982.

Millett, Larry R, *A Touch of Here and Beyond*. Salt Lake City, Utah: Hawkes Publishing, Inc.

Moody, Raymond A., Jr., *Life After Life*. New York, N.Y.: Bantam Books, 1988.

Moody, Raymond A., Jr., *The Light Beyond*. Bantam Books, New York, N.Y., 1988.

Moody, Raymond A. Jr., M.D., *Reflections on Life After Life*, New York, N.Y.: Bantam Books, 1983.

Morse, Melvin with Perry, Paul., *Closer to the Light*. New York, N.Y.: Villard Books, 1990.

Morse, Melvin with Perry, Paul, *Transformed by the Light*. New York, N.Y.: Villard Books, 1992.

Murphet, Howard., *Beyond Death*. Wheaton, Illinois: Quest Books, The Theosophical Publishing House, 1990.

Nelson, Lee, *Beyond the Veil—Volume I*. Orem, Utah: Cedar Fort Inc., 1988.

Nelson, Lee, *Beyond the Veil—Volume II*. Orem, Utah: Cedar Fort Inc., 1989.

Rawlings, Maurice, *Beyond Death's Door*. N.Y.: Bantam Books, 1979.

Ring, Kenneth, *Heading Toward Omega*. N. Y.: William Morrow Inc., 1985.

Ring, Kenneth, *Life at Death*. New York, N.Y.: Quill, 1982.

Ritchie, George G. with Sherrill, Elizabeth, *Return from Tomorrow*. Old Tappan, New Jersey: Spire Books, Fleming H. Revell Co., 1978.

Ritchie, George G., *My Life After Dying—Becoming Alive to Universal Love*. Norfolk, Virginia: Hampton Roads Publishing, 1991.

Sorensen, Michele R.; Willmore, David R., *The Journey Beyond Life, Vol. One*. Orem, Utah: Family Affair Books, 1988.

Storm, Howard. Unpublished document in possession of author; transcribed from taped experience recorded in 1989 at The NDE Research Institute, Fort Thomas, Kentucky.

Wilson, Ian, *The After Death Experience*, William Morrow and Company, Inc., N.Y., 1987.

Wren-Lewis, John, "Avoiding the Columbus Confusion: An Ockhamish View of Near-Death Research;" *Journal of Near-Death Studies*, Vol. 11, No. 2, Winter 1992. 233 Spring St., New York, N.Y.: Human Sciences Press, Inc.,

Zaleski, Carol. *Otherworld Journeys*. N.Y. and Oxford: Oxford University Press, 1987.

Other Literature

Gibson, Arvin S. *In Search of Angels*. Bountiful, Utah: Horizon Publishers and Distributors, Inc., 1990.

Moody, Raymond A. Jr. *Coming Back—A Psychiatrist Explores Past-Life Journeys*. N.Y., London: Bantam Books, 1991.

Spanos, Nicholas P.; Menary, Evelyn; Gabora, Natalie DuBreuil, Susan C.; and Dewhirst, Bridget; "Secondary Identity Enactments During Hypnotic Past-Life Regression: A Sociocognitive Perspective;" *Journal of Personality and Social Psychology*, 1991, Vol. 61, No. 2.

Index